D0801732

DATE DUE		
F 10/73		
MAY 7 1975		
F 6-77		
JUL 7 '82		
APR 23 '85		
SEP 13 '89		
MAY 17 '04		

TEACHING ENGLISH

AS A SECOND LANGUAGE

Teaching English as a Second Language

REVISED AND ENLARGED

By MARY FINOCCHIARO

HARPER & ROW, PUBLISHERS

1817

NEW YORK, EVANSTON, AND LONDON

Contents

Acknowledgments

In the original textbook, I acknowledged my gratitude to Professor Mario Pei of Columbia University, who first introduced me to linguistics, to Mr. Paul Bisgaier and Mr. Adrian Blumenfeld of the New York City Board of Education, and to Mr. Adrian Hull of the Department of Education of Puerto Rico for their reading of the manuscript and their valuable suggestions. I expressed my appreciation to Mrs. Cynthia Bonomo for her care in typing the manuscript.

Mr. Bisgaier, principal in the New York City schools and lecturer at Hunter College, has also contributed to this revision his wise counsel and his many years of experience as supervisor. Mr. Henry Pascual, Supervisor of Modern Languages in the schools of New Mexico, has read this manuscript and has suggested valuable additions. Mrs. Jeanne Levie of New York University reviewed the Appendix materials. I am grateful to these eminent colleagues for their sincere cooperation.

I appreciate the patience of my secretary, Mrs. Eileen Wholey, who has deciphered the manuscript and its many afterthoughts with great attentiveness.

I am deeply indebted to Virginia Hilu, my editor at Harper & Row, for her confidence in the revision project, for her untiring good-natured patience and help during the preparation of the manuscript, and especially for her inspiring personal and professional attitude.

I wish to acknowledge again the testing and sharpening of

my ideas which contact with my students in seminars in the United States and abroad has made possible. My many colleagues in the fields of education, language teaching, psychology, sociology, anthropology, and English will recognize my many debts to them. Reading the results of their thinking, listening to them at conferences, visiting their classrooms, and exchanging points of view have stimulated me to continue the unending search for the most effective ways of teaching and guiding speakers of other languages.

M. F.

Casoli di Camaiore, Italy
June, 1968

Foreword

Anyone who attempts to trace the development of the teaching of English as a foreign language in the United States is struck by two distinguishing features: first, in its beginnings, it involved only small numbers of foreign students, usually on the adult college level; and second, it was inextricably intertwined with the field of linguistics.

Dr. Mary Finocchiaro has long been a leader in the field of language teaching in general, and in English as a second language in particular. Even before the National Defense Education Act of 1958, she had published *Teaching English as a Second Language,* which, though useful in teaching students of any age, was designed primarily for teachers of English on the elementary and secondary school levels. Yet it was not until December 1963 that the Foreign Language Institutes Section of the NDEA was amended to include the words "English to speakers of other languages." In October 1964, Congress repealed that section and enacted an entirely new institutes title (Title XI) in its stead. Thus federal support was further extended to English as a second language. The federal government had given official recognition to the fact that English is not the mother tongue of a growing number of students in elementary and secondary schools, and that this lack of competence was creating major social and economic problems for the nation as a whole.

The NDEA Institute Program was primarily a *domestic* program, designed to improve instruction in the United States —in *American* elementary and secondary schools. The pendulum of governmental activities seemed to have swung entirely in the opposite direction. The problem of teaching English as a second language, which had been so critical abroad and which concerned *international* educational programs and *foreign* students, had come home to roost—and with a vengeance. The demand for properly trained teachers of English as a second language had become acute.

Leaders in the field had long advocated courses in the structure of English, introductory linguistics, and methods and materials for teaching English as a second language as the minimum ingredients for teacher training programs. Accordingly, such courses were offered in nearly all the NDEA English-as-a-foreign-language institutes and in many of the institutes for teaching English and for disadvantaged youth.

There is a desperate need for textbooks and reference manuals for teacher training. Dr. Finocchiaro anticipated the need for such books long ago and produced an excellent one. But the indefatigable Dr. Finocchiaro has kept abreast of theoretical and practical developments in the past decade. We are fortunate indeed that she has decided to share her wisdom and experience with us in this new and revised edition. It should prove a welcome addition to the libraries of teachers of English as a second language—as well as to teachers of the disadvantaged—at all levels of instruction. It is linguistically sophisticated and pedagogically sound. It combines theory and practice, content and method.

At the 17th Annual Conference of the National Association for Foreign Student Affairs in April 1965, I introduced Dr. Finocchiaro as a "vivacious, dynamic, warm human being . . . one of those rare creatures for which there is such a dire need in our society today—a master teacher, a scholar-administrator and administrator-scholar." All these attributes are reflected in this revised edition of her book.

JAMES E. ALATIS
Associate Dean
School of Languages and
Linguistics
Georgetown University

Preface

Dear Colleagues,

So much has happened in the field of language teaching and learning since this book was first published in 1958 that the publishers and I have felt a responsibility to incorporate the many current insights and research findings in a completely revised edition.

The past ten years have seen an increased awareness that our primary concern is teaching *people* rather than teaching subject matter. We recognize that each individual is unique and that many forces determine the pace and rate of his learning or, indeed, whether learning will take place at all.

There is growing concern, too, about the loss to the nation when speakers of other languages, because of their inability to function in the English language, do not reach their full potential and do not avail themselves of the possibilities for upward social mobility which the country offers. Moreover, it is now generally recognized that in the past we have not utilized sufficiently the gift of other tongues which speakers of other languages can offer to English-speaking members of the community and which could be used to great advantage in meeting national and international responsibilities.

With regard to language learning, there have been found new ways of describing the English language, of comparing it with other languages, of helping to develop communication skills—all knowledges that the teacher will bring to bear in teaching speakers of other languages.

In addition, there have been published many studies of regional dialects within English-speaking countries and of the differences that exist between standard and nonstandard English. Research points to the fact that numerous principles, methods, and techniques which have been used successfully in teaching English as a second language can be applied effectively in the teaching of a *second dialect* to native English speakers. It is hoped, therefore, that persons concerned with this educational problem will also find something of value in the following pages.

Finally, the last decade has witnessed an explosion of technological knowledge resulting in the more widespread use of audio-visual materials and equipment of all kinds. These should become familiar to teachers of speakers of other languages, since their skillful use will enhance the learner's prospects for success.

This volume still remains a practical textbook born of my many years of experience in classrooms as a teacher and supervisor of programs for speakers of other languages and other dialects both in the United States and abroad. It is the result of soul-searching questioning of my own that arose when I realized that pupils were making little or no progress toward learning English even though teaching was based on a prescribed "system" or "method." It is the result, too, of seeking answers in cooperation with teachers and administrators in my courses at universities and at language seminars in the United States and abroad.

This book is a synthesis of principles and procedures that have worked in actual practice for me and for many others. As advocated by educators and linguists, these have been subjected to the test of practicability with literate and illiterate students ranging in age from four to eighty, in both English-speaking and non-English-speaking communities.

Many excellent books have appeared in the United States and abroad on the subject of teaching English as a second language. Some have been concerned primarily with descriptions of English, some with the teaching of English at various levels and in various situations, and some with the advantages and disadvantages of using certain methods. If this book has any merit, it lies in the fact that it brings together in nontechnical terms applicable theories in general education, in foreign language teaching, and in the teaching of English, so that teachers will recognize many points of similarity within them and their inherent interrelationship. It aims to help teachers or language specialists make the transition from linguistic and educational theory to actual teaching practice, whether the school situation is one in which 1) one specialist teacher is responsible for the teaching of the pronunciation, the structure, the vocabulary, and the cultural aspects of English to groups of language learners; 2) specialists in different areas are responsible for the teaching of one or more phases of language and culture; 3) the regular teacher is responsible for developing language skills as well as knowledge in all curriculum areas in the language learners in classrooms which also include native speakers of English. As the reader will note in Unit III, this book also stresses that while the teaching of English to speakers of other languages is a discrete discipline, it embodies all the principles of good teaching.

Since I felt that the teaching of English could not be discussed apart from many other related factors in the school and the community, the base of this book has been broadened to include topics not usually found in a book concerned with the teaching of English as a second language. However, the treatment of important facets of the educational program, such as the role of the supervisor or school-community relations, is by no means exhaustive. It is suggested that further reading be done on subjects of personal interest or responsibility.

Having been myself a learner of English as a second language and, later, as teacher and administrator, having viewed with frustration and some despair the well-meaning but often futile efforts of my colleagues to teach English as a second language, I sincerely hope that some of the approaches and insights suggested in these pages will enable teachers to accelerate the personal-social integration of newcomers into the mainstream of the English-speaking society. Such integration can only profit both the newcomers and the society in which they have chosen to create a new home and a new life.

M.F.

UNIT I

PLANNING FOR LANGUAGE TEACHING AND LEARNING

CHAPTER 1

Guidelines for Language Teaching and Learning

Educators are well aware of the fact that no two programs for teaching English to speakers of other languages will ever parallel each other in all respects. They will differ from country to country, from community to community, from school to school, and from teacher to teacher. The general objectives sought may bear some similarity, the outcomes of the programs may be equally as good, but the routes by which these outcomes are reached will vary appreciably.

The reasons for the differences are varied and many. Although we all recognize that there are inherent differences in learners, in teachers, and in schools which will bring about modifications in the program, perhaps the fundamental cause for the diversity may be found in the fact that there is often no clear-cut agreement as to "What are we trying to teach?" and "Is what we are trying to teach attainable in the *time* available, with *these students,* in *this community?*"

OBJECTIVES

Of primary consideration, therefore, is the necessity for a clear definition of basic objectives. No intelligent discussion of procedure and materials is possible unless there is some agreement as to the outcomes desired or attainable. Any generaliza-

3

tion made here or anywhere as to "the most effective way" or "the most desirable method" would have to be studied and modified in terms of the language goals we are seeking and in the light of other factors related to the learners themselves.

The problem of determining objectives of language teaching has been the subject of innumerable studies. For years, most authorities favored the reading objective as the ultimate goal, contending that it was the most easily obtainable in language programs (as they were organized) and that it allowed for more advanced, independent study without the help of a teacher or of additional courses. The residual nature of the reading skill was emphasized. In most such programs, the study of other language skills such as understanding and speaking was considered subsidiary to the attainment of reading ability. The stress was placed on the wide reading of graded materials.

Today, research results in linguistics and psychology, as well as empirical observation of learning situations, point to the overwhelming necessity for developing the learners' understanding and speaking skills *before* introducing them to reading and writing. Not only are these competencies more self-motivating to the learner as he recognizes their usefulness in his everyday world but they will later contribute to and facilitate his ability to read and write as the teacher emphasizes the correspondences between the oral and the graphic symbols.

Some confusion still exists, however, in discussions of objectives because of the manner in which terms such as "mastery," "automatic control," and "bilingualism" have sometimes been used or misinterpreted.

The term "mastery," when used with relation to objectives in language teaching, brings us to a well-nigh unanswerable question: "When does a person know a second language or when can one say that a person has mastered a language?"

Various definitions have been advanced by authorities in the field. Most are in agreement about the importance of knowing the sound system (or the phonology) of the language, of using appropriate words and correct grammatical structures habitually in speaking and in writing, and of being able to read with facility.*

For practical purposes, however, what can be considered mastery? Can any of us say, for example, that we have mastered English? Are there not words and expressions in special fields of interest which are completely incomprehensible to us? By the same token, when may we say that our students have mastered a second language? Should not our definition depend upon such matters as the use the students will want to or have to make of the language and the varying language standards of people with whom they will have to communicate?

There is growing recognition in the field of language teaching that not all language learners will have the capacity or the need to become expert users of English. The *functional* use to which they will need to put the English they are learning should be considered in planning a program. This does *not* imply that we will lower our expectations, but it does mean that we will be aware that while some of our learners may become great writers, others will learn only enough to function satisfactorily in school and to participate meaningfully as members of their communities. Individual differences with relation to the mastery of English will exist in language learners as they do in native English speakers.

Automatic control, that is, the ability to use *habitually* a correct sound, a word form or word order, will be attained, if at all, at varying rates by individuals. For example, while some

* Charles C. Fries, *Teaching and Learning English as a Foreign Language* (Ann Arbor, University of Michigan Press, 1948): "A person has 'learned' a foreign language when he has thus first, within a limited vocabulary, mastered the sound system (that is, when he can understand the stream of speech and achieve an understandable production of it) and has, second, made the structural devices (that is, the basic arrangement of utterances) matters of automatic habit" (p. 3).

Peter Hagboldt, *Language Learning* (Chicago, The University of Chicago Press, 1935): "We have a mastery of language when our comprehension by ear is spontaneous, our reading effortless and fluent, our use of words, idioms, and sentences in speech and writing habitual and skillful" (p. 2).

students will need two years to learn to pronounce the *he* and *she* forms of the simple present of verbs with a sound of (s), others may learn to do so within two weeks.

Automatic control is a result we hope to achieve *after* intensive and extensive practice. In the meantime, we should be gratified by reasonable progress—with daily, sometimes nearly imperceptible progress. Nor should we wait until pupils have "perfected," "mastered," or attained "automatic control" of one feature of language before proceeding to another. Not only would boredom result, but also waiting is often unnecessary. Since language learning is cumulative, previously taught language items are gradually shaped toward the "native" English standard as they are reviewed and used in conjunction with other language items that are constantly being introduced.

And now, a few words about "bilingualism"—ideally, the ability of a person to use his native language and a second language interchangeably in all circumstances. Unless the study of a second language is begun in early childhood and unless both languages are practiced within the same areas of experience, true bilingualism will be difficult to achieve. Students who may have little or no occasion to use English "school" vocabulary at home will not learn it in their native tongue. This would be equally true in the reverse circumstances. It is not likely that students would learn the English vocabulary related to certain aspects of their native culture unless the school planned special activities in which this would be taught. Research has demonstrated that real bilingualism is achieved by relatively few second-language learners.

Closely related to this is the subject of "bilingual education." Four current trends are noteworthy and warrant attentive consideration by educators everywhere: (1) The effort to make non-English speakers literate in their native tongue through school *language* programs; (2) The desire to teach pupils to read in their native tongue *before* teaching them to read in English; (3) The teaching of curriculum areas such as science, social studies and mathematics in the native tongue so that non-

English-speaking pupils—upon entering the mainstream of the school—will not lag behind their age peers; (4) The increasing attention to the teaching of foreign languages to English speakers (with emphasis on the language spoken by the non-English speakers in the community) so that early communication between the groups will be possible.

Controlled experimentation is needed, however, particularly with reference to the first three trends noted above. Recurring questions throughout this text which are applicable here and which need to be answered include: (1) How old are the learners we are talking about? (2) What proportion of students in the school and in the community are non-English-speaking? (3) How many native languages are involved? (4) Does the native language have a written language? (5) What proportion of time will be spent on the development of the native language and on the development of English? (6) Should the same curriculum areas be taught *concurrently* in the native language and in English (adapted, naturally, to the level of the learners' ability) or should there be a time lapse between the knowledge given in the native language and similar knowledge given in English? If so, how long should the English component be deferred?

Projects should not be delayed pending the results of research. Anything which fosters a positive self-image in a learner while increasing his linguistic competency so that he can function in the school and in the community can only redound to the benefit of the learner, the school, and society.

While it is obvious that we still have much to learn in relation to the ways in which human beings learn languages, there is nonetheless general agreement on certain fundamental principles and objectives. Since the procedures, practices, and materials in this book are predicated on these principles and on the results of their application in the classroom, a number of them are stated here.

GUIDING PRINCIPLES IN FORMULATING OBJECTIVES

1. The aim of the English-teaching program should be to develop in the learner the four basic aspects of communication —understanding, speaking, reading, and writing—within the social and cultural situations normal to persons of his age level.

2. Long-range objectives should include a) the *gradual* perfecting or shaping of the language skills needed for everyday communication and for the learning of other curriculum areas; and b) the development of an increasing insight into the culture of the English-speaking community, including an appreciation of its art, music, and literature.

3. The teacher's objectives at any learning level should be to develop in the pupil (in consonance with his age, of course) :

   a. the increasing ability to understand a native speaker of English in any situation
   b. the progressive ability to sustain a conversation with native English speakers
   c. the progressive ability to read any material in English with comprehension, ease, and enjoyment
   d. the progressive ability to write correctly, functionally, and creatively in English

4. These four fundamental aspects of the language program should be developed concurrently, in an integrative reinforcing manner *after an initial* listening-speaking period.

5. Formal reading from textbooks is generally deferred for a *flexible* period of time, depending on such matters as the *age* and *literacy* of the pupils in their native tongue and the duration of the program.

6. Although the ultimate goal of language teaching is the integration of all the communication skills, each skill should be practiced separately.

7. Increased ability in any language skill will be in direct proportion to the amount of meaningful practice given in that skill.

8. Of vital importance in communication—understanding, speaking, reading, and writing—are a knowledge of, and a facility with, the pronunciation and intonation patterns of English.

9. The cultural context in which the language is used is also of fundamental importance for full understanding. Often comprehension of material heard will depend upon the learner's anticipating or supplementing what is being said. Reading comprehension is increased by knowledge of sociocultural allusions or implications in the material.

10. The cultural and social situations in which features of language are normally used should be clarified and taught concomitantly with the feature of language. This is best done by simulating real life, everyday situations in the classroom, thus allowing students to practice language in its cultural context.

11. The degree of mastery sought or obtained in a language is always relative. Assuming that the stream of speech in the second language is intelligible, standards of "mastery" will vary in accordance with factors other than the knowledge of a certain number of words, of structures, or of a fixed number of sociocultural patterns. The philosophy and objectives of the program as set by the school and community will influence the degree of mastery sought. The capacity of the students will determine to a great extent the level of achievement attained.

12. English should be presented and practiced in the following sequence: listening with understanding, speaking, reading, and writing.

13. Features of pronunciation should be practiced with the language items that are being taught. They should not generally be practiced with words or sentences that have little or no immediate utility for pupils.

14. Any program, regardless of duration or scope, should aim at giving pupils the knowledge, skills, and attitudes which will prepare them for further study.

15. English should be taught not only as a vehicle for school learning but also for personal expression and self-realization.

16. Learners should be made continuously aware through planned activities that they can use English to express the same needs, desires, ideas, and frustrations they voice in their native tongue.

17. Since our learners speak another language, they already appreciate the function of language in their everyday life. They should be engaged in numerous shared activities which will not only aid them in grasping meanings and limitations of meaning in the new language but will also encourage and facilitate its use.

18. Except for very young children, language is *not* learned merely by imitation and repetition. Specific guidance in every facet of language cognition, imitation, reception, and production will be needed for most learners.

19. Special efforts should be made through its reentry and review to ensure consolidation and integration of previously taught material on which the new material being introduced is based.

20. It is imperative that speakers of other languages feel that English is being *added* to their language skills and *not* that it is intended to replace their native tongue.

We will have occasion to examine each of the principles above in greater detail.

FACTORS AFFECTING THE PROGRAM

Even after consensus has been reached about objectives and principles, many specific factors in the teaching situation will determine the program which will evolve. These factors reside within the pupils themselves, the teachers, the school, and the community. The elements within each of these supposedly disparate entities will together influence the formulation and implementation of the instructional program in the classroom.

Let us examine a number of these factors briefly, noting as we proceed some of the many implications each may hold for actual teaching practice.

The Language of the Community

Where English is taught in an English-speaking community or country, students will naturally have many opportunities for direct contact with the language outside the classroom. Community resources will be utilized to give students an added store of experiences. The language taught in the classroom will acquire increasing meaning since it will have an immediate functional application outside the school. Students can be expected to learn some language incidentally by speaking with their peers, reading signs, listening to conversations on buses and on the radio, going to movies, watching television, and attending classes or going to places where English is the medium of communication.

The pace of learning will vary of necessity in the English-speaking situation since the teacher of English will undoubtedly feel impelled to prepare his pupils for immediate participation in the full school and community life. The structural items, vocabulary, and concepts in all curriculum areas needed by the learner at his age or grade level or both will be woven into the English lessons as quickly as feasible. The focus on the basic features of English as well as on the language items needed in the curriculum areas will enable the learner to experience success in the school program of his age peers.

On the other hand, where English is not the predominant native tongue of the community, the teacher will have to create an intensive English-speaking environment in the short time his class is in session. He will have to organize many practice activities to furnish the listening, speaking, and reading opportunities which will not be found outside the classroom. He will have to provide for frequent reviews to counteract the pupils' natural tendency to forget the language unless, as is true in any other skill, it is practiced regularly in a variety of situations.

The Pupil

The factors within the pupil are many and varied. His native language is of fundamental importance. Whereas native speakers of languages such as French, Spanish, or Italian find similar alphabets and cognate words to facilitate learning, speakers of some other languages will have to learn new alphabets and writing systems and will find fewer similarities in vocabulary items.

Depending on his age (the younger the pupil, the less ingrained will be his native language habits), the pupil will experience conflict and difficulty in hearing English sounds; in moving his mouth muscles in ways which will produce these sounds; in pronouncing certain word endings; or in placing words in phrases or sentences in the order required by the English language system. Since each language has its own system, each will cause different kinds of difficulties. On page 371 will be found a brief chart indicating the major points of difficulty in pronunciation which students of different language backgrounds may experience. An awareness of the probable points of interference will enable the teacher to anticipate problems as he presents certain features of the English language and to plan techniques and materials for helping to overcome them.

Intrinsic motivation comes to mind when discussing the major language of the community where English is taught, since it may be assumed that most learners of English in a predominantly English-speaking situation will feel a greater urgency for acquiring the language of the community. Where this strong intrinsic motivation is lacking, the teacher will have to stimulate learning through varied appeals and approaches. The kind of motivation or stimulus which will be effective will hinge strongly on the pupil's age. Whereas play activities may be desirable with younger pupils, older pupils may want to plunge immediately into reading matter which is close to their social or vocational interest. Approach, development, materials of instruction, and language habits to be inculcated or changed will vary depending on the pupil's age, his level of literacy, and his social maturity.

The pupil's attitude and that of his parents toward English speakers is of paramount importance in determining motivation. Research indicates that prejudice or active dislike diminishes motivation and interferes with learning. While this is true of students of all ages, it is even more so in cases of older students who ascribe their lack of academic success to their inability to speak or read English and thus to compete on an equal basis with native English-speaking classmates.

This feeling is reinforced in schools where pupils are not permitted to hear, speak, or study their native tongue because of the school's zealousness in having the pupils use English. The fact that their native tongue seems to be avoided may make the pupils feel that it has little status. Since they are not yet comfortable or fluent in English and are ashamed of their native language, they find themselves in a temporary no man's land. This feeling, termed "anomie," affects their entire attitude. In addition, some parents may resent the greater language knowledge of their children—which allows them to participate in activities from which they, as non-English-speaking adults, are excluded.

Many interesting studies by Fishman, Herman, and Lambert* underscore the crucial role of attitudes in learning languages. Herman's study conducted in Israel identifies five steps through which the speaker of other languages proceeds in learning the language which he has to use in his new environment: anticipation, initial conformity, discouragement, crisis (fear of losing one's personality), and, finally, adjustment and integration.

The pupil's literacy in his native language will affect teaching techniques considerably. If the pupil is illiterate, is below the age of eight or nine, and is placed in a group where *all* pupils need help in building experiential concepts, the problem is generally not one of great magnitude. If, on the other hand, he is illiterate, about fourteen years old, and is placed with a group of English-speaking pupils who have had the advantages

* J. Fishman, "Bilingualism, Intelligence and Language Learning," *Modern Language Journal,* April, 1965, pp. 227–237; S. Herman, "Explorations in the Social Psychology of Language Choice," *Human Relations,* No. 14, 1961, pp. 149–164; W. Lambert, "Psychological Aspects to the Study of Language," *Modern Language Journal,* 47, 1963, pp. 51–62, 114–121.

of schooling, the problem assumes tremendous proportions. Unless the teacher is extremely skillful and unless the school has organized special programs for this pupil, he will not have the opportunity to acquire the concepts, knowledge, and skills necessary for effective participation in school and community life and for gainful employment.

The students' learning potential will also play a leading role in determining the content of each lesson, the review needed, the type of approach used, the variety of graded materials to be prepared, and the outcomes that may be expected.

Whether English is a second language or one of several languages that the student has studied should also be considered. If the foreign languages are similar and have been studied within a short period of each other, there may be danger of confusion in such matters as vocabulary or verb endings. On the other hand, knowledge of several similar languages may aid the pupils in making analogies and in grasping generalizations more quickly.

We shall not go into detail about the more obvious factors within the pupils such as socioeconomic level, interests outside school, parent encouragement, or out-of-class time devoted to study. These influence the teaching of any area or discipline.

The Teacher

The teacher is the most important single element in any teaching situation. It has been frequently said: "There are no good or bad methods; there are only good or bad teachers."

The personality of the teacher coupled with his attitude towards his pupils, his colleagues, his supervisors, and his work will determine the extent to which any program, no matter how well formulated, will be carried out. Naturally, the general teaching skill of the instructor, his special training in the field of language teaching, and his linguistic ability will also affect the teaching-learning situation. But, whereas it may be more difficult to modify personality and attitude, teaching skills and language ability *can be acquired*. Any teacher is capable of teaching English as a second language, particularly at the beginning level, provided he is willing to devote some time to attentive reading in the fields of anthropology, sociology, psychology and linguistics, to taking pertinent courses, to attending lectures, and to observing more experienced teachers so that he will master not only the essential teaching techniques but also the fundamental features of the English language—its sound system and its structure.

Other more specialized studies by the teacher are also desirable. For example, the teacher who himself is not a speaker of his pupils' language should allocate time to study the broad characteristics of that language. He should familiarize himself with such matters as word order, special pronunciation and intonation features, and inflection (of noun and verb endings, for example) in order to: 1) emphasize *similar* or *contrasting* elements in *both* languages in his teaching, 2) prepare appropriate approaches and materials based on these similarities or contrasts, and 3) appreciate the difficulties the students face.

Although a functional knowledge of the students' language is not essential to teach English effectively, the instructor who knows the language may utilize this special knowledge in establishing rapport, in making wide use of cognates (if the language lends itself to such a possibility), in clarifying concepts, in broadening the vocabulary base of discussion, in giving grammatical explanations to older students, and in knitting the school and community closer together. *All* teachers of beginners will find it desirable to learn the following six words in their students' native tongue: Look, Listen, Repeat, Say, Ask, Answer.

We repeat, however, that knowledge of the students' native tongue is an *added* asset. Skill in teaching, the willingness to prepare a wealth of instructional material, a knowledge of the broad characteristics of the pupils' language and of English structure, awareness of cultural similarities and differences, and a warm, friendly attitude will more than counterbalance the lack of knowledge of the students' native tongue.

The School

The school or center in which the English language is taught will also affect the instructional program. Of primary consideration is the philosophy of the supervisory staff. If the objectives, the curriculum, and the evaluative procedures are the result of *joint* supervisor-teacher thinking and planning, the attitude of cooperation will be reflected in the classroom instructional program. The teacher who feels secure in the understanding and cooperation of the supervisor will experiment with new practices, will modify the curriculum, will feel free to develop one facet of a topic more thoroughly because of pupil interest, and will prepare special instructional materials.

This statement *does not* imply that supervisor-initiated practices such as observations, conferences, reports to teachers containing recommendations for improvement are not valuable or essential. All teachers, the beginners and the more experienced, welcome the evaluation of supervisors whose broader experience and more extensive training may enable them to note the effectiveness of teaching procedures and to make constructive suggestions. The statement *does* mean that the curriculum, teaching techniques, and evaluative procedures cannot be arbitrarily imposed from above. Teachers who are more familiar with the needs and interests of their pupils should be free to suggest, to modify, and to adapt the curriculum in the light of this more intimate knowledge of their pupils.

School classification and organizational practices will definitely influence classroom proceedings. Because of these practices, the teacher may find it necessary to change the number and size of his groups often, to prepare materials for varying ability levels, and to modify his teaching practices in numerous ways. This aspect of school management as it impinges on the classroom situation will be discussed more fully later.

The school-wide program, including, as it may, assemblies, clubs, guidance facilities, and other areas of study, will influence the English class program. A well-rounded school program, in which pupils who are learning English can participate, will permit the teacher to broaden the experiential base of learning. He will be enabled to draw from the activities of the school to motivate and develop language skills. The teacher will not find it necessary to create vicarious situations constantly since real, functional activities will exist all around him.

The physical plant itself (auditorium, club rooms, cafeteria, language laboratory, nature-science room, gymnasium, and storage space for supplies) may also assume a certain importance. The skillful teacher, however, will know how to use the assets and overcome any serious deficiencies in this quarter.

The amount of money available for school equipment and supplies will also force the teacher to modify or to curtail certain teaching activities. A series of film strips to motivate the lesson, sets of books at various reading levels, or a tape recorder to evaluate pupils' progress, would undoubtedly permit a more varied approach. However, *none of these educational aids is essential in teaching.* As a famous educator once said, "All that is needed to teach is a teacher, a pupil, and a log."

The Community

The community in which the school is located cannot be ignored in any discussion of the forces which affect the curriculum of a school or class. In addition to the implications inherent in the language spoken in the community, other factors must be taken into consideration. The socioeconomic level of the community very often influences the aspirations of parents and students and determines the amount of pressure which parents may place on school authorities to make changes in the curriculum, to buy materials, and to organize co-curricular programs.

If there exists only a small language island of non-English-speaking persons, the composition and the size of the English-speaking community may affect teaching practices. A recent study showed that where non-English-speaking pupils were in the minority in an English-speaking community of high socio-economic level, they learned English much more quickly, since

English was the language of the stores, of the movies, and of all other community agencies. It must be noted, however, that some English-speaking parents in this type of community may feel that their children may be handicapped because the instructor will have to devote time to teaching English to a small non-English-speaking group in his room.

On the other hand, where the non-English speakers are the majority group in a lower socioeconomic community, and where the younger English-speaking pupils may have poor experiential and language backgrounds, the instructor may not have to divide the class into small groups. *All* pupils in the class will have to be given a rich background of experiences to "ready" them for language activities.

Unfortunately, pupils in this environment may have little opportunity to practice English outside the classroom; nor do many of the working parents, sometimes linguistically handicapped themselves, encourage the use of English either in the home or on the outside. Let us not forget, however, the importance of other factors that have been mentioned in relation to pupils—namely motivation, age, maturity, and native ability, which can and do offset environmental influences. Above all, let us not forget the role of the interested, sympathetic, and skillful teacher who will help pupils overcome initial handicaps.

The discussion of factors affecting teaching and learning has been kept brief deliberately. The aim of this book is not to point up problems but rather to suggest positive ways to teachers and supervisors of leveling initial handicaps and of organizing effective English programs.

FUNDAMENTAL NEEDS OF SCHOOLS

Certain needs with relation to schools and teachers are basic. We refer to the need for ensuring proper classification and placement of pupils; for setting up fundamental, attainable objectives; for preparing materials; for developing specific techniques to teach language skills; and for overcoming problems in teaching such as that of the older pupil with little or no schooling.

Reception and Placement of Pupils

Let us assume that we are dealing with a situation in which English is the native tongue of the community and where pupils intend to remain in the community as active, participating members.

How can we help these pupils in our schools?

We can *welcome* them cordially

We can *place* them in specially organized classes

1. with pupils

   a. who also need to learn English as a second language
   b. who are nearest their age group
   c. who are at similar stages of language learning
   d. who have been prepared to accept them

2. with teachers

   a. who are friendly, understanding, and accepting
   b. who have a knowledge of the native cultural and language patterns of their pupils
   c. who make use of this knowledge in curriculum planning
   d. who know the system of English and methods of teaching it to language learners

We can *orient* them to the school and to the community by means of

1. trips and excursions
2. simple talks by resource people (specialists in various fields) in their native tongue where feasible
3. judicious use of audio-visual aids
4. graded instructional materials

5. materials containing information about community resources

We can *provide* for their immediate participation with native English-speaking pupils in subject areas and in activities where English language competency is not absolutely necessary. For example, in

1. assemblies
2. shops
3. clubs, recreation periods, and other co-curricular activities
4. art, music, and physical education lessons

We can *develop* their ability to communicate with others by giving them

1. increasing control of the essential features of the pronunciation and grammar systems of English
2. practice in sentence patterns which contain the vocabulary items of everyday situations
3. a functional vocabulary that they can use *immediately* in the school and in their home and community and that will enable them to function in the social and cultural situations of the English-speaking community
4. experiences in numerous activities in which they participate as listeners and/or speakers

We can *prepare* them for educational and vocational opportunities available to them by giving them

1. basic concepts and vocabulary in all needed curriculum areas
2. knowledge and skills required for the world of work
3. educational and social guidance

We can *give* them status by

1. developing pride in their cultural heritage (including their language)
2. providing instructional materials (suitable to their achievement and maturity levels) which will ensure success

3. bringing about a mutual accepting relationship between them and other community members (native English speakers or others)
4. utilizing and providing a setting for their creative abilities in the school and in the community.

Organization of Classes

In English-speaking countries and in bilingual areas where there are large numbers of pupils who need to learn English as a second language, various patterns of organization are emerging. In one large section of the United States, for example, such pupils are placed in a pre-first grade until they have acquired basic oral skills, a vocabulary of several hundred words, and a large number of concepts. In another area outside the continental United States, all pupils learn English as a second language from the first grade.

In other school districts, pupils are placed with their age peers whether or not they have had previous schooling. In some schools in these areas where large numbers of pupils warrant their formation, pupils are placed in homogeneous classes with other pupils (of varying ethnic backgrounds) who need to learn English as a second language. They remain in such a class, commonly called a reception or orientation class, for a flexible length of time, that is, until they are considered ready (by tests and other evaluative techniques) to enter the regular stream of the school.

In another type of organizational pattern, pupils are placed in regular classes and either assigned a bilingual assistant, or "buddy," or taken out of the regular class for one or two hours a day for special English instruction. In still another, pupils are programed for English for half the school day and receive instruction in their native language for the other half.

With adolescents and young adults, problems of programing are even more complex. With beginners in English, illiterates (in the native tongue) may be placed in one group, while literates may be placed in another. There may be classes at the intermediate or advanced level for those who know some English.

A problem to be considered with relation to organization is that pupils in most schools are usually permitted to register at any time during the semester. This places on the teacher the obligation to provide individual and group teaching with specially prepared materials which will enable these newcomers to "catch up" with the other class members so that they can participate in regular class activities as quickly as possible.

The initial placement of pupils is one of the thorniest problems faced by schools. A fourteen-year-old adolescent who has never been to school and who is illiterate in his native tongue is generally doomed to failure if he is placed in classes with his age peers. On the other hand, he cannot be placed in the first grade.

Placing children at all stages of literacy in their native tongue or in English in regular classes creates numerous problems for teachers who are forced to prepare differentiating activities for these pupils as well as integrative activities in which the language learners could participate with the entire class. If the teacher takes too much time from teaching the whole class in order to help the newcomers, many parents will object to the shortened program for their children. Teacher aides (sometimes called "paraprofessionals"), "buddies," or pupil assistants can be trained for certain chores but this is not always a satisfactory solution. Parents feel that their children are missing valuable instruction if they help newcomers during their music, art, or physical education periods. By the same token, newcomers feel they are being punished when they have to learn English during recreation periods or during periods in which their lack of knowledge of English does not place them at a total disadvantage.

There are other problems too. If the teacher does spend a half-hour with newcomers during the day, what do the latter do for the other three or four hours (assuming they participate in music, art and physical education activities for part of the day)? If students are placed in special classes for a protracted period of time without *specially trained teachers,* a *specially prepared curriculum,* and a *continuous evaluation* program, might not the charge of "segregated" instruction justly be leveled against the school? If students are illiterate in their native tongue and about fourteen or fifteen, can educators in all conscience feel they can ever really enter the regular school stream without preparation in special programs?

One answer to this serious, persistent problem is to place the newcomers—those above the ages of eight or nine—in *special* classes with *experienced, trained* teachers, with *special intensive programs* in English and in their native tongue, with safeguards for the children in terms of *frequent evaluation* which indicates when they are "ready" to join the regular school track. Three points are worthy of mention: (1) The students should participate in all school-wide activities and in school periods where a knowledge of English is not of paramount importance. (2) *All* the teachers in the schools should be oriented and encouraged to accept these language learners as quickly as possible even though they still make "errors" in English. (3) Parents of newcomers as well as older children who would understand its advantages must be reassured that such placement is for a flexible period of time and that intensive work in English leading to academic and vocational success should not be mistaken for "segregation."

Numerous communities are experimenting with various placement and teaching patterns. In some areas of Texas, for example, newcomers are placed in a special preschool program of forty days with intensive English instruction for two hours a day. In some California counties, steps are being taken to give speakers of other languages two years of special assistance in English. In others, bilingual programs have been organized. In Miami, bilingual schools enable the younger children to learn the same curriculum content in English and in Spanish during the school day. In New York, there are special programs in science and mathematics in Spanish and English.

The national "Head Start" program for young children holds promise for developing concepts and related vocabulary in young preschool children. Other nationwide efforts include the placement of school-age speakers of other languages in non-graded classes where various levels of English curriculum are provided without regard to age or grade level. Pupils move to the next higher curriculum level on the basis of performance alone.

Training of Teachers

Regardless of the organizational scheme, the teacher will find wide variations in ability, in interests, and in ages among his pupils. It is obvious that materials will have to be adapted and that teachers will have to be specially trained to meet these wide ranges in pupils' backgrounds. The following competencies are recommended for teachers who wish to become skilled in the teaching of English as a second language. Teachers need:

1. To gain insight into the linguistic and cultural backgrounds of their pupils as a bridge to understanding and acceptance.

2. To study the educational and cultural backgrounds of their students as a springboard for curriculum planning.

3. To gain conscious familiarity with the features of the English sound, grammar, vocabulary, and cultural systems.

4. To learn methods of teaching English as a second language or a second dialect.

5. To learn how to embody principles and/or procedures of related disciplines (linguistics, psychology, sociology, and anthropology) in the teaching of English to speakers of other languages.

6. To understand the dynamics and techniques of grouping. These are important not only in providing for wide ranges in ability level, but also for meeting a situation which is common. We refer to the fact that teachers find themselves compelled to provide a program in English and in school-community orienta-

tion to the pupils whose native language is not English while teaching English-speaking pupils (in the same classroom) subject areas such as mathematics, social studies, science, and language arts.

7. To learn how to utilize and/or develop instructional materials in harmony with program objectives and students' goals and learning problems.

8. To learn how to evaluate pupil progress for possible corrective teaching, for regrouping in the class, or for placement in another class.

9. To provide a classroom environment conducive to successful learning and to ego enhancement.

Preparation of Materials

The following materials, prepared by a teacher alone or preferably by a committee of teachers, are necessary for an effective educational program:

1. *Materials for teaching and reinforcing pronunciation, sentence patterns and vocabulary.* Wherever possible, these should be based on a knowledge of the points of similarity and contrast in the English language and in the native language of the pupils. If no scientific research study exists, a curriculum committee in the school can prepare materials after analyzing the language difficulties which pupils seem to encounter in using structural patterns or in imitating the teacher's speech. A bilingual person in the community or a bilingual teacher may be asked to help in the preparation of the materials by indicating the structures in his language which differ from English and which may be at the root of the pupils' difficulties.

Since no two languages differ from English in identical respects, ideally certain materials for each ethnic group should be specifically designed to furnish language practice to that ethnic group in the aspects of language in which practice is needed. This is often impossible. It will therefore be found desirable to prepare materials which emphasize the important features of English structure and pronunciation with language items selected from among those words which have the greatest immediate utility for pupils, which are useful in more than one communication situation, and which are suitable to their age and interest level.

2. *Orientation materials to be used in orientation classes, in special English classes, and in regular classes* (or self-contained classrooms as they are sometimes called). This material should include worksheets, drills, and where feasible reading selections with self-checking devices which can be used by students themselves or with a teacher or student assistant. The center of interest in these materials should be the sociocultural patterns or experiences of the English-speaking community.

3. *Materials with the curriculum areas as a nucleus* to be used by the special teacher of English, the regular class teacher, or by a teacher or student assistant, in mathematics, social studies, science, language arts, etc. The activities provided should be in the form of simple exercises based on the units of work in the regular school curriculum. After the initial orientation period, when pupils have acquired some language competency, the regular teacher, for example, may present a unit topic to the entire class, making provision through these materials for exercises on the language level of the non-English group.

4. *Materials for the illiterate student;* for example, tapes, records for listening reinforcement, letters, words, and sentences to be traced.

5. *Simple audio-visual aids* such as flat pictures and duplicated materials.

All the materials should be on appropriate levels of reading ability and *social maturity,* and should include the vocabulary, the sentence patterns, and concepts from as many curriculum areas as possible. Thus, pupils will be better equipped to participate now and in the future in a school program where all classes are conducted in the English language.

Although the problems outlined above will not be found to

the same extent in all communities, teachers of English anywhere will still have to provide for the wide range of individual differences found in any classroom in any subject area. Techniques of grouping, varied instructional materials such as those described above, multiple sensory appeals in presentations, and systematic evaluation techniques to diagnose difficulties and determine progress will be needed by all teachers of English as a second language.

Formulation of Goals

The need for setting up attainable objectives is imperative and should precede any other step. Supervisors or directors, working with interested community members and teachers, must first determine the long-term goals that are desired and that can be attained. Realistic over-all goals will depend upon numerous related considerations in addition to the factors cited above:

1. The number of months or years the program or course will run. (Certainly, the short-term and long-term objectives will differ in a one-year program that is intended for adolescents and one for young children which may be of six or eight years duration.)

2. The number of hours a day for each English-as-a-second-language session.

3. The availability of trained teachers.

4. The use to be made of other native English speakers (buddies, teacher aides, or informants; that is, speakers of the pupils' native tongue) or of language laboratory facilities to supplement the work of the teacher in furnishing intensive language practice.

The broad general goals need to be broken down further into steps or "minima" which can be reasonably taught in specific time segments within the over-all time allotted. It is essential, however, that the program provide for continuous review and integration of all previously taught material with new learnings. Language study is cumulative. Learning will depend to a large extent on the pupil's realization that bits of vocabulary and language items fit together to make a logical, unified whole which is increasingly useful to him for communication purposes in the school and community.

SUMMARY

In this chapter, we have discussed the importance of defining realistic objectives and of recognizing the factors within the pupils, the teachers, the school, and the community that influence the formulation of the objectives and the framework of the instructional program. We have indicated, too, the needs that we consider basic in teaching English to speakers of other languages irrespective of the nature of the pupil population or of the dominant language spoken in the community.

It is important to recognize that the language learners who have had some instruction in English may be at various points on the continua of language skills. Some may be able to say some stereotyped sentences but have little or no understanding. Some may be able to call out words in reading. Some may be able to do some printing of letters.

Each student will have to be helped to move along the continua of skills as rapidly as possible. In order to do this, educators must prepare materials in pronunciation, structure, and vocabulary—the major features of the language—but in consonance with the age and interest levels of the learners.

We hope through the material in the following pages to lighten the burdens of our colleagues in the field. We propose to give concrete illustrations of many procedures that have been advocated by language authorities as a result of their extensive research in linguistics and other disciplines. We will give only those that we have attempted, or that we have seen attempted, and that have withstood the test of actual classroom practice.

CHAPTER 2

The Curriculum and Its Content

All the experiences which learners have both in and out of school and which contribute to the desired terminal behavior are included in the term curriculum. Let us examine this statement in more detail. What are the principal goals in the teaching of English to speakers of other languages? What experiences should we give our students which will further these aims? What knowledge and skills should we develop?

The two fundamental objectives for learners in our program are so interrelated that it is difficult to say which should be given precedence. The first is the progressive development of the ability to communicate. The second is the fostering of an insight into the cultural patterns and social values of the English-speaking community. It is obvious that this second objective becomes of vital importance when the language of instruction in the schools is English and students live in the English community.

The interrelationship of language development and cultural orientation—since language is the central feature of culture—warrants continuous re-emphasis in the curriculum planning of teachers and supervisors. A conscious effort needs to be made to ensure that language will be presented and practiced in appropriate cultural contexts and that pupils will be made aware of the cultural implications of the language item. For example, in English, *you* is used for both *familiar* and *formal, singular* or *plural*.

Although the springboard for all teaching is the "here and now" of the students' immediate environment, the teacher will provide illustrations, activities, and experiences which simulate as closely as possible the experiences of native speakers of English. For example, in presenting a moviegoing experience with concomitant language activities, the point of departure or motivation will be the moviegoing experience with which the learner is familiar. The new lesson might be based on a conversation between a boy and a ticket seller in the English-speaking community.

The two main currents in the teaching of English to speakers of other languages are, therefore, linguistic and cultural. In actual teaching practice these will be integrated, as will be noted in later discussions. For the sake of clarity and emphasis, however, we will list essentials under each of these areas separately. We will then give a number of illustrations of the language-culture integration which should be planned in the presentation of any item or topic.

DEVELOPING CULTURAL INSIGHTS

The list of topics given below is not all-inclusive nor should the sequence in which the themes are given be followed mechanically. If the teacher will think of them as "minimum essentials," he will add to them those learnings which are of particular interest in the school-community in which he teaches. He may also omit certain patterns which he may consider of little real immediate value in *his* teaching-learning situation. The basic fact to remember is that the starting point is the student in his immediate environment.

Students of all age and ability levels will profit, however, from some essential concepts in each area. The depth and breadth of the presentation will depend upon the age and social maturity level of the class members, as well as upon the community in which English is being taught. The teacher will have a dual responsibility in the teaching of the sociocultural patterns. For language-building purposes, he will have to give pupils practice in understanding and saying the English names for the various items whether they exist in the immediate environment or not. He will also have to select and give practice in those language patterns which fit best in the sociocultural topic being developed. In addition, he will have to point out, with older students especially, the contrasts or similarities between sociocultural patterns in English-speaking communities and those with which the students may be more familiar. He will also be obliged to encourage the acceptance of necessary social or cultural patterns which will help the pupil adjust to his new environment.

It goes without saying that understanding and tact are necessary if pupils are to develop an attitude of acceptance of English and of English speakers and, perhaps of greater importance, if pupils are to be made to feel that "different from" does not mean "better than" or "worse than." To help pupils retain a pride in their own cultural heritage while helping them to accept and appreciate other values is the hallmark of the real teacher.

SOCIOCULTURAL PATTERNS

1. Introductions and identification
   a. Greetings, leave-takings, introductions
   b. Various ways of expressing one's name (*My name's, It's,* the name alone)
   c. Identification of self and others
   d. Address and age

2. The immediate classroom
   a. Names of instructional materials
   b. Names and location of parts of the room
   c. Identification of activities (reading, writing, etc.)
   d. The program (hours for various subject areas, activities in and out of class)

3. The school

   a. Location of rooms and special places (auditorium, principal's office)
   b. People in the building (names, functions, special services)
   c. Rules and regulations (fire drills, time of arrival, use of stairs)
   d. School activities such as club programs, general organization, assembly programs, newspaper, magazine
   e. Parent associations

4. The family

   a. Members
   b. Relationships and ages
   c. The home

      1) Various rooms and their uses
      2) Furnishings for each
      3) Cleanliness
      4) Safety

   d. Occupations of various members
   e. Meals
   f. Health practices and problems
   g. Clothing (including seasonal changes necessary)
   h. Recreational activities

5. The surrounding community

   a. Homes
   b. Non-residential buildings (offices, movies, library, etc.)
   c. Transportation facilities (directions, tickets)
   d. Communication facilities (telephone, mail, newspapers, TV)
   e. Consumer services (stores, banks, etc.)
   f. Local government agencies such as post office, police station, fire house
   g. Places of recreational interest such as parks, libraries, community centers, movies and theaters

h. Educational opportunities (for parents as well)
i. Places of worship

6. The wider community

   a. Health services
   b. Customs
   c. Transportation and communication
   d. Government—city, state, national
   e. Rural or urban centers

7. The cultural heritage of English speakers

   a. Holidays
   b. Heroes and history
   c. Historical documents and speeches
   d. Songs
   e. Music, literature, and art forms

8. Guidance (This area is treated more fully because of its importance to the new arrival)

   a. Social

      1) Recreational facilities (addresses, special features, fees, or qualifications for admission)
      2) Social relations—living together, working together, and playing together with other people in the school and community
      3) Customs

         a) Greetings and leave-takings
         b) Foods—time for meals, types of restaurants, special habits
         c) Holidays—dates, gifts, visiting, greeting cards
         d) Dress—seasonal, formal, informal, special occasion
         e) Communication—letters, telegrams, telephones
         f) Transportation—reservations
         g) Business forms and legal practices
         h) Courtship and marriage
         i) Behavior patterns in various situations

j) Consumer education—installment buying, credit, borrowing
k) Social courtesies in different situations

b. Educational

1) Opportunities for advanced study (e.g., college orientation)
2) Requirements for admission to institutions of higher learning (physical, educational, other)
3) Scholarships available
4) Educational and specialized training for certain careers
5) Adult education or general studies program
6) Library and museum facilities

c. Vocational

1) Opportunities for employment after graduation; part-time employment
2) Requirements for various types of employment
3) Means of finding employment—agencies, newspaper, governmental agencies, letters, etc.
4) Filling out forms such as applications for employment and social security
5) Getting a job—dress and conduct at interview
6) Holding a job—punctuality, performance, human relationships
7) Labor laws, withholding taxes, pension, rights and responsibilities

d. Avocational

1) Community facilities such as community centers and exhibits
2) Hobbies—kinds (indoor, outdoor)
3) Arts, crafts, dancing, sports—where to learn, cost, etc.
4) Private recreational facilities and clubs
5) Popular sports in the community or city (participant or spectator)
6) Club programs in schools

e. Moral and spiritual

1) Principles of human rights
2) Individual rights and responsibilities
3) Places of worship—addresses, denominations, special language service

9. Miscellaneous

a. Expressions of time
b. Days of week
c. Months of year
d. Weather and safety
e. Seasons
f. Weights, sizes, measurements, money
g. Formulas of courtesy, agreement, disagreement (e.g., of course; not at all; if you don't mind)

Special areas may be added, of course, according to the known interests of the students or of the community members. With older students these may be based on their vocational or professional leanings.

Only limitations of time and the maturity level of the pupils will determine the end limits of the curriculum and the amount of time which will be devoted to each broad unit of work. As you will observe, the daily lessons which may be drawn from each topic are countless. Let us take a few broad topics and note the variety of individual lessons or lesson series possible under each.

Clothing

1. Names of items worn by adults, children, babies
2. Seasonal changes
3. Fabrics
4. Sizes and measurements
5. Where to buy (specialty or department store)
6. Home care (washing, ironing, repairing)

Meals

1. Number, name, and time of meals
2. Names of foods
3. Typical foods for various meals
4. Utensils, glassware, dishes
5. Table settings
6. Nutritional facts
7. Special occasion meals

Clothing

7. Community cleaning services
8. Community repair services
9. Storing clothing (moth protection)
10. Special occasion clothing (beach, school, parties)
11. Consumer education facts
12. Manufacturing or making clothing
13. Patterns of clothing
14. Origin of certain fabrics
15. Clothing in other lands

Meals

8. Typical menus
9. Restaurants and cafeterias
10. Picnic lunches
11. Buying foods
12. Weights and measures; containers
13. Preparing foods
14. Storing foods
15. Recipes
16. Formulas appropriate at mealtime; e.g., Please pass the_____; May I have another_____.

Even these suggested lessons may be broken down further. Either a review or a new presentation of numbers and money would be essential before many of the lessons listed above—buying foods, for example—could have meaning for the students.

There should be flexibility, logical sequence, and linguistic gradation in the presentation of individual lesson topics. A topic such as "How are fabrics made?" would be among the last lessons introduced in a unit on clothing since (1) the industrial concepts involved would not be as important to pupils as learning to speak about the items they are wearing; and (2) talking or reading about the making of fabrics would necessitate a knowledge of vocabulary and structural items—the use of the passive voice, for example—which beginning language learners do not possess.

DEVELOPING LANGUAGE SKILLS

Basic principles for teachers to bear in mind include the following:*

* Many of these principles are derived from the science of linguistics. (See p. 96 for further discussion.)

1. In order to acquire the abilities to *understand, speak, read,* and *write,* pupils must learn to use the *system* of the English language. The *pronunciation, structure,* and *vocabulary* of English all follow a definite pattern of recurring forms and sequences of forms which signal meaning to English speakers. The four major signals in the English system are: *word form, word order, function words,* and *intonation.* Following are brief examples of each:

a. *Word form: boy* means "one boy," *boy's* means belonging to the boy; *boys* means more than one boy; *boys'* means belonging to more than one boy; the (t) sound at the end of *walked* signals past time; the prefix *dis* signals negation in *disagree, dissimilar,* etc.

b. *Word order:* Notice the meaning difference in *The man bit the tiger* and *The tiger bit the man;* in *I have it done* and *I have done it;* in *pocket watch* and *watch pocket;* in *race horse* and *horse race;* in *arm chair* and *chair arm.*

c. *Function words:* There are about two hundred of these words—sometimes referred to as structure words—which have little or no meaning of their own but which signal the relationship of other words to each other. Function words are distinguished from content words, which include "nouns," "verbs," "adjectives," and "adverbs."
Among function words are
determiners such as *the, a, some, each;*
auxiliaries such as *be, have, will;*
prepositions, such as *on, in, of, to, with, for;*
modals such as *may, can, must, should;*
conjunctions such as *because, since, although, and, but.*

d. *Intonation:* This term includes:
1) *Stress* (accent): présent, presént
2) *Pitch* (the melody of the voice):
John has a headache.
John has a headache?

3) *Pause:*
> The *night rate* is cheap.
> The *nitrate* is cheap.

2. Understanding and oral production of the structures and patterns of language should *precede* reading and writing. Pupils should understand words and word groups and be able to produce them with *reasonable fluency* before being asked to read or write them. It goes without saying that the pronunciation (sounds, rhythm, intonation) of all patterns requires continued attention and, especially with older children, systematic drills.

3. Language learning is cumulative. Pupils must be engaged in continuous review of previously taught items with new vocabulary and sentence patterns in varied meaningful communication situations.

4. New items should be developed and practiced with limited *familiar* vocabulary and with *known* sentence patterns.

5. We should proceed from what pupils know, either from their native language background or from previous lesson presentations, to the new language item. Comparison and contrast, with the native language and/or the English contrasts (e.g., he, it; walks, walked), facilitate learning.

6. We should start with demonstrable items before proceeding to more abstract or complex features of language. To illustrate, the classroom situation affords natural opportunities to teach patterns of identification and items related to the actual routines and activities of the classroom. Directives such as "Say," "Repeat," and "Ask him (her)" may be among the first language items taught.

7. We should select patterns for beginning teaching on the basis of their greatest utility in manipulating other language items. The statement pattern "This is" and "It's" and the question pattern "What's this?" fall into this category.

8. We should select language items, also, because they follow a definite pattern, mold, or "rule." An illustration of such a pattern for beginning students would be the use of simple

adjectives of color in front of a noun (the red book, the blue hat, etc.) or the question-word questions such as

Where do you live?
How do you come to school?
When do you eat lunch?
What do you eat?

Here the position of the interrogative word and "do" remains constant while meeting the criterion of utility.

9. Where possible, language items for beginning learners should be selected because of similarity with language items in their native tongue, provided the items have wide utility in English and provided their form follows a well-defined, recurring, easily perceived pattern.

Not all linguists would agree with this statement. Some feel that *contrasting* features should be taught first so that pupils will have longer periods in which to practice them. We have found repeatedly, however, that the teaching of similar patterns in the early stages gives learners a feeling of security and success which has a decidedly favorable psychological effect on them.

10. Pupils can be made aware of the fact that there may be more than one way of expressing the same idea; for example, "Where do you live?" or "What's your address?" For production purposes, however, only the form most commonly used in normal speech—that is, "Where do you live?"—should be taught initially. Important, too, is to teach first the form the teacher normally uses (e.g., It isn't or It's not). Later, practice will be given in both forms as needed.

11. Language patterns should be taught within cultural "situations." For example, in teaching expressions such as "to the right" or "to the left," it would be desirable to present them in a table-setting situation: "A knife is placed to the right of the plate." Or in a context of direction or location: "Turn to the right at the corner."

12. Pupils must be led to understand through the study and

practice of basic patterns that English follows a well-defined systematic pattern in its word order, its inflections (word forms), its use of function words, and in its other features.

13. We must strive for the attainment of habitual, spontaneous, unconscious control of basic patterns of language so that the student can ultimately give his full attention to the idea and meaning he is trying to convey; that is, to real communication. This is only possible through intensive practice which will help learners internalize the language patterns and understand and generate variations of the basic patterns.

14. Features of pronunciation should be developed wherever possible as concomitants of the structural patterns and vocabulary which are being taught. They should also be introduced and practiced systematically, however, in a manner which will ensure increasingly more "native" comprehension and production.

At Level I, for example, students should be able to *hear, distinguish* and *produce* all the vowel and consonant sounds in English, the two basic intonation patterns (see page 106), and the stress and rhythm of the patterns being taught.

At Level II, in addition to reinforcing and further "shaping" the pronunciation features taught in the preceding level, emphasis should be placed on word stress and on the intonation of tag (attached) questions and responses (see page 107 for examples). The intonation of two-word verbs used with nouns or with pronouns should also be taught intensively.

Put your | coat | on.   Put it | on.

At Level III, all the above should be reinforced, along with intonation patterns in emphatic speech (see page 108); rhythm in complex and compound sentences and word stress in contrasting words; e.g., présent, presént.

15. The proportion of time* devoted to the practice of

---

* These percentages will vary according to the grade and age levels. In the early childhood grades, for example, reading and writing are introduced only after the children have had numerous listening and speaking activities. The period of deferment may be of one or more years. In the middle and upper grades, reading and writing *of familiar material* are introduced much earlier in the program.

understanding, speaking, reading and *writing* skills may be divided as follows:

Level I		Level II		Level III	
Understand-ing	40%	Understand-ing, Speak-ing	50%	Understand-ing, Speak-ing	40%
Speaking	40	Reading	30	Reading	30
Reading	15	Guided Writing	20	"Freer" Writ-ing	30
Guided Writing	5			(Summaries, letters, guided essays.)	

16. The curriculum should provide for the continuous progress of the pupils toward understanding, speaking, reading, and writing with native or near native control. The instruction in skills is determined *not* by the pupil's chronological age but by the point on the continuum within each of these four language arts strands at which the pupil is found. The experiences or materials provided to introduce, practice, or reinforce the skills, will differ, however, according to the pupils' chronological age and social maturity.

You will notice that the term "level" was used above and not "grade" or "age." Since the study of English may be begun in the primary grade, in the upper elementary or in the secondary grades, it is desirable to think of learning in terms of level rather than of a specific grade. Instruction on Level I may be necessary for pupils in grades 1, 2, and 3, or grades 5 and 6, or grade 9 or indeed in any school grade in which speakers of other languages are placed upon admission. The duration of time spent on each level will depend on the age, capacity, and rate of progress of each pupil. For example, in early childhood programs, the language patterns listed under Level I below may need two or three years of instruction.

Nor is it feasible to think only in terms of the pupil's language development level. Young children should be taught *only those language patterns which children of their age level normally use.* The vocabulary used within the sentence patterns will also be concerned with items children like to talk about. Children of six, for example, are interested in pets, dolls, blocks. Older learners would be interested in ball games, friends, and clubs.

Some Useful Structures

Level I

Note: The *italicized* words and expressions are those to be taught intensively. Words in *parentheses* are those which can be substituted for by other words which may be useful in other situations or more interesting to your pupils because of their age, the community in which they live, their more immediate needs, etc. The interrogative and negative should be practiced with all structures.

My name's (Mr., Mrs., Miss) (Smith).
What's your name? It's (John).
My name's (John).
How are you? I'm fine, thank you. How are you?
Where do you live, (John)? *I live (at)* (22) (Grand Street).
This is a (desk).
That's a (window).
It's a (desk).
What's this? It's a (desk).
What's that? It's a (desk).
Is (this) a (desk)? Yes, it is. No, it isn't or *No, it's not.**
It's not a (desk). *It's a* (chair).
This (desk) is (big). It's big.
This (table) is not (small). It's not small.
These are (windows). *They're* (windows).

* Both negative forms—so common in English—should be taught, although not necessarily in the same lesson.

What are (these)? They're (windows).

Are the (windows) (closed)? Yes, they are; No, they aren't.
(No, they're not.)*

Is the (door) (closed)? Yes, it is. No, it's not.

This (pencil) is (long). That (pencil) is (short).

These (pencils) are (long). Those (pencils) are (short).

This (pencil) is (yellow). It's (yellow).

What color is the (pencil)? *It's* (green).

These (pencils) are (yellow). They're (yellow).

What do you have? (I) (have) a pencil.

Do you have a *(pencil)? Yes, I do. No, I don't.*

What color is it? It's (red).

What color are (these)? *They're* (black).

Is this (book) (brown) *or* (black)?

This is (Harry). He's a boy. He's a pupil in this class.

This is (Mary). She's a girl. She's a pupil in this class.

(Harry) and (Mary) are pupils. They're pupils.

What's (his) name? It's (Harry).

(Harry)*'s tall.*

Are you a pupil? Yes, I am.

Are you the teacher? No, I'm not. I'm a pupil.

What's (Mary)? (She's) a pupil.

What is (she)? (She's) a pupil.

Who's (he)? (He's) the (principal).

Who's (Mr. Smith)? He's the *(English teacher).*

Where's the (auditorium)? *It's on the (first) floor.*

Where's the (book)? *Here it is.*

Is there a *(clock) on the (wall)? Yes, there is. No, there isn't.*

Are there (pictures) on the (wall)? *Yes, there are. No, there aren't.*

Are there (books) *in* the desk? *Yes, there are. No, there aren't.*

What time is it?

It's (three) o'clock.

It's *(half past* eight) *in the morning.*

It's (eight o'clock) *at night.*
What's today? It's (*Tuesday*).
What's tomorrow?
What's today's date? It's (*January 4*).
What's the weather today? (It's sunny.) (It's raining.)
How old are you? I'm (ten).
I'm (ten) *and he's* (*ten*) *too.*
He's (fourteen). *So* (am I).
How many (pencils) do you have?
How many (*pencils*) *are there* in the box?
I (*need*) a (pencil).
How many (pencils) *do you* (*need*)?
How much does a (*pencil*) *cost?*
How much is a (pencil)?
What time do you come to school? *At* (half-past eight).
I need a (book). *I need it.*
I (need) *some* (pencils). *I need them.*
Do you walk to school every morning?
I *don't walk* to school. I *ride* to school.
I (*always*) (walk) to school.
I (walk) to school *but* (*he doesn't*).
I *come* to school at eight but he doesn't.
Which book is (*yours*)? This one or *that one?*
Whose book is this? *It's* (*mine*).
It's (*my*) (book).
It's (*my friend's*).
It's (*John's*).
What kind of (book) is it? It's a (*history*) *book.*
What do (you) *have for* (*lunch*)?
Do (*you*) *have* (milk) for lunch?
What *do you like* for breakfast?
I *like* (coffee) *and* (*Mary*) *does too.*
I *don't like* (coffee) and (Mary) doesn't *either.*
I'd like some (water).
I'd like (a glass) of (water).
I'd like *another glass* of (milk). *I'm thirsty.*

I *like* milk *very much.*

Do you like milk? *Very much.*

I (drink) *lots of* (milk).

I (*always*) (drink) lots of (milk).

Open the door.

Please open the door. (Open the door), please.

Don't open the door.

Let's open the door.

Let's not open the door.

What are you doing?

I'm (*opening*) the (door).

Is (*John*) (*opening*) the (*door*)?

Who's (opening) the door? (*John*); or (*John*) *is;* or (*John's*) *opening the door.*

(*John and Mary*) *are* (*opening*) the (door). They're (opening) the (door).

Where are you going? I'm going to (*my grandmother's*).

How long are you going to stay?

Only (four) days.

When are you *coming back?*

I'll be back *in four days.*

I'll be back *in an hour.*

I'll be back *at seven o'clock.*

I'll be back *on* (May 26).

How are you going?

I'm going *by* (*bus*).

Who(*m*) are you going *with?*

I'm going *with my* (*family*).

When are you going? *I'm going* (next week).

Tomorrow's my birthday.

Are you going to have a party? Yes, I am. No, I'm not.

What are you *going to have at the party?*

(Ice cream) *and* (cake).

What are you *going to do* at the party?

We're *going to sing and play games.*

What a (lovely) (cake)!

What are you *going to study?*
I'm going to study (Spanish).
What are you *going to be?*
I'm going *to be a (butcher).*
I'm *going to tell you* a story.
Please *tell us* a story.
Were you ill yesterday? *Yes, I was. No, I wasn't.*
Was (he) at home? Yes, (he) was. No, (he) wasn't.
What was yesterday? It was (Monday).
Were they absent yesterday? Yes, they were. No, they weren't.
When (were you) born? I was born on (*June 5, 1958*).
(Mary) (*washed*) her (blouse yesterday).
Did Mary *wash* her (blouse) yesterday? *Yes, she did.*
What *did* (Mary) *do?* She washed her blouse.
Who washed her blouse? *Mary did.*
I (*got up*) early this morning.
What time *did you get up?*
(I) (got up) *an hour ago.*
(Mary) is *taller than* (Joan).
(Mary) is *as tall as* (Bob).
(John's) *the tallest boy in* the class.
How tall is John?
He's *four feet, two inches.*
How much does he weigh?
He weighs (eighty) *pounds.*
He weighs (eighty) pounds, *doesn't he?*
I didn't go to the circus. *Neither did (John).*

Level II

Can you speak (English) ? *Yes, I can.*
Your (brother) can speak (English), *can't he? No, he can't.*
He's only a baby.
I can speak (English) *but (my brother) can't.*
He can speak (English). *So can I.*

I can speak (English) *and* (*Henry*) *can, too.*
Please *put your* (*coat*) *on* or Please *put on* your (coat).
Please *take your* (*coat*) *off* or Please *take off* your (coat).
Will you play (baseball) with me today?
You'll play (baseball) with me later, *won't you?*
I don't know. I (*must*) see *a friend of mine.*
(*Someone*) (came in).
(*Everyone*) is (happy).
If I get the money, *I'll buy* a (bicycle).
If they do their homework, *they can go* to the movies.
If you go to the movies, *when will you* go?
Did Mary eat *all of* the (cake)? No. She only ate *some of it.*
(She) (ate) *less than* (John).
Who ate *all the* (*cake*)? (*John*) *did.*
Why can't you (play)?
I *have to do* my homework.
I *must do* (the laundry).
Why can't you (play)? *Because* I'm (tired).
I'm *very tired.* I'm *too* tired to (play).
It's very (*hot*). *It's too* (*hot*) *to* (drink).
If I had money, *I'd buy* a (dress).
I'd go, if I could. So would I.
I *couldn't go* there (yesterday). *Neither could I.*
I *should go* there (later). *So should I.*
I *ought to speak* to the (teacher).
Would you lend me that (book)?
May I borrow this (book)? *Yes, you may. No, you can't.*
I (*hope*) you'll like (it).
If (you're) not careful, (you'll) hurt (*yourself*).
Do you *know how* to speak (Spanish)?
How old is he? *I don't know how old he is.*
Where will I put these? *I don't know where to put* these.
How long have you lived here?
I've lived here *for two years.*
I've lived here *since 1965.*

Have you *ever* (lived) here? I've *never* (lived) here.

Have you been working hard? Yes. *I've been working all (day)*.

The book *was written by* (Fields).

This (house) *was built by* my (father).

The (house) *is made of* (wood).

That house *with the* (*red*) *roof* is (mine).

(*England*) is (lovely) in (spring).

(*Tokyo*) is a (large) city.

Gold is (expensive).

The gold in this (ring) is 14 carats.

(*Everything*) is for sale. (*Nothing*) is free.

I *hardly ever* see you.

Are you going *anywhere*? No. I'm *not going anywhere*.

I'm hungry. I'm going to get *a* (*ham*) *sandwich*.

You must speak *slowly*. You *mustn't* speak quickly.

You *should* (study). You *shouldn't stay* out late.

I *used to live* here.

I *used to go* (*swimming*) *every day*.

I'd *rather* go (swimming).

You'd *better* (study).

I *may go* to (Jeff's) (house) (tonight).

I *might go* to (Jeff's) (house) (tonight).

(Jeff) *looks like* his (brother), doesn't he?

(John) (sings) *well*.

(Jeff) (sings) *better*.

(Rose) (sings) *best of all*.

After singing, Jeff *always feels* tired.

It's *fun to* (*sing*).

(*Singing*) is fun.

This is *the same as* that.

I've (*been*) (there) *many times*.

I've *just* (*been*) (there).

I've (*been*) there (*already*).

Have you (*been*) there (*yet*)?

I've *never* (*been*) (there).

You've (been) (there), *haven't you? No, I haven't.*
I've eaten there *many times.* I *ate* there *yesterday.*
I haven't (been) (there) *for a long time.*
I haven't (been) (there) *since last* (Tuesday).
I've *just* (been) there.
I know (*him*).
I know (*who*) (*he*) is.
I *don't know who* he is.
Whose (*book*) is (it)?
I don't know *whose* (*book*) *it is.*
Won't you (come in)?

Level III

I have *so much to do.*
I have *so much to do that* I can't finish.
I'm *so tired that* I can't (eat).
The man who is speaking is the (doctor).
The man you saw is (my) (teacher).
The boy whose father is ill just came in.
I saw him *myself.*
(*While*) *I do* this, you can do that.
As I do this, you can do that.
He *spoke* English well.
They *talked* together for a while.
They *talked about* sports.
He *told me* to go.
He *asked me* to go.
I *told* (*her*) *not to* go.
He *asked me if I get up* early every day.
He *asked me if I got up* early.
He said, "Good-bye."
She said, "I can do that."
He *said he could* do that.
She *said that she had seen* him before.
He *told her where it was.*
He got dressed *before he had* breakfast.

He went out *after he had had* breakfast.

Don't (go) *until I get back.*

Don't (go) *unless I come back.*

I'll go with you *although* I don't like that (movie).

I'll go *whether or not* it rains.

I could have done that myself.

I *would have done* that.

I *should have done* that myself.

He *must have done* that himself.

You *might have told me* you were tired.

He *should have been working.*

I want you to study this *until you've learned* it.

(Mr. Mack) left *just as* the lights *went out.*

(Rose) washed her hair *before she went* to the party.

(Rose) washed her hair *before going* to the party.

She'd *no sooner* finished her homework *than* she had to wash the dishes.

The more (she) (read), *the more* (she) (understood).

The (boy) *to whom* you spoke is (ill).

The (boy) *about whom* you are speaking is my brother.

Why are you changing your seat? *Because I* want to see better, or *In order to* see better.

I prefer *not to be* a doctor.

May I *have a* (skirt) *made?*

May I *have* my picture *taken?*

May I *have one taken too?*

Your (skirt) is *too long.* You *should have* it *shortened.*

I don't have *much money. Neither does* my mother.

What's this called? It's called a "refrigerator."

What's this called? It's a (windshield wiper).

Get on your (sweater) or (*Get* your sweater *on*).

Get on the (ladder).

Run up the street.

Is (*this*) why you're (late)?

I'll go there *as quickly as* (I can).

Notice the difference between some separable and inseparable two-word verbs. We say, "He ran down the street," but either "He ran down the man" or "He ran the man down." (Moreover the last example can have two different meanings depending on the context.)

THE TIME NEEDED FOR DEVELOPING THE LANGUAGE STRUCTURES

There will be wide variations in the time needed to give pupils reasonable control of each structure, depending on their age and ability levels as well as on the active, intensive, spaced practice provided. For instance, if Level I structures are taught in the primary grades, five or six lessons may be needed to teach the names and position of adjectives of color in the singular alone; ten or more lessons may be needed to teach the past of certain common verbs such as "went" and "saw" and the interrogative forms with "did" requiring answers in the simple past.

The problem is not simply teaching the forms of the words or the word order. Each sentence or utterance must be taught with its characteristic pronunciation—sounds, intonation, and rhythm. Moreover, with each, pupils should gain increasing facility in manipulating the pattern (substituting other words within it and deriving or generating other sentences from it; e.g., questions, negatives) and in using it (or its derived form) in any social or cultural context in which it can logically fit. How this might be done is discussed in more detail in Chapter 3.

THE PLACEMENT OF LANGUAGE ITEMS

As has been indicated, the learning of the structural items above may take anywhere from two to five or more years depending upon the age group and the program time allocated to the study of English each day.

After the duration of the program and the length of each

session have been decided upon, the supervisor, teacher, or a curriculum committee should plan for the inclusion and *sequential* placement of these items within the time allowed for the complete English program. This should be based upon the criteria of utility and uniformity to which we have alluded.

The sequence of presentation should always go from *the simple to the more complex*. Note these examples of sequence:

It's a coat.
It's a green coat.
It's a green coat with a silk lining.
It's a green coat with a red silk lining.

He's tall.
He's as tall as John.
He's as tall as John and Jim.
He's taller than John.
He's the tallest of the boys.

I get up at six.
I usually get up at six.
I usually get up at six when I go to work.
I usually get up at six except on Sundays.

It goes without saying that before introducing the new structure, the teacher will provide review in the structure on which the more complex one is built. Pupils should be given the feeling, conscious or unconscious, that each bit of the new language is a building block which culminates in the ability to express the same wants, desires, ideas, and doubts that one can express in one's native tongue.

Language items in addition to those listed should be taught if they appear with any frequency in the available instructional materials. The placement of items, at least for purposes of recognition, may also have to be modified if they appear in reading materials used in the school or if they are needed by learners in other curriculum areas.

Naturally, in harmony with the spiral approach, the same item may appear a number of times throughout the program. To illustrate, the interrogative "who" may be placed in the first year in patterns such as "Who's the principal?" and later in patterns such as "Who did that?" or "Who do you think did that?" or "Do you know who might have done that?"—always from the simple to the more complex.

Even within a specific grade or level in the program, the teacher may find it impractical to set a definite time limit for the learning of each item. In fact, he may be forced to decide, if pupils reach a plateau of little or no return, to set an item aside for awhile and to present it through a new approach at a later date. Between the presentation of an item for active use and its use by pupils in any communication situation, there will be many intermediate steps ranging from the pupils' being able to (1) repeat the item after the teacher; (2) produce it consciously after much guided practice; (3) substitute other words within the pattern; (4) select it from among other choices; and (5) use it habitually without conscious choice, concentrating on the meaning rather than on the structure. These procedures will be treated in more detail in Chapter 3.

With any structural item, the teacher should make sure that he is teaching its form, meaning, function and position in the utterance. Of course, not all meanings and functions of an item need be given or should be given at one time. The teacher will need skill and experience to determine just how much his pupils can absorb during one session and which use of the item he will want to emphasize for that particular lesson. For example, in teaching "to," only its use in directions might be emphasized first. The teacher would scrupulously avoid illustrations like "He likes to dance" or "He goes to the store to buy candy" during the active development of the initial lesson with "to" used in directions. To illustrate further, in teaching "too," only its meaning as "also" might be emphasized during the initial development. The use of "too" in sentences such as, "I was too ill to study" would certainly not be presented at the same time or even on the following day since many additional language items and difficulties are involved in this type of sentence pattern.

INTEGRATING THE LANGUAGE AND CULTURAL ITEMS

Since a systematic approach is essential in language learning it is recommended that the school or district curriculum committee analyze which language and cultural items will best be taught together and in which school grade or level of the program they should be placed. It will be found helpful to set up a regular format or schematic arrangement for the teachers' use. This will ensure placing proper emphasis on important aspects of language and it will avoid the "lumping together" of too many similar items which may conflict with each other; for example, the prepositions *in, at, on, for, by, with,* etc. Let us repeat: specific suggestions as to content at any level are not given here, since the curriculum in any school will depend upon the native language background of the learners and all the factors in the school and community cited in Chapter 1. An example, however, of a course of study developed in one school for pupils of varied ethnic backgrounds will be found at the end of this chapter.

The format may use either a cultural (experiential) item or a language item as its initial emphasis. The former is preferred by many schools. Two possible examples of formats are given here. Other longer illustrations of ways in which language and culture may be integrated will be found at the end of the chapter.

> *Type A* (with a cultural item as the point of departure)
>   *Aim:* To teach about buying food in stores in a community
>   *Review items:* Names of food stores and the pattern,
>   "Where do you buy _____?"
>   *New structures:* I need _____. May I have _____?
>   How much is _____? It's (twenty) (cents) a (pound).*

* Words in parentheses are those which may be substituted by other similar words as, for example, forty, eighty, dollars, box, can, dozen.

Vocabulary: Names of foods (known). Names of weights, measurements, and coins.

Pronunciation emphasis: The "tsh" sound in *much*

Materials needed: Pictures; scale; word cards; containers; money

Type B (with a language item as the point of departure)

Aim: To teach comparisons of adjectives

Review: Statements such as: (John) is (tall) and/or questions such as: Is (John) (tall)? Is the (chair) (small)?

Situations: Compare 2 pupils in class; 2 books; 2 chairs; 2 pictures, etc.

Patterns: _____ is (taller) *than* _____. _____ is the (taller) *of* the two.

Vocabulary: Known vocabulary

Pronunciation practice: The "th" sound in *than*

Materials needed: Word cards; pictures; real objects of different sizes

If a box arrangement is preferred, sheets can be ruled with either Type A or Type B in mind. Any other item of course can be added such as *Outcome Expected.*

Unit	Aim	Review	Sentence Patterns	Vocabulary	Pronunciation Emphasis	Materials	Assignment
II							

The preparation of this over-all format should *precede* any attempt to differentiate materials for the intra-class groups which may have to be organized because of varied language abilities or individual pupil needs.

It is only by selecting the language material carefully, by presenting it sequentially and systematically, and by furnishing varied practice activities to the point where material is *overlearned* that we can help our pupils progress towards meaningful communication in full English.

PROVIDING EXPERIENCES FOR LANGUAGE PATTERN TEACHING

The skillful teacher will provide many experiences which will foster personal-social adjustment and cultural orientation and from which language learning will naturally arise. The teacher may decide, however, that a certain language pattern should be taught immediately because it is needed in a communication activity. He will then, as we have demonstrated in Type B format above, build situations or meaningful sentences around the language pattern which needs practice. *Both approaches—that is, the experience giving rise to language and the language pattern around which situations for presentation and practice are built—are correct.* What is important to remember in either approach is that language should be taught sequentially in a context which has meaning for the *age* group and the *ability* level of the learners.

The same experience or "life" situation may be used many times to present a new language pattern or to practice a variety of language patterns and vocabulary items. The pupils should not feel that the names of family members if taught originally in the pattern, "This is" or "That's," for example, can be used *only* with "This is" or "That's." Note this illustration of some simple language pattern combinations and cultural insights which are possible with names of family members:

1. With study of *This is:*
   This is my mother.
   This is my sister.
2. With *home activities* and *third person singular of the present:*
   My mother *cooks in the kitchen* every day.
   My sister *sets the table* every day.
3. With *numbers* or *adjectives* or *expressions of age:*
   My mother is *pretty.*
   My sister is *fourteen.*
4. With a study of *occupations* and/or *two-word verbs*:

My mother is a *dressmaker*. She sews dresses.
My older sister is a *nurse*. She takes care of the sick.
5. With *recreational facilities* and uses of *like*:
My mother *likes* the movies.
My sisters *like to* dance.

All classroom activities should lead to the development of language competency and to an understanding of the cultural values of the English-speaking community. Although games and other forms of creative activities should be used for the emotional and social values which we realize to be important, they should also be made to contribute to various phases of language growth.

A movie-going experience for pupils of any age may serve to review and reinforce vocabulary and sentence patterns such as:

What was the name of the movie?	It was _____.
What was the name of the heroine?	It was _____.
Was she young?	Yes, she was.
What was the name of the hero?	It was _____.
Where did the heroine live?	She lived in _____.
What did her father do?	He was a _____.
What did her mother do?	She was a _____.

To illustrate further, an experience in dancing can be used with older students to teach new vocabulary and to practice a variety of language patterns such as:

1. Who played the music?
   _____ and _____ played the music.
2. Who directed the dance?
   Mr. _____ directed the dance.
3. Where did you dance?
   We danced in the _____.
4. Who was your partner?
   My partner was _____.
5. Did you enjoy the dance?
   Yes, very much.

There is another kind of integration which is of vital importance in any discussion of teaching or learning English. We refer to the essential integration of the various aspects of a language program, that is, the understanding, speaking, reading, and writing phases which are integral facets of the process we call communication. This form of integration is discussed in the next unit.

UTILIZING RESOURCE UNITS IN LANGUAGE TEACHING

The term "resource unit" is found frequently in current textbooks on curriculum planning. The resource unit, briefly defined, is a compilation of experiences and materials centered about an area or problem whose study helps pupils meet definite sociocultural and language needs. Since a problem is to be solved, the title of the resource unit is usually couched in question form. Any of the sociocultural areas found in this chapter may properly be considered subjects for resource units. For example, a broad topic such as "People in the Community" can be stated simply as, "How can the people in our community help me and my family?" The topic found under "School Rules and Regulations" may be stated as, "What do I need to know about the school so that I can become a responsible school citizen?" Broad areas or problems are then subdivided into daily lesson units by the teacher or the teacher and pupils planning together.

Resource units, as they are found in textbooks and brochures, usually *contain much more material than any teacher can cover with one class*. The material in resource units is often designed for pupils of varying ability levels. Activities in all curriculum areas and in all aspects of the language arts are included for teacher selection.

It is not expected that the teacher will utilize all the approaches, activities, or materials suggested in the unit. He will select only those activities that he feels the class is able to do, both with respect to time and to ability level. He will then decide upon the length of time that the class can spend on the unit and make tentative divisions of the material into daily lesson units. Examples of daily lesson units which are based on resource units are given below.

One of the many ways in which the topic of personal and community health, for example, may be divided is illustrated here. Please note that topics within this broad topic of health can again be subdivided into many additional subtopics.

How Can I Guard My Health and My Family's Health?

1. Personal cleanliness
2. Common illnesses and care
3. Daily routines (sleep, meals, etc.)
4. The doctor
5. The drug store
6. The dentist
7. Clothing
8. Nutrition
9. Safety cautions in the home or in using recreational facilities
10. First aid
11. Clinics
12. The school nurse
13. Hospitals
14. Traffic safety
15. Dangers in alcoholic beverages
16. Consumer education (shopping for food, etc.)
17. Preparation of food
18. The work of the sanitation department
19. Cleaning up the community
20. Cleanliness of the home (detergents, spring cleaning, etc.)
21. Dangers of narcotics

Another broad topic which arouses interest and enthusiasm is one related to recreation outside the school. In developing such a unit of work, it is suggested that information be included about such items as appropriate clothing, fees, specialized vocabulary needed (if any), and changes in activities and clothing because of season.

How Can We Enjoy Ourselves in Our Community?

1. All sports (both as participant and spectator); safety
2. Movies
3. Radio; television
4. Hobbies
5. Indoor games (cards, chess, checkers)
6. Dances
7. Leisure reading
8. Trips to points of interest
9. Free play in public parks
10. Community centers
11. Clubs
12. Concerts
13. Art exhibits
14. Libraries
15. Theater and ballet
16. Conferences, forums
17. Zoos, aquarium, botanical gardens
18. Museums

Generally, the resource unit is outlined in the following manner:

1. *Title:* Broad area of study stated in question or problem form.

2. *Objectives:*

   a. *General:* In our program, these would be the development of language items and an appreciation of cultural values.

   b. *Specific:* Stated in terms of the habits, attitudes, knowledge, and skills (linguistic and cultural) that the learners would develop.

3. *Duration:* Approximate number of days or weeks. (This should be flexible.)

4. *Approaches:* Possible sources of motivation so that pupils would become personally interested in helping to find the answers to the problem. Approaches may include trips, the viewing of films or slides, listening to speakers or stories, reading stories, following up pupils' or parents' questions, or following leads from preceding units of work.

5. *Activities and experiences:* This section would include *whole class, subgroup, or individual* activities or experiences in which the pupils engage in order to achieve desirable linguistic and cultural outcomes. Experiences would be centered around any area of the curriculum (art, music, science, social studies, mathematics, health education) and should be designed to further growth in *comprehension, reading, speaking,* and *writing.*

6. *Subject matter learnings:* Knowledge, information, vocabulary, and language patterns that would result from the study of the unit.

7. *Outcomes:* Work habits, attitudes, skills, appreciations, and interests initiated and developed as the result of the study of this unit; greater facility in communication; knowledge gained.

8. *Materials:* Audio-visual aids, recordings of pupil reports, realia, and other instructional materials needed in the development of the units. In addition, community resources should be used.

9. *Bibliography:* Reference books for the teacher and for pupils.

10. *Culminating activities:* Activities, such as a class newspaper, which sum up the learnings that have been developed and which (preferably) are shared with other classes, parents, or community members.

11. *Evaluation:* Informal testing (oral and/or written) and observation procedures to determine degree of mastery of sub-

ject matter; growth toward desirable attitudes; and language competency.

Because of the interest that teachers have expressed in finding culminating activities to meet the needs of varied groups, some suggestions are offered below.

Group members, individuals, or the class as a whole may prepare culminating activities at the termination of each broad unit of work or as a result of the study of a number of related units. These activities, if well planned, should include both linguistic and cultural learnings and should provide for an audience situation, leading again to the feeling of status and success so important to language learners.

Pupils, with teacher help, may prepare:

1. Labeled photographic displays indicating the high points of a visit to a place of interest.

2. A picture dictionary containing labeled pictures of articles of clothing, of foods, or of other items related to a unit.

3. A current events scrapbook which can be donated to the library.

4. Maps showing the location of the business establishments and/or government agencies in the community.

5. A chart illustrating means of transportation such as buses, trains, automobiles, ships, and airplanes.

6. A diorama depicting the various rooms of a house and the furniture in it; illustrating a story event; or showing some phase of history.

7. A colored clay relief map of the city indicating its various sections.

8. Captioned cartoons or pictures of famous people in the field of entertainment or the field of sports.

9. Paintings and drawings depicting important holidays.

10. Papier-mâché models or puppets of community helpers such as the policeman, the fireman, and the postman.

11. Captioned posters stressing safety in the school, in the home, and in the community.

12. Charts listing pupils' responsibilities in daily health rou-

tines (brushing teeth, bathing, eating nutritious meals); in working as members of a group; or in some other facet of school work.

13. Games made of cardboard or wood, such as word games and jigsaw puzzles.

14. A class newspaper about activities in the school and in the neighborhood.

15. A class magazine issued at the end of the term describing the various activities of the class, such as trips taken during the year or class hobbies.

16. An auditorium program consisting of a play, a quiz, or a speech by an invited speaker.

17. A school-community project such as a clean-up drive.

18. Recordings of pupils' research reports.

19. A play or a story on some aspect of a unit of work.

20. An open house in which parents and community people are invited to see displays related to the current unit, to hear the pupils' reports or dramatizations or to ask questions of the pupils on the unit just completed.

SUMMARY

A well-rounded curriculum necessitates the careful selection and conscious integration of both linguistic and cultural materials which will contribute to the attainment of our dual fundamental objectives. It requires also the careful planning of meaningful situations and experiences which will simulate or duplicate life situations. Its implementation demands an approach and a sequence which will help pupils gain increasing mastery of language and cultural patterns.

The basis for the selection of language materials is found in the careful study of the important features of the English language. Where possible, a comparison should be made of the points of similarity and contrast between the learner's native language and English in order to facilitate learning. By becoming aware of those aspects which require less concentrated teaching because they exist in the same pattern in both languages, and by noting those which create difficulties because there exist no points in common, teaching can be made more systematic and direct, and thus more effective.

Although in the elementary and secondary schools many experiences are given to children for their inherent social values, the English teacher would be wise to utilize and "exploit" fully these same experiences to motivate or to practice language.

Definite arrangements of experiences and materials are extremely helpful to teachers in planning their work and in ensuring the proper allocation of time to important items of language or culture.

Language should be developed in the cultural context of the English-speaking community. Understanding a native speaker of English and getting meaning from reading in English will depend upon familiarity with the pronunciation, structural patterns and vocabulary of the language as well as upon the sociocultural concepts reflected in or inferred from language. Such knowledge is essential for pupils who are learning English as a second language as a basis for active participation in an English-speaking community.

In sum, the curriculum should include the development of the skills of *understanding, speaking, reading,* and *writing,* all of which require the progressively more habitual *control* of the system of English (its sound system, its structure [word form and word order] and its vocabulary) and *a knowledge of the context*—the social or cultural situation—in which the structures and skills are normally used.

The content of the curriculum should (a) reflect the objectives of the program; (b) ensure continuity in learning; (c) embody flexibility and yet be systematic in scope, sequence, and method of presentation; (d) provide whole class integrative experiences; (e) make provision for differentiating experiences according to special needs of pupils. Finally, and of major importance, the curriculum should be evaluated continuously.

All this is necessary to make sure that the desired terminal behavior is achieved in terms of each pupil's needs, age, intellectual ability, and social maturity level.

A Course of Study for Beginning Language Learners*

(*Age level: for pupils twelve and above*)

The following course of study designed to cover a two-year period was prepared for use with children twelve years of age or above for intensive study of English two hours a day. They had had no previous English instruction. This is one illustration of the many combinations of language-cultural programs which can be formulated by school systems.

The same course, spread over a much longer period of time, may be adapted for use with younger children; that is, children between the ages of eight and twelve. A special course of study, however, may not be necessary for young children in the primary grades. The emphases in these grades on the experiential approach and on a "readiness" program in the language arts and mathematics curricula will generally meet the needs of the children. *Individual help, however, should be provided even for very young pupils* when these come to school with limited concepts and vocabulary in their native tongue. All the considerations noted in Chapter 1 should guide administrators and teachers in deciding whether special placement and a special curriculum are needed for the very young children.

Where time is a factor, particularly with older students, the same course may be telescoped into a three- or six-months course of more hours a day. No course of study prepared for one school should be taken over *in toto* by any other school. Adaptations and modifications are always advisable to meet the local situation.

Please notice that terms needed in other curriculum areas are emphasized toward the end of the program. These should be introduced much earlier when learners need them to function in classes other than the Special English class.

* Sample lesson plans will be found on p. 398.

Also, possible items for pronunciation emphasis are included under Language. It is important to remember, however, that even when the course of study recommends that [i] be taught, for example, the teacher should give practice in any other sound which impedes communication at that point of language development.

The sequence for the presentation of vowel sounds in the following pages is one which approximates the Vowel Triangle (page 396), enabling the teacher to review the preceding sound and then to make statements such as "Now just open your mouth a little more" or "Round your lips more." The Triangle also permits a quick warm-up drill in which pupils are made aware that the tongue moves further back or the jaw drops as each succeeding vowel is pronounced. (These considerations are important for the older pupils who cannot imitate readily.) While this sequence has advantages, the teacher should feel free to change it to suit the needs of *his* pupils.

The items under each category are for *special* emphasis and intensive practice. It is perfectly possible that some language items will have been met, understood, spoken or read, *before* they are introduced and practiced for active use by the pupils. It is also expected that expressions needed for immediate use—in the classroom and in social and cultural situations ·of the school and community—will be explained and practiced as they are needed. Last, but not least, review and re-entry of previously taught items should be provided in each lesson.

LEVEL I (FIRST YEAR)

WEEKS 1 AND 2

Language Items:

Interrogative with *do*; e.g., "Where do you live?"; who
Possessives: my, your, his, etc.—with name
Pronouns: I, you, me, your, his

Present of verb: "to live"; some forms of "be"
Pronunciation:* [i] as in "leave" and [ɪ] as in "live"

Sentence Patterns:

What's your name? (address, school, etc.)† Where do you
   live? Who lives with you? My (brother) [lives with me].

Vocabulary:

What, where, who, name, Mr., Mrs., Miss, address, various
   names of fellow pupils and school personnel

Miscellaneous Items:

Common classroom expressions such as "Please stand up,"
   "Please sit down."
Numbers 1–100

WEEKS 3 AND 4

Language Items:

Negatives: It's not a _____. It isn't.
Short answers: Yes, it is. No, it's not.
Differences among *this is, that's* and *it's*
Pronunciation: [e] as in "say" and [ɛ] as in "set"

Sentence Patterns:

What's this? This is _____. That's _____. It's a _____.
It's not a _____. Is this a _____?

Vocabulary:

Names of classroom objects

* The pronunciation symbols used will be found on p. 368.
   † Words in parentheses are those which can be substituted by other similar
words.

WEEKS 5 AND 6

Language Items:

Ordinals 1–10
Interrogatives: *who, where, which*
Pronunciation: [æ] as in "hat"; [ɑ] as in "hot"

Sentence Patterns:

On which floor is the _____? It's on the _____ floor.
Where's the _____? Who's Mr. _____? He's the
_____.

Vocabulary:

Names of people and places in the school building.

WEEKS 7 AND 8

Language Items:

Simple present of *to come* including the negative and interrogative forms
Intensive practice with prepositions such as *near* and *far
from*
Pronunciation: [ə] as in "fun"; [ɔ] as in "all"

Sentence Patterns:

I come from _____. I live in _____. Is it near _____?
Is it far from _____?

Vocabulary:

Orientation to the new community: such words as map,
place, city, town, street, country, come, live, from, in,
near, far

WEEKS 9 AND 10

Language:

Present of *to be*
Present of *to have*
Use of verb *do* in context below; e.g., short answer to question
Use of negative in full and contracted forms
Pronunciation: [o] as in "boat"

Sentence Patterns:

How old are you? How old is your _____?
Do you have a (brother)? Yes, I do, or Yes, I have a (brother). No, I don't, or No, I don't have a (brother).

Vocabulary:

Names and relationships of family members; expressions of age

WEEKS 11 AND 12

Language:

"ing" form of the present
Simple past of regular verbs
Use of *did* in short answers
Interrogative: *what*
Pronunciation: contrast between [ɔ] and [o]

Sentence Patterns:

What are you (studying) in _____? (I'm) studying _____. Did you study _____ in _____? Yes, I studied _____. Yes, I did. No, I didn't study _____. No, I didn't.

Vocabulary:

Subject areas with emphasis on words such as *study, read, learn*

WEEK 13

REVIEW AND COMPREHENSIVE TEST

WEEKS 14 AND 15

Language:

Adjectives of size, color, etc. (position, forms, function)
Present of verbs such as *wash, clean*
Interrogative in sentences such as Is the room large? Do you
always eat in the _____ ?
Frequency words such as *always, usually*
What a and *what* plus adjective
Pronunciation: [ʊ] as in "full"; [u] as in "food"

Sentence Patterns:

What do you do in the (kitchen)? I (eat) in the (kitchen).
I (always) eat in the kitchen. Is the _____ (large,
comfortable, sunny, airy, etc.) ?
What a pretty room! What large rooms!

WEEKS 16 AND 17

Language:

Plurals of nouns
There is (*There's*) and *There are,* in unstressed position
Is there _____? *Are there* _____?
Yes, there is (are). *No, there aren't*
Marked infinitive (*to* cut)
Pronunciation: [ɛ:r] as in "there"

Sentence Patterns:

There's (a stove) in the (kitchen). There are four chairs
in the (kitchen). We use (a knife) to cut (bread).

Vocabulary:

Articles and utensils in the home

WEEKS 18 AND 19

Language:

Use of *how many* and *what color*
Possessive pronouns
Pronunciation: [ɑi] as in "tie"

Sentence Patterns:

How many (eyes) do you have? I have _____.
What color (are) (his) (eyes)? (His) (eyes) are
(brown); hers are (blue). They're (brown).

Vocabulary:

Parts of the body; items needed for personal cleanliness
and health

WEEKS 20 AND 21

Language:

Past tense of *have* and *be* (including interrogative and
negative)
Interrogative word: *why*
Pronunciation: [au] as in "brown"

Sentence Patterns:

Why were you absent? I had a (head)ache. My (teeth)
hurt. I was (ill).
Did you take (medicine)? Did you call a doctor?

Vocabulary:

Names of common illnesses and possible remedies
Time words such as *yesterday, last week*

WEEKS 22 AND 23

Language:

The letter names of the alphabet*
Prepositions *in, into, on*
Interrogative *who(m)*
Pronunciation: [ɔi] as in "boy"

Sentence Patterns:

Who(m) are you calling? I'm calling the _____.
What are you doing now? I'm putting a dime in the slot.
What number are you calling? I'm calling Lo 4-2345.

Vocabulary:

Parts of the telephone, the phone booth, the directory; uses
of the telephone
Courtesy expressions such as "May I take a message?"

WEEK 24

REVIEW AND COMPREHENSIVE TEST

WEEKS 25 AND 26

Language:

The future with "going to" (including negative and in-
terrogative in contracted form)
The "will" future
Pronunciation: [s] as in "wants"; [z] as in "needs"

Sentence Patterns:

When are you going? At what time are you going? He
won't (go).

* The alphabet could also have been taught with the spelling of pupils' names.

Vocabulary:

Expressions for telling time; days, months, concept of century
At night, in the morning, in the afternoon

WEEKS 27 AND 28

Language:

Requests
and
Passive construction (for example, It is made of or by)
Two-word verbs; e.g., *put on; take off*
Pronunciation: [b] as in "bat"; [v] as in "vat"

Sentence Patterns:

What (do you wear) in the (winter)? What size (do you) wear?

Of what is the (coat) made? Put on your (hat). Take off your (shoes), please. Please give me (your) (coat). Put on your (hat) and (coat).

Vocabulary:

Articles of clothing; materials; seasons of the year, months

WEEKS 29 AND 30

Language:

Imperfect with *was:* I was (eat)ing; It was snowing.
Present perfect with auxiliary verb *have*
Expressions of time: *now, yesterday, all (day); in (January)*, etc.
Pronunciation: [d] as in "do"; [t] as in "to".

Sentence Patterns:

How's the weather today?

It's (rained) all day. It was (raining) yesterday.
Does it (rain) in (January)? Is it (hot) in (January)?

Vocabulary:

Expressions of weather

WEEKS 31 AND 32

Language:

Direct and indirect pronouns with requests in affirmative
and negative; for example, Give them to him. Don't
give him the butter (eggs) (apples).
Count nouns and mass nouns; e.g. (names of things which
are generally not counted), *butter, bread*
Interrogative: *How much?*
Quantity words: *some, any*
Pronunciation: [ʃ] as in "shoe"

Sentence Patterns:

Please give (me) a (pound) of (sugar). Please give (it)
to (me).
I need a (box) of (salt). How much is (butter) a
(pound)? How much (butter) do you (need)? Do you
have any (milk)? I'd like some (bread).

Vocabulary:

Names of food stores; food, weights, measures

WEEKS 33 AND 34

Language:

Expressions and symbols re money and costs
Forms, meanings, and use of modals *may* and *can*
Demonstrative pronouns in singular and plural
Pronunciation: [tʃ] as in "chew"

Sentence Patterns:

> When will this (coat) be ready? When should I come back for these (shoes)? How much will this cost? It will cost (it will be) (five) dollars. May I have this (right away)? Can you (do) this?

Vocabulary:

> Services and items needed to keep clothing clean and wearable; for example, laundry, dry cleaner, shoemaker, washboard, soaps, etc.

WEEK 35

REVIEW AND COMPREHENSIVE TEST

Required reading:*

> Intensive: 20 or more pages
> Extensive: 40 or more pages
> Supplementary: according to pupils' individual ability

Memory work:

> Songs needed in assembly exercises and other favorites
> Poems and other material such as speeches and proverbs; some dialogues

LEVEL II (SECOND YEAR)

WEEKS 1 THROUGH 4

> Systematic review of vocabulary and other language items in Level I
> Reading, dictation, aural comprehension,* songs

* See pp. 149 and 178 for a discussion on when to introduce reading and for procedures in developing both reading and writing skills.

WEEKS 5 AND 6

Language:

Past tense of irregular verbs; for example, (I came)
Expressions related to travel; for example, *on foot; by car,*
etc.
Have to
but
Pronunciation: contrast among [s], [ʃ], [tʃ]

Sentence Patterns:

How did you come to _____? I came by (train).
I had to go to visit (him). I went to (see) (my aunt).
I took the (bus). I paid (ten) cents. I changed to the (bus).
I take the (bus) but he (walks).

Vocabulary:

Transportation (kind, fares, transfers) within the community and outside the community or city

WEEKS 7 AND 8

Language:

Should
Use of interrogatives: *when, where, how, why,* etc.
Time expressions
Pronunciation: [ʒ] as in "pleasure"

Sentence Patterns:

Where's the pain? When should I come again?
Your appointment is on _____. It's marked on the (card).
Take this (twice) a day.

Vocabulary:

Community resources: hospitals, clinics, day centers, etc.

WEEK 9

REVIEW AND COMPREHENSIVE TEST

WEEKS 10 AND 11

Language:

Review of interrogative with known verbs
Use of marked infinitive after verbs such as *need, want,* etc.
Pronunciation: [ð] as in "this"; [θ] as in "thick"

Sentence Patterns:

May I have (five) stamps? How many stamps does this (letter) need?
Where should I write the (address)? I want to send this (special delivery). How can I get an (ambulance)? Where can I report this (accident)?

Vocabulary:

Community resources: the post office; the police station

WEEKS 12 AND 13

Language:

Modals: *should, can, may*
"If" clauses
Use of indefinite "we"
Pronunciation: [ə] as in unstressed "can"

Sentence Patterns:

We should save each (week). We should spend (carefully). If you earn _____, you should spend _____, for (food). If you go to the _____, you'll save (money). If you go, you can save (time).

Vocabulary:

Banking and budgeting (consumer education)

WEEKS 14 AND 15

Language:

"Like" followed by "to" or followed directly by singular and plural nouns
Modals: *must* and *have to*
mustn't
Pronunciation: [y] as in "yellow"; [dӡ] as in "jello"

Sentence Patterns:

Do you like to (dance)? Yes, I do. No, I don't. I must see (the program). You mustn't watch that program. I like this program.

Vocabulary:

Recreational facilities in the home (television, radio, parties)

WEEKS 16 AND 17

Language:

How long in expressions of time
How (meaning "manner")
Pronunciation: initial [l] as in "late"

Sentence Patterns:

Where is _____ playing? How do I get to _____ Beach? How may I become a member? How long may I keep this (book)?

Vocabulary:

Recreation outside the home (library, movies, beach, community center)

WEEKS 18 AND 19

Language:

Negatives (*never, nothing, anything*)
Words expressing quantity (*some, a few, a little, a lot, another,* etc.)
Pronunciation: [l] as in "fall"

Sentence Patterns:

What do you have for (dessert)? Please bring another (glass).
I don't want (anything).

Vocabulary:

Eating out (restaurants, cafeterias, automat, etc.)

WEEK 20

REVIEW AND COMPREHENSIVE TEST

WEEKS 21 AND 22

Language:

Do as a main verb
'd like; 'd like very much; *Would you like?*
Pronunciation: contrast between [v] and [w] as in "vine" and "wine"

Sentence Patterns:

I'd like to be a (doctor). I'd like to be a doctor very much.
Would you like to be a carpenter? What does a (carpenter) do? What must I do to become a (nurse)?

Vocabulary:

Occupational activities: working papers, employment agencies, etc.

WEEKS 23 AND 24

Language:

(I)*'d rather; Would you rather?*
Contrary-to-fact conditional sentences
Pronunciation: [ŋ] as in "sing"

Sentence Patterns:

Would you rather be a (dentist)? Where can I study (dentistry)? What (marks) do I need to go to (high school)? If you (studied), you could (go) to (college).

Vocabulary:

Educational opportunities

WEEKS 25 AND 26

Language:

Sentences with *who, which, in which* (e.g., the community in which I live _____)
Practice with passive in context below
Pronunciation: Contrast among [t], [d] and [ɪd] as in "walked," "combed," "wanted"

Sentence Patterns:

The (mayor) is the head of the (city).
People are protected. The legislature makes the laws.

Vocabulary:

Social studies: government of city, county, state, nation

WEEKS 27 AND 28

Language:

Form, meaning, and function of regular and irregular adverbs

Intensive practice of punctuation and capitalization
Pronunciation: [h] as in "hot"

Sentence Patterns:

What type of (novel) do you prefer? He writes (well).
She left the room (quickly).

Vocabulary:

Terms and symbols used in English

WEEKS 29 AND 30

Language:

Comparison of adjectives and adverbs
"Superlatives"
Pronunciation: contrast between [p] and [b] as in "pat"
and "bat"

Sentence Patterns:

This is more (important) than that. The volume is
(greater). This is the (most important) result. This is
as _____ as that. This is the same as that.

Vocabulary:

Terms used in science; for example, experiment, micro-
scope

WEEKS 31 AND 32

Language:

Conjunctions: *although, since, unless, while,* etc.
Compound words: *deposit slip; bankbook*
Prefixes: *in*correct, *un*true, *dis*agree
Derived words: agree*ment,* agree*able*
Pronunciation: clusters with [s] as in *school, stop, splash*

Sentence Patterns:

How do you find the percent of _____? Although (even though) you added _____ and _____, the answer is incorrect. We're not in agreement. She's disagreeable.

Vocabulary:

Mathematical terms and symbols

Reading:

Intensive: 50 or more pages
Extensive: 100 or more pages
Supplementary: according to level and interest

Examples of Language-Culture Lesson Units

Below are two illustrations of lesson units for adolescents in which language and orientation learnings are fused together in a number of meaningful activities. It is obvious that many more than two lessons could be developed under each broad area.

I

1. Topic: Recreation outside our home
2. Duration: Two or more sessions
3. General objectives for the pupil
    a. To learn to understand and use the vocabulary and language patterns related to recreational activities; to grow in communication skill
    b. To become aware of the recreational facilities offered in the community

4. Specific aims

    a. To learn the forms, meanings, and functions of:
        1) *Vocabulary*—park, grass, tree, flower, playground, community center, ball, team, club, member, dues
        2) *Sentence patterns*
            a) There's a park (community center, playground)*
               on _____ Street.
            b) *I belong* to a club (team, band).
            c) *I'm* a member of the _____ club.
            d) *I go* to a (meeting) every (Tuesday).
            e) *I pay* (ten cents) dues.

    * Words in parentheses are those which may and should be substituted by other similar words. Italicized words are those which should be practiced with all other known pronouns and verb forms.

5. Possible pupil-teacher activities: used in the *approach*, during the *development*, or as a *culmination* in addition to language practice activities (see page 164).

    a. A visit to the park, to the playground, or to the community center
    b. The preparation of an experience reading chart* using the new vocabulary
    c. Aural, oral, reading, and writing activities based on the chart
    d. A talk by the director of a community center. His talk (arranged after conference with the teacher) should include information about special facilities, dues, meeting nights, the role of parents, etc.
    e. The showing of a film strip, slides or a film
    f. Pupil-made pictures related to activities in a center
    g. Preparation of a list of community resources
    h. Research by committees on facilities in each resource studied
    i. Preparation of a neighborhood map
    j. Research and discussions about ball games and other sports in the students' communities or native lands
    k. Gathering of clippings related to the items above
    l. Development of original pupil materials based on individual membership on teams (taped or in writing)
    m. Dramatization and role playing

6. Materials gathered by teacher (in addition to text and worksheets)

    a. Crayons, graph paper, drawing paper, composition paper, maps
    b. Literature from community centers telling about their facilities and activities
    c. Pictures, films, filmstrips, slides, tapes, recordings.

* The preparation of experience charts is explained on pp. 146–148.

II

1. Topic: Some job opportunities in this community
2. Duration: One or more weeks
3. General objectives for the pupil

    a. To understand and use the vocabulary and patterns related to work processes; to grow in communication skill
    b. To become increasingly aware of the fact that people engage in a variety of occupations to earn their living and that there is dignity in all types of work

4. Teacher aims: To present and give practice in

    a. Vocabulary: work, job, carpenter, painter, barber, grocer, baker, butcher, shop, factory, etc.
    b. Sentence patterns
        1) (*He*) *works. He's* a (baker, carpenter, etc.)
        2) (*He*) *makes* (furniture).
        3) (*He*) *uses* a (hammer).
        4) (*He*) *works* in a (shop) (factory) (office) (hospital).

5. Possible pupil-teacher activities: used in the *approach*, as part of the *development* or as a *culmination* in addition to language practice activities (see page 164).

    a. The teacher shows pictures of people at work and develops the appropriate vocabulary (name of person; name of trade; tools used; end products, if any; place in which work is done; etc.)
    b. The pupils are asked to tell about jobs of friends.*
    c. Experience charts are developed under various occupations; e.g., "She's a nurse; She works in a hospital," etc.
    d. Pupils prepare drawings or paintings illustrating job activities
    e. Pupils prepare picture charts showing tools used in various occupations

* Jobs of family members should not be included if the teacher knows his pupils will be reluctant to talk about them.

f. A list of safety precautions under several occupations may be drawn up

g. Committees of pupils may prepare a list of occupational opportunities within a radius of two or three blocks of the school

h. The teacher and class discuss the prerequisites for certain occupations

i. Pupils do research (by asking parents or others) on ways of finding jobs

j. The teacher and class discuss community, state, or country-wide laws relating to after-school work

k. Parents or other community people are invited to tell about their jobs

l. Pupils engage in appropriate oral, reading, and writing activities such as letters of thanks to speakers or talks about their aspirations

m. Visits are made to bakeries, etc.

n. Scrapbooks are prepared with pictures, charts, and stories

o. Language games are prepared and played such as:

1) Telling about the activities of a workman.
   I'm a carpenter.
   What do I use? I use a _____.
   What do I do? I make _____.

2) Telling who uses certain tools.
   This is a hammer.
   It's used by _____.

3) Guessing who a person is from a description; e.g.,
   I take care of the sick.
   I'm a _____.

6. Materials needed:

a. Pictures of workmen performing various jobs

b. Flashcards with names of workers

c. Flashcards with names of tools

d. Forms (employment); charts of safety precautions or job qualifications

e. Maps showing the location of factories in the community

UNIT II

TEACHING ENGLISH

AS A SECOND LANGUAGE

CHAPTER 3

The Development of Basic Aural-Oral Abilities

GENERAL CONSIDERATIONS

Many "methods" or "systems" of teaching English and other languages as second languages have been developed and used for varying periods of time in one country or another. In most instances, their creators have had specific ethnic groups in mind and have based their methodology on a knowledge of the linguistic and cultural patterns of the people studying the new language. Many "systems" or "methods" were often formulated to meet linguistic and social needs of a given society at a given moment. Other "methods" have been prescribed as the panacea which would make communication among all peoples in the world possible and easily achievable. Each of the methods has had some value. In the hands of competent teachers, each one has been able to produce second (or foreign) language speakers or readers of varying degrees of competency.

In writing this section on the teaching of English as a second language, we recognize our indebtedness to Agard and Alatis, to the Allens (Harold, Robert, Virginia, Walter), to Bowen, to Dunkel, to Fries, to Gouin and Hagbolt, to Harris, Huebener, to Jesperson, to Kaulfers and Kitchin, to Lado, to Laubach, to Marckwardt, McIntosh and Ogden, to Palmer, to Pei, to Prator, Richards, Rojas, Smith, Tireman, Trager, Troike, West, and to a host of other eminent scholars. The work of each in turn has furnished a frame of reference for succeeding scholars and has given impetus to increasing research in the teaching of English as a second language. Each has contributed principles from his special field of linguistics or methodology which have given meaning and direction to English teaching programs.

We wish to state from the very outset, however, that we advocate no one method or system. We do recommend that an eclectic method be used—a method which utilizes results of recent research in psychology, sociology, anthropology, and linguistics; a method which fuses the successful and non-conflicting elements of the many systems or methods that have been developed for teaching English as a second language; a method which includes successful approaches in the teaching of any foreign language; in other words, *a method which will work with your student population, with your school organization, with your personality, and in your environment.*

We would strongly urge that all materials and procedures that have been prepared *anywhere* for teaching English as a second language be consulted and even utilized in the preparation of instructional materials. Our plea, however, is that caution be exercised. Adaptation and modification of materials must be made if they are to serve your pupils in attaining the two major purposes of the program: (1) the acquisition of those abilities and skills necessary to communicate needs, interests, and ideas and to participate in the total school program; and (2) an understanding of the sociocultural patterns of the English-speaking peoples.

The attainment of these two fundamental goals in teaching English to speakers of other languages is furthered by the utilization of psychological principles of learning and teaching. Educators believe, for example, that:

1. The experiences which are part of the learner's background should serve as the springboard for all new learning. Learning takes place when it is related to the needs, interests and immediate environment of the learner.

2. The teacher should start at the students' own level of achievement as a basis for further development.

3. Pupils learn at different rates and in different ways.

4. Pupil activity is basic to learning.

5. Many repetitions are needed to develop habits of using sounds and word forms and word sequences correctly. Learning should result in a change in the pupil's linguistic behavior.

6. Repetitions should be spaced at increasingly longer intervals.

7. Knowledge that a response is correct leads to the learning of that response.

8. Learning is facilitated when students understand the basic concepts and meaning of what they are repeating.

9. Older students, particularly, will learn not only through intensive repetitive practice but through the understanding of the "rule" or "recurring" feature of the material being taught which they can then apply in generating new sentences in new language situations.

10. Learning should be functional and have relevance for the students in terms of their needs and values.

11. Transfer of learning does not generally take place automatically.

12. The sequence of learning requires careful planning.

How can we apply some of these fundamental principles of psychology to our everyday classroom teaching of English?

1. The teacher should familiarize himself with the major language features and the socioeducational background of his pupils in order to relate the new teaching-learning activities to the pupils' native language and culture and to their previous educational experiences.

2. Students may be at different levels of linguistic development in the four basic language skills. Some may be able to hear sounds and yet not be able to produce them; others may be able to manipulate or vary a pattern during practice and yet not be able to use it in a real language situation; some may be able to

call out words in reading and yet not be able to get meaning from the printed page. The teacher will have to provide specific practice in these and other skills on an individual or group basis in order to bring the pupils up to grade or age level and to overcome weaknesses in these or other aspects of language.

3. Individual differences that exist normally among learners are emphasized with pupils who may come from different cultures and who may not have had the advantages of formal schooling. All teachers should prepare files of pictures, flashcards, experience charts, and worksheets to help pupils to progress at their own rate. A multi-sensory approach should be used. Listening, looking, saying, seeing, smelling, touching, writing or reading should be utilized to ensure that the different learning modes of individuals are taken into account.

4. Language or sociocultural items should be repeated, re-entered, and practiced consistently by pupils in a variety of situations. The ratio between teacher and pupil activity should be changed gradually so that as soon as pupils gain some security and ability, the teacher will speak twenty per cent of the time to the pupils' eighty per cent.

5. Not only should the pupils hear and say a new language item or pattern thirty or forty times on the day it is presented, but the teacher should plan to reintroduce and practice the same item in many subsequent lessons. If a new item is introduced on Monday, for example, it should be reviewed on Tuesday, re-entered into the lesson on Thursday, then perhaps on the following Monday.

6. Any item, if worth teaching at all, should be kept alive by using it in all logical situations with as many other items as possible with which it fits.

7. Through praise, or some reinforcing sounds, gesture or action, e.g., asking a pupil to repeat another pupil's correct response, pupils should learn when their response is satisfactory. When a pupil's response is not satisfactory, the teacher should give the correct response and ask the pupil to repeat it, and, where desirable, engage the class in repetition. *Teaching* and *testing* should never be confused.

8. Students should not repeat anything whose meaning is not clear. Through pantomime, pictures, paraphrase, or other technique, e.g., the use of the students' native language (where this is possible), meaning should be clarified and sounds associated with concepts *before* repetition and practice. Nor is it enough in teaching a new item to point to only one chair or one fish, for example, and to engage the students in repetition of the one word. Pupils may mistake the part the teacher's hand has touched for the whole. Many examples of the same object, animal, or person are needed to avoid confusion of meaning in the pupils' minds. Moreover, the individual word should be inserted in several sentences or utterances which will clarify its meaning even further.

9. After several examples of the new pattern being taught are given, the teacher should *elicit* from the pupils the recurring feature of word form or word position which they have heard or which they can see (if examples are placed on the board). This is particularly important with pupils over about the age of ten.

10. Those language and sociocultural learnings which the pupil can use immediately in his school, in his work, and in his community activities should take precedence in teaching.

11. The teacher should help students make any logical transfer from one language feature to another or one skill to another (listening or speaking to reading, for example) by pointing out their similar elements. Moreover, the teacher should always review for comparison or contrast the language feature on which the one to be taught that day is based.

12. Material for presentation should be carefully graded proceeding from the known to the new and from the simple to the more difficult.

Other behaviorial sciences also contribute to the teaching of English to speakers of other languages. We have already touched upon several sociological factors. Two others warrant further mention: (1) The attitudes of both the learner and his parents or peers toward English speakers and toward school, as well as the concept of parental authority, may affect learning. In addition, a child's feeling that because of his race or socio-economic background he cannot be "upward bound" in the society in which he lives may reduce his motivation. (2) Learning to interact with other human beings is fostered in the classroom as the teacher provides numerous experiences in which pupils ask and answer questions; react to her or to classmates' requests; and make comments to each other.

Principles within the anthropological sciences also have immediate application in the teaching of English to speakers of other languages. Culture is defined as the sum total of the customs and mores of a group of people. *There are no people without culture.* In the basics of life, all people have the same needs and aspirations. It is important that in teaching we emphasize the basic similarities existing among peoples and that we foster an understanding among our pupils that cultural differences can often be explained by different geographical or historical factors. It is essential, too, that we clarify—through illustration in many situations, dramatization, etc.—the different dimensions of a cultural item when one exists. For example, speakers of other languages will need to understand, to internalize and to use "you" numerous times before they can speak of one or more people—older, younger, newly introduced, or family members—with reasonable fluency.

Anthropologists have underscored the concept that language is the central feature of a community's culture. We will unwittingly foster the feeling of "cultural deprivation" if we discourage students from using and perfecting their native language or if we make them ashamed of it by not allowing them to use it or to master its literature.

We realize that this is a knotty problem in some cases.

1. If classes are composed of students of many ethnic backgrounds, it is the rare teacher who is able to use the languages of all his pupils.

2. Moreover, the question of teacher morale often enters the

picture in large schools where all have to teach English as a second language and where only some teachers know the native tongue of the pupils—Spanish, for example. Those teachers who do not know Spanish feel that their more fortunate colleagues have special advantages which affect their rapport with pupils and which facilitate their teaching.

3. It is also argued in favor of not allowing the use of the native language that students may take advantage of the fact that the teacher speaks their language and thus make less of an effort to understand and to be understood in English.

We wish to emphasize again that although the ability of the teacher to speak the pupils' language is not important, a knowledge of the broad characteristics of the structure and sound of their language is essential for good teaching. This knowledge can be easily acquired.

Where needed, the native language of the students should be used *judiciously*. For example, in teaching, in order to clarify or reinforce an item or concept, the native word may be given *once and only once* in a low voice immediately followed by the English in a normal tone. To illustrate further, students may be permitted to speak their native tongue during the morning snack period, during part of the lunch hour, or during the recreation period. No harm will come from permitting them to do so. On the contrary, the students' feeling of status and pride engendered by the obvious acceptance of their culture will undoubtedly encourage them to "add" another culture.

In practice, of course, the amount of the native language used in the English classes will depend upon such factors as the knowledge and skill of the teacher, the age of the pupils, the number of prior years of schooling in English they have had, the needs of the students, the policy of the school, and the community in which the language is being taught. The well-trained teacher in any community (English-speaking or not) will use as much English as possible in the classroom and will try to ensure the carry-over of English outside the classroom.

Linguistic science has a major role to play, of course, in the teaching of English to speakers of other languages. Principles and practices gleaned from linguistics underlie much of what has already been said in this book (see this chapter, page 92 particularly) and much of what will follow. The brief outline below of some of the pertinent results of linguistic research relating to language and language learning will indicate our indebtedness to the linguists:

1. *The spoken language is primary.* All human beings can speak. Many of them cannot read and write.

2. *Writing is a secondary,* often imperfect, *representation of speech.*

3. *Language has system;* that is, it has a recurring set of arrangements of sounds and words which permit people who know the system to communicate and to interact.

4. *Language is learned behavior.* Human beings are born with the capacity to produce unlimited noises. The noises are shaped and become meaningful language sounds only if they are reinforced by speakers of the language community into which the child is born and grows up.

5. *The meaningful signals of a language can be discovered, analyzed, and described through contrasts.* With relation to sounds, for example, we know that /p/ and /b/ contrast in English because we can find pairs of words (called minimal pairs) in which only the /p/ and /b/ make the difference in meaning; e.g., pat, bat; pit, bit; pet, bet; pear, bear. (The units of sounds which make the meaning difference are called "phonemes" and are enclosed in slant lines.)

6. *The native speaker uses the meaningful arrangements* of sounds and words in his language *without conscious awareness.*

7. *The ingrained language habits of the native speaker may interfere* or conflict with the learning of the second language.

8. *Language is the central feature of culture* of any community.

The implications of these findings will become increasingly apparent in the following pages as we discuss the approaches and techniques which lead to language development.

THE SEQUENCE OF LANGUAGE DEVELOPMENT

Full communication between two speakers can take place only where there exists reciprocal understanding of the features of pronunciation, of language structure, of vocabulary, and of sociocultural patterns. Words have little meaning in themselves unless the context or the experience in which they are used is familiar to the listener or reader. The order in which words are put together, as we know, will also alter an entire concept. Furthermore, a sentence, although it may be correct structurally, may have little meaning to a listener unless the intonation or the rhythm of the speaker approximates one to which the listener is accustomed.

It is necessary, therefore, that in teaching we give equal importance to the development of pronunciation, language items, and cultural meaning in order to develop language competency among our students. It is also essential to remember that vocabulary, structure, etc., are not taught as ends in themselves but that they are integrated in actual use in the four basic communication skills: understanding, speaking, reading, and writing. These four fundamental activities, through which we learn language and for which we need language, should serve as the bases of a well-rounded, comprehensive communication arts or language arts program.

The sequence of development of language skills, if it is to conform to natural language development, will proceed from *the listening to the speaking, to the reading* and, last, *to the writing* steps. If we remember four key words in teaching language, the words *hear, say, see, do,* which indicate a logical sequence of presentation and practice, we will find that we are helping our pupils develop important linguistic skills both naturally and functionally.

Although the language arts activities are interrelated in actual use, concentrated practice should be given in each aspect separately. In addition to lessons emphasizing pronunciation, structure, and vocabulary practice, certain fundamental language activities will be found especially appropriate to the growth of listening, speaking, reading, and writing. These will be discussed separately in the following pages.

INTRODUCING LANGUAGE ITEMS

There are many ways of introducing the teaching of the sounds, structure, and vocabulary, as well as the normal forms of conversation of English. Some teachers prefer to start having students learn a conversation or dialogue; some start by telling well-known stories or fairy tales; some start by dramatizing an action series such as, "I get up every morning, I wash, I have my breakfast, I get dressed," etc.; some teachers start directly by giving the new structures in normal, everyday sentences. At later levels, reading materials such as letters, news articles, advertisements, and autobiographies may also serve as a starting point for the intensive study of some features of structure.

The "stimulus" used should depend on the age of the students, on their interests, and on the length and major aims of the program. Each approach to learning has merit. Many teachers today favor the conversational approach in which students hear, say, and perhaps memorize a short dialogue. They feel that the dialogue duplicates most closely the normal speech of native speakers. Whichever approach is used to introduce any feature of the language, provision should be made for giving learners practice in the normal forms of conversation, i.e., in listening to questions and answers, in formulating questions, in making short or long responses, and in participating in conversational exchanges of varying lengths.

The procedure may be varied, depending on the structure to be taught. With one structure it may be most desirable to start with a dialogue,* with another, to start with a structure and then to incorporate it with previously taught material into a real everyday conversation. Certainly, with every cultural theme or structure, two or more dialogues of four to eight utterances

* See p. 174 for discussion.

should be studied and dramatized. These dialogues should not be confined to questions and answers alone, but should include other forms of normal speech such as statements, short and long responses, requests, suggestions, formulas (expressions such as "How do you do?"), complete sentences, and one-word utterances.

BASIC STEPS IN LANGUAGE DEVELOPMENT

Whatever the procedural approach—conversation, story, etc. —the teaching of any language item should proceed in five sequential steps:

1. The pupils should be led to *understand* the material. This may be done through pictures; paraphrases; pantomime; dramatization; through a brief explanation in English; or (as a last resort) through the equivalent expression in the pupils' native language. This may be termed the step of "cognition."

2. They should be led to *repeat* the material after the teacher models it as often as necessary. The repetition is done first by *the entire group,* then *by smaller groups,* then by *individuals,* always preceded by the teacher model.

3. They should be led to *practice* the material in as many ways as possible. Practice exercises are suggested on pages 113-124.

4. They should be helped to *choose* the correct structure, word, or expression from several alternatives, in statements, responses, or questions. This is often called the step of "discrimination."

5. They should be encouraged to *use* the new material in any communication situation in which they can express ideas, wants, or desires without conscious concern for inflections, word order, stress, or any other feature of the English language system. This step is often labeled "production."

This sequence of development is equally desirable in teaching pronunciation, structure, vocabulary, or cultural aspects. A few comments should be added with regard to steps 1 and 4. Learners must be made aware of the relationship between the sound and the meaning of a language item being taught before they are asked to engage in repetition of that item. Planning for the situations, examples, and materials through which understanding of structures and concepts will be brought about should be given top priority. Repetition of material that is not understood will not lead to real learning and retention.

Learners should not be asked to choose between two language items (e.g., *in, on*; *he, she*; *went, have gone*; *walks, is walking*) until each item has been practiced to the point of reasonable control. With some sets of items, days or weeks may have to elapse between the separate introduction and practice of each item in the set and the inclusion of the contrasting items in an activity requiring the learners to choose between them. The time, of course, will depend on the age and ability of the learners, the thoroughness of presentation, and so on.

Teaching Pronunciation

Correct pronunciation, including intonation, rhythm, stress, and pause, is of primary importance in developing any of the communication arts. The sounds and melody of the language need constant attention and practice from the first day of the program.

Practice in the early stages of learning should generally be limited to the sounds in the structural patterns or vocabulary which are being taught for active production, particularly if the incorrect pronunciation of a sound would confuse the meaning. An example of this might be the pattern "I live at ———," which might be confused with "I leave at ———," since the /ɪ/ in "live" and the /i/ in "leave" are phonemes. "Get me the map" might be mistaken for "Get me the mop."

This attention to early elimination of errors does not preclude the teacher's giving systematic intensive practice on one sound (or two contrasting sounds) during each lesson. Indeed, with older pupils who cannot *imitate* pronunciation easily, intensive practice on one feature of the sound system should be made an integral part of each language lesson. The sounds to be taught, however, should *not* be determined by "What is the next letter in the alphabet?" or "What comes next in the speech book?" Long practice periods of isolated sounds or of meaningless words and sentences often deaden interest in the new language at the very time when initial interest should be maintained and heightened.

The sound system of the language, that is, the pronunciation of its sounds, its intonation, and its rhythm, should not be taught as something apart from the other language arts skills of understanding, speaking, and, later, reading and writing. The pupils' *initial* experience with the flow of speech will come from hearing the sentences the teacher says, by repeating them without seeing them, and then by repeating them with the words in a text. In teaching English, it is strongly recommended that the visual image *never* be given first because of the confusion which may ensue from our often difficult English spelling (cf., cough, enough, through, bough, etc.).

Hearing, identification, discrimination, and *repetition* are the key words to be remembered in teaching correct pronunciation and intonation. Teachers need not be phoneticians to give pupils correct pronunciation and melody patterns. By a downward or upward gesture of his arm the teacher can indicate stress and the rise or fall of the voice. When the class or individual pupils repeat, he can again indicate stress and intonation by the sweep of his hand. In addition to this gesture approach, it may be desirable with older pupils to represent the melody pattern and stress by a system of dots or lines. *After* the oral repetition which has been accompanied by gestures, the teacher can indicate the intonation pattern at the board by using some simple scheme he has worked out or by using one of the systems of markings prepared by scholars in the field.*

* For a more detailed treatment of types of intonation markings, you may wish to consult the following studies:

H. Klinghardt, M. Fourmestraux, and M. L. Barker, *French Intonation Exercises* (Cambridge, England; W. Heffer & Sons, 1928).

The dots or lines representing the stress and intonation will later enable the students to practice in groups or to study independently. Only with very literate and mature students should the teacher present rules of stress and intonation.*

Pronunciation practice must be planned carefully so that growth in the ability to *hear, identify, discriminate,* and *pronounce* sounds and to recognize the same sound in other words and in normal utterances will be systematic and continuous.

All approaches—visual, kinesthetic, aural, and oral—should be utilized in teaching pronunciation. Two main sources should be tapped to determine the sounds for initial intensive pronunciation practice: (1) the sounds that appear in the vocabulary and structures that are being taught for active use; and (2) the sounds which differ from, or do not exist at all, in the native language of the pupils and which therefore cause difficulty. The illustrations within this second group should be selected from among words, structures, or idioms that the pupils are learning or that they will need to learn shortly for production purposes.

A few minutes should be set aside each day even in the primary grades for drills in pronunciation and intonation. When teaching vowel and consonant sounds, it is desirable that the teacher ascertain that the meaning of the vocabulary used for the presentation and drills is clear to pupils. Some language authorities feel, however, that since it is essential that pupils hear and recognize the difference among sounds before they can be expected to produce them, the teacher may occasionally ask pupils to distinguish minimally contrasting sounds (the sounds in the verbs "live" and "leave," for example) even among nonsense words. In this way, he will be able to diagnose the cause of the speech production difficulty if one exists. If he finds that pupils are incapable of *hearing* the two contrasting sounds, he will give additional specific *hearing* practice.

Kenneth L. Pike, *The Intonation of American English* (Ann Arbor: University of Michigan Press, 1945).

Betty J. Wallace, *The Pronunciation of American English for Teachers of English as a Second Language* (Ann Arbor: George Wahr Publishing Co., 1951).

* Rules of stress, intonation and rhythm will be found in many excellent texts on the subject listed under *Bibliographies,* page 458.

The teacher can prepare short lists or pictures representing contrasting words such as *live, leave; ship, sheep; pick, peek; chick, cheek.* He can then ask pupils to raise one finger when they hear the short sound and two fingers when they hear the long sound, or he can ask individual pupils to go to the board or picture to point to the word that he pronounces, or he can ask learners to indicate whether the words (or utterances) are "the same" or "different." The same procedure may be followed with longer phrases or utterances such as "I leave the sheep" or "I leave the ship" to give further practice in *hearing* and *distinguishing* sounds. If, on the other hand, he ascertains that pupils *hear* the differences but are incapable of *producing* the sounds, he will provide more intensive practice in the actual *production* of the sound through some of the techniques suggested below.

The teacher may motivate the pronunciation lesson by a statement such as, "Yesterday when we were talking about _____, we had difficulty in saying the word *boys*. Let's practice saying that word now. Let's also learn how to say other words that begin with the sound 'b' " (or end with the "z" sound, depending upon the pronunciation emphasis for the day).

The mnemonic *fan* should be kept in mind at this point. In pronunciation, *focalization of attention, attentive repetition,* and *no exception* should be the rule. One sound should be taught at one time. Only after the *individual* sounds have been drilled thoroughly should attempts be made to contrast sounds. To illustrate, Spanish-speaking peoples have difficulty in pronouncing "y" initially, often confusing it with "g" or "j." Intensive practice should be given with English words beginning with "y" alone and "g" or "j" alone, before expecting pupils to differentiate *among* the sounds in lists of words or in speech utterances.

When you are ready to contrast two sounds, you may wish to use the following procedure:

Use simple pictures illustrating the words, or (when learners can read) place the words themselves on the board in print or cursive writing.

I	II
eat	it
beet	bit
feet	fit
heat	hit
meet	mitt
seat	sit

1. Say *all the words* in Column I or in the first row of pictures several times.

2. Say *all the words* in Column II several times.

3. Say the words across a few times.

4. Give two words from either list and ask the students to indicate whether they are the "same" or "different."

5. Give three words from either list and ask the students to indicate which two are the same or which one is different. They will say, for example, "two and three" or "three."

6. Give a word and ask students to hold up a finger or two fingers depending on the list in which the word appears.

7. Say each word in Column I. Ask the students to repeat each word after you.

8. Do the same for Column II words.

9. Say the words across. Have students repeat each pair.

10. Say a word in one column and have *individuals* give the *same* word.

11. Say a word in one column and have *individuals* give the *contrasting* word.

12. Turn your back to the students. Say a word and have them give you the same or the contrasting word.

13. Have able *individual* students come up, turn their back to the class, give a word and ask their classmates to give the same or the contrasting word.

14. Insert the new words in sentences. Model them and ask for group and individual repetition.

Pronunciation lessons should follow the developmental steps of any lesson. After motivation and statement of aim, the teacher will present the sound—initial "b" for example—in words familiar to the pupils; for example, boy, bus, book, boat. In addition to the techniques of discrimination, imitation, and repetition, the teacher will use a multiple sense approach to develop correct habits of pronunciation of sounds. Since, particularly for older pupils, a knowledge of point and manner of articulation and voicing are essential, he may in teaching any sound:

1. Sketch a profile of a face at the board and indicate the position of the lips, tongue, and teeth when forming the sound.

2. Tell the pupils where to place their tongues with relation to their teeth or palates.

3. Ask the pupils to watch him closely, shape their lips, or drop their jaws in the same way.

4. Direct them to touch their throats to get the feel of the sound. (Voiced and voiceless sounds are distinguished in this way.)

5. Ask the pupils to use small pocket mirrors to study the position of the observable vocal organs.

6. Ask the students to place their hands before their mouths to note the amount of breath escaping in pronouncing an initial "p" or a "t," for example.

7. Review a *known* English sound (by modelling or diagraming) and indicate that to produce the new sound, the mouth is more open or more rounded or the tongue is further back. Notice /æ/ as in *hat;* /ɑ/ as in *hot;* /ɔ/ as in *all,* and /o/ as in *old.*

8. If he knows the learners' native language, suggest the "approximate" sound in their native tongue, and help them isolate the sound and use it in English.

9. Where this is reasonable, the teacher may also produce sounds made by well-known animals or vehicles and ask the students to imitate him; for example, a fly for "z" and a train for "tsh."

A generalization or "rule" in the pupils' own words *may* follow the choral and individual repetition if the pupils are capable of making it. For example, the pupils may say, "We make _____ by placing _____." *Rules are not necessary,* however, but correct habits of articulation (placing the movable parts of the vocal organs in the proper position) *are* important. Extensive practice, that is, use of the newly studied sound in utterances with other familiar words, should follow the generalization immediately.

The "next" step in the pronunciation sequence will vary depending upon the age, the native language and ability levels of the pupils, and the related language work that is being taught. To illustrate, the next lesson may be devoted to the letter "b" in other positions (intervocalic, preceding a consonant, as a final letter, etc.) or, if the need is more urgent, the teacher may leave "b" and proceed to another sound which is causing difficulty either because it does not exist in the pupils' native tongue or because it exists in different positions in the pupils' tongue.

Whether or not phonetic transcriptions should be used depends upon the knowledge and training of the teacher, the maturity of the pupils, and their degree of literacy. Many teachers who have not studied phonetic symbols find learning them and using them to teach their pupils a rather difficult task. Others feel that to learn phonetic symbols places an added burden on pupils when their primary need may be to master a new alphabet and a new writing system. Some authorities, on the other hand, have found a pronunciation alphabet or phonemic transcription extremely effective with literate older students.

In general, it may be preferable in the elementary and secondary schools to avoid the use of the International Phonetic System or of any other pronunciation system with students and to use the multiple-sense approach mentioned above. The knowledge of the International Phonetic System is extremely useful for teachers, however. (See page 368.)

The two principal intonation curves of English should be introduced and practiced as early as possible in the program.

1. *Rising-Falling* intonation is used in:
   a. Simple statements

      It's a ⎤pen⎦.

   b. Requests

      Give me your ⎤pen⎦.

   c. Question-word (*Wh* questions)

      Where is your ⎤pen⎦?

   d. Attached or tag questions (when confirmation is sought)

      You lost your ⎤pen, didn't ⎤you?

   e. Tag answers

      Yes I ⎤do.
      So am ⎤I.

2. *Rising* intonation is used in:

   a. Inverted questions (those which do not begin with *Wh* question words)

      Is it a ⎡pen?

      Does he have his ⎡pen with him today?

   (Notice that all the words following the first high pitch are also on that same pitch.)

   b. In a series

      I have a ⎡pen, a ⎡pencil, and a ⎡ru⎡ler.

   c. In attached or tag questions when information is sought

      You have a ⎤pen, don't ⎡you?

   d. In direct address and in introductions

      Miss ⎡Smith, this is my brother ⎡John.

Intonation is taught through the imitation of many similar sentence patterns. In addition, the teacher may wish to raise or lower his arm to indicate rising or falling intonation; he may place arrows on the board, ↓↑ or ⌒ ⌎ ; or he may use musical notes or dots on a scale.

We would reserve for the intermediate or even advanced level the placement of stress on different parts of a sentence to show varying emphases. For example:

<u>Did ╱Harry study yesterday?</u>	or his brother?
<u>Did Harry study ╱yesterday?</u>	or this afternoon?
<u>Did Harry ╱study yesterday?</u>	or did he do something else?

The typical rhythm of English is learned by imitation and through practice in saying increasingly longer sentences—using the words in the first sentence in combination with other words to make the longer sentences: I like that coat. I like that brown coat. I like that pretty brown coat. I like that pretty brown coat in the window.

Pupils should be helped to gain increasing awareness that English has *phrase timed rhythm*. This can be done by giving them practice in emphasizing the stressed syllables in thought groups and in utterances and by tapping out the regularity of stress *of the thought groups* in utterances of varying lengths. (Stressed syllables are held a little longer and spoken louder. Unstressed words and syllables are usually pronounced with the sound /ə/.)*

With older students the teacher may also wish to teach the symbol /ə/, and to write it over words or syllables which are weakened or which are reduced due to a shift in stress—e.g., "Can [kən] I have my dinner now? Yes, you can [kæn]." The vowel sound in the short answer is different from that in the question. Notice also [prəzɛnt] (verb) and [prezənt] (noun); [rəkɔrd] and [rekərd]; [rəbɛl] and [rebəl].

To help students produce the characteristic rhythm of English,

---

* For example, in the sentence "John and Mary went to the movies," the teacher would tap in pronouncing *Mary, went* and *movies.* He would indicate, too, that *and, to* and *the* are unstressed.

they should also be given extensive practice in recognizing thought groups; in pausing between them in longer sentences; and in blending final sounds of words with the initial sound of the following word *within the same* thought group.

The effectiveness of pronunciation drill should be measured mainly by the improvement made by students in their daily language activities—conversing, reading, summarizing, engaging in varied practice, etc.

Perhaps of the three major facets of language learning—pronunciation, structure, and vocabulary—mastery of pronunciation is the most difficult to achieve. Older pupils, especially, even after intensive training in a sound, tend to revert to the more familiar approximate sound in their native tongue. This is more evident during "free" discussions or during structural pattern practice, where the attention of the student is not focused on pronunciation particularly but on meaning or idea.

A world of patience is needed by the teacher to try to develop in pupils the aural acuity needed for pronunciation and to overcome their inhibitions in saying sounds which may be completely new to them. The same sentence may have to be practiced over and over again for months before progress is obvious. The necessity of concentrating on one sound makes it extremely difficult to hear a perfect or near-perfect utterance at one time, but the teacher will have occasion—or create occasions—to practice the same or a similar utterance many times during the semester with noticeable improvement each time it is said. If the teacher will look for and commend good pronunciation as well as structural facility during all phases of language work, if he will insist on the complete repetition of an utterance that has been given in small parts, improvement can be effected.

We wish to emphasize again in connection with pronunciation that the teacher or assistant should serve as the model before pupils are asked to say or read anything. It is important also that pupils *not be* asked to read orally to other class members unless they have attained a very high degree of competency. Since the acquisition of good pronunciation depends primarily upon listening to and imitating good oral models, learners should not be exposed to anything but perfect or nearly perfect speech in the classroom situation.

It is important, too, that the teacher not exaggerate or distort speech sounds or intonation in the mistaken notion that this will aid pupils in comprehension or production. (Other English speakers will generally not do so for the pupils.) *The teacher or assistant should speak normally at all times.* Sounds may be isolated for intensive practice but, as quickly as possible, they should be inserted in normal utterances and spoken with authentic intonation and rhythm.

When an utterance is too long for easy initial repetition, it should be practiced in logical segments (thought groups) and then in its entirety. The utterance may be divided from the beginning or from the end:

I see || Mr. Jones || every day.

The teacher should say the entire utterance twice; then (if it is divided from the beginning) students should repeat in chorus *after* the teacher's model in the following way:

I see
Mr. Jones
I see Mr. Jones
every day
I see Mr. Jones every day.

If divided from the end, the order would be:

every day
Mr. Jones
Mr. Jones every day
I see
I see Mr. Jones every day.

The emphasis on language learning today is on achieving understanding. Most authorities recognize that the complete elimination of a "foreign" accent is impossible in the majority of older students without a tremendous expenditure of time and effort. This effort might better be given to helping them acquire more habitual control of the structure system of English and greater fluency in the language. The practice of structure patterns and of vocabulary will automatically contribute to more accurate sound production. It is important, however, that the teacher strive for comprehensibility at all times, even during those periods in the lesson when he is not giving concentrated practice on elements of the sound system.

TEACHING STRUCTURES AND VOCABULARY ITEMS

The same five basic steps (*recognition, repetition, practice, conscious selection,* and *production*) are essential in presenting and practicing structures and vocabulary. Let us assume that you wish to teach the names of colors and the position of adjectives of color in front of the noun. You would first motivate the lesson and then review the names of the objects which you will use in developing the new structure. For example, you would elicit, "This is a pencil—a book—a notebook—a scarf—a hat, etc.," all of which had been previously taught.

These sentences would be placed on the *front left* board (*only if the students can read,* however). You would then say, "Now let's learn something (or Let's talk) about the pencil, the scarf, (etc.). Look. Listen. 'This is a red pencil.' Listen again, 'This is a red pencil.' " Your model would be followed by unison and later by individual repetition, students saying, however, "That's a red pencil." A short question-answer drill could take place at this point or you may prefer to present, in the same way, one or two more nouns preceded by *red* before giving a substitution drill in which the name of the object is varied while the word *red*—the item being taught—is kept constant.

It is desirable during the first presentation of the concept that the adjective and the basic structural pattern remain unchanged. The repetition, for example, might take the following form:

Teacher: "This is a red book."
Pupil(s): "That's a red book."
Teacher: "This is a red scarf."
Pupil(s): "That's a red scarf," using the names of the assembled objects of "red" color.

In order that pupils who can read *see* the structural arrangement with the adjective, the new sentences, with the adjective *red* underlined, are placed next to the original review sentences. Better still, the sentences can be boxed or framed as follows showing the position of *red* more graphically:

This	is	a		book.
This	is	a		pencil.
This	is	a	red	book.
This	is	a	red	pencil.

That's	a		book.
That's	a		scarf.
That's	a	red	book.
That's	a	red	scarf.

Depending on the age of the pupils (after sufficient practice with *red,* for example) one or two additional colors may be introduced in the same structural pattern on the same day. Later lessons on colors may be devoted to structures such as, "The book is red"; "The books are red"; "Is the book red?"; "Are the books red?"; "Is the book red or blue?" etc. Whether one or more of these patterns are taught in one lesson will depend on the age and learning level of the pupils and the language items with which the pupils are familiar because they have been previously taught.

The same procedure is followed in presenting any vocabulary item or sentence pattern. For example, in teaching a more complex pattern such as, "I eat breakfast at (eight) o'clock," the teacher would have available a large clock with hands indicating the hour (eight o'clock) and a picture of someone eating breakfast. After an *appropriate* motivation he would review numbers and expressions of time. Then, pointing to himself, he would say, "I eat breakfast at (eight) o'clock every day." He would ask the learners to repeat, while pointing to themselves, "I eat breakfast at (eight) o'clock every day." Repetition by individual members would follow.

After much oral repetition this sentence is placed on the board, spoken by the teacher, and repeated first in chorus and then by individual students. The same procedure, aided by pantomime and dramatization, would be used in presenting *you, we, he, she,* etc. The teacher's models are followed by extensive choral and individual repetition. After repetitive practice, a substitution drill and a replacement drill should be given. (See page 117 for discussion.) These drills—during the same lesson (only if time permits, of course) or in subsequent lessons—may be followed by a *sequential* series of question-answer drills; for example,

Teacher (to many individual learners)	*Individual Students*
1. Do you eat breakfast at eight o'clock?*	Yes, I do.
2. Do you eat breakfast at seven or at eight?	At eight.
3. Do you eat breakfast at seven or at eight? ("A complete sentence, please.")	I eat breakfast at seven.
4. (At) what time do you eat breakfast?	At seven, *or* I eat breakfast at seven.

Each of these questions and responses may again give rise to substitution drills and to replacement drills.

Subsequent lessons may be devoted to giving pupils practice in using the same sentence pattern with other hours for meals. "I eat lunch at 12 o'clock" or "He eats dinner at 7 o'clock."

"What are the next steps?" is a question often asked. There is no one best step. For example, you may wish to develop and give practice as next steps in:

I cook (breakfast) at _____ o'clock.

    or

* Teachers are reminded to exercise care in asking questions which elicit the verb forms in a natural manner. It is recommended that interrogative words be used such as "When" or "Where" in front of "Do you eat breakfast" in order to practice the *verb* form. (The natural answer to "Do you eat breakfast?" is "Yes, I do.")

I wash at ———— o'clock.
> or

I get up at ———— o'clock.
> or

I come to school at ———— o'clock.
> or

I eat a large (breakfast).
> or

I eat a small (breakfast) of (bread and butter) at ————
o'clock.

Any one of the above next steps is possible and logical, provided the sentence arrangement is retained so that pupils can
gain security and some degree of flexibility in generating new
sentence combinations without varying the basic pattern. Often,
the next steps are determined by the textbook being used or by
the needs of the learners in other curriculum areas.

Two important facts to remember in *introducing* a language
item are that (1) the other language items to be used in presenting it should be familiar to the pupils; and (2) only the
familiar items which are most appropriate to the new item
should be reviewed in various drill activities immediately prior
to the presentation of the new structure. In *practicing* a language
item, the teacher's model is followed by pupil repetition and
then by a *single slot* substitution or, where feasible, by a replacement drill.

BASIC PRACTICE ACTIVITIES

The structures, sentence patterns, and vocabulary items presented should be practiced intensively so that they can be understood by the pupils with ease and spoken with increasingly
greater control of pronunciation, word form and word order.
Moreover, pupils have to be helped to gain insight, through
varied practice, into the types of words or expressions which

fit into the various slots of an utterance or sentence. For example, words such as *the, a, some, each,* can be fitted into the determiner slot. *Nouns, noun phrases,* and *pronouns* can be fitted into the noun slot. Pupils also have to be helped to learn—and this is by far the most important and most satisfying step—how the *entire* sentence or utterance fits into an actual communication situation. Both phases of language learning—habituation and communication—are essential. Effective communication is impossible without the preliminary step of habituation leading to control of features of pronunciation, word form and word order. Habituation, on the other hand, becomes a meaningless, sterile exercise unless it results in normal, authentic communication.

The intensive drills suggested below are designed to give students the progressive skill needed to understand and to use the meaningful signals of English in listening and speaking and, eventually, in reading and writing.

These drills have been called by different names by different writers but the name has no intrinsic importance. There are, however, several fundamental guidelines with which most educators are in agreement:

1. The drills should be preceded by repetition drills—whole class, sub-groups, individuals.

2. Two or three models of the response desired should be given by the teacher *before* students are asked to respond.

3. Unless half-class question and response is required, preceded by a teacher model (see page 256 for the procedure), *all responses should be given by individual students.* Confusion results even with a simple question such as, "What's today?," which may elicit three or four different responses.

4. Drills are usually carried out with four kinds of cues or stimuli: a) The teacher gives an oral word and, where possible, indicates the object or picture to which it refers in order to reinforce sound and concept; b) the teacher gives the word orally; c) the teacher points to a picture or object; d) the teacher shows

the written word on a cue or flashcard or on the chalkboard.

5. Various types of pupil participation may be required with each of the cues: The teacher may call on a student to respond; a pupil may ask the teacher to respond; a pupil may ask another pupil to respond.

6. The directions to the pupils are made very clear. For example, in a substitution drill: "Now I'll give you some words. Use them in place of the word 'book.' "

In a replacement drill: "I'm going to give you some sentences beginning with a boy's *name*. Use *he* in place of the boy's name."

7. As noted above, the step of *conscious selection* (between two or more items) is attempted only *after* many repetition and substitution drills have been practiced with *each* specific item. This step may have to be deferred for several days or more; that is, until the learners can use each of the individual items—for example, the simple present and "ing" present—with reasonable fluency.

8. Hand signals should be used in conducting drills so that a definite rhythm is established. Oral directions such as "The whole class," "This half of the class," or a pupil's name interspersed between the teacher's model and the pupil response interrupt the response of the pupil to a given stimulus.

9. Every drill should contain a model, a cue, and a response.

10. The slot fillers, particularly in beginning practice activities—those not demanding conscious selection by the learners—must be carefully chosen. Note, for example, that the verb "enjoy" cannot be used as a *substitute* verb in the pattern "I want to eat," since it is obligatory in English that "enjoy" be followed by the "ing" form. Verbs like "need" and "like," however, could be used.

Note, too, that although the *surface* structure is alike in the two sentences "John is easy to please" and "John is eager to please," the *deep* structure of the sentences is quite different. The two sentences are derived from different base (or kernel) sentences. Moreover, whereas the first sentence may be *transformed* to "It is easy to please John," the second cannot.

Substitution

In this, students are asked to use another word of the same class; that is, *the same part of speech* in the place of a word in the model sentence. A noun is replaced by another noun, a verb by another verb, an adjective by another adjective (cf. 10, above).

As noted above, the teacher may utilize various stimuli. For example, let us assume that the pattern to be drilled is "I have a _____."

1. Say, "I have a book." Repeat it. Pause for a moment. Say the cue word "ruler" and show a ruler. The student called upon will say, "I have a ruler." Say "notebook" and show one. The student called upon will say, "I have a notebook." Continue in this way, practicing about ten sentences.

2. Use the oral word alone as a cue.

3. Instead of saying the word, show the object. As above, say the sentence, show an object for the word to be substituted, then call on a student.

4. Instead of saying the word or showing the object, point to a picture of it. Give the model sentence, then point to the picture. At times, have pupils come up and point to the pictures. They can then ask you or one of their classmates to give the new sentence.

5. Instead of the spoken word, object or picture, use flash-cards on which are written individual words or write the words on the blackboard *under* the one to be substituted. Use this fourth cue only *after* reading has been taught.

Replacement

The students will be expected to replace one part of speech or one type of modal by another, e.g., nouns or names by pronouns; *must* by *have to, ought to* by *should*.

1. Give the model sentence; e.g., "Harry has a dog." The students will be expected to say, "*He* has a dog." Do not change

the object; e.g., dog, in any of the sentences in this type of drill in the beginning stages of learning. In the drills we will describe, only *one* element in the sentence is to be changed at one time, except for the Progressive Replacement Drill (explained below).

2. Give sentences such as "I know the boy." Students will say, "I know him." Please notice the change of intonation in the second sentence, or, as it is called, in the "derived" sentence.

3. Give sentences such as "I *must* study now." Students will be expected to say, "I *have to* study now."

4. At more advanced levels, students may be asked to replace verbs not followed by the marked infinitive (with to) by those that are; e.g., "Make him eat." "Ask" (cue).

Paired Sentences

In this drill, give a sentence and then ask a question. For example, say "Rose likes spinach. What about you?" A student would say, "I like spinach, too."

Negatives can also be practiced. Give sentences such as "Rose doesn't like coffee. What about Harry?" A student would say, "He doesn't like coffee, either."

Combined sentences such as the following could be drilled: "Mary doesn't like to study but John does"; "We don't like to swim and Harry doesn't like to swim either."

Transformation (Sometimes Called Conversion)

Students will be given practice in deriving *plurals* from *singulars* or vice versa; *negative* or *interrogative** sentences from *affirmative* sentences; sentences in the *past* or *future* time from sentences in the *present; passive* sentences from *active* sentences; *full* forms from *contracted* forms; *complex* or *compound* sentences from *two simple* sentences.

As always, the teacher will give the model sentence and ex-

* The derived interrogative sentences should be of two types: *inverted* and *Wh* questions. Thus, the interrogative sentences practiced with "George went to the park" could be, "Did George go to the park?" (inverted question), "Who went to the park?" and "Where did George go?" (*Wh* questions).

plicit directions, saying for example: "Now we're going to make questions from these sentences. Listen, 'He has a pencil.' Now listen to the question, 'Does he have a pencil?' or 'Has he a pencil?' " (depending on the form which has been taught).

It is not necessary to use words like negative, future, etc. Instead, say something like, "Let's start each sentence with *No*" or "Let's use *tomorrow* in these sentences."

Expansion

The students will be given a word or expression to be *added to* a sentence you give them. For example, say, "Let's add the words *very well* to the sentences I give you. 'I know the lesson.' " A student would say, "I know the lesson very well."

At later levels of learning they may be asked to add elements such as *I'm sure, I think, I know* before other sentences. They may also be required to insert adjectives into the proper place. For example:

I have a dress. (model)
Pretty (cue)
I have a pretty dress. (response)
White (cue)
I have a pretty white dress. (response)
Two (cue)
I have two pretty white dresses. (response)

After giving intensive practice in sentences in which the addition does *not* change the word order or the word forms of the sentence, ask students to expand sentences which will necessitate changes in either word form or word order. For example, say, "Use *later* in these sentences. 'I'm studying.' " The student would say, "I'm going to study later." Say, "Place *I don't know* in front of these questions; for example, 'Where is he?' " The student would say, "I don't know where he is." You may say, "Place '*He asked him*' in front of these questions: 'Where are you going?' " The student would say, "He asked him where he was going."

Reduction

This drill may be considered a form of replacement drill because a sentence is "reduced" by changing an expression to a word. For example, "I'm going *to the store*" becomes "I'm going *there*." "Come *to this restaurant*" becomes "Come *here*."

Later, substitute expressions can be introduced and practiced. "I'd like one of the books in the window" may become "I'd like one of those"; "I see all the people" is reduced to "I see everyone." "I believe it's raining" becomes "I believe so." *It is important to practice intonation changes* in sentences such as these.

Directed Practice

A student is directed (asked) to ask another student a question. The second student is directed to answer. The drill is usually practiced in three stages:

1. Teacher: X ask Y, "Do you have a sister?"
   Teacher: Y tell X, "I have a sister" or ("Yes, I do").
2. Teacher: "X, ask Y if he has a sister" and whispers to X, "Say, 'Do you have a sister?'"
   Teacher says to Y, "Y, tell X that you have a sister" and whispers to Y, "Yes, I have a sister" or "Yes, I do," which student Y says aloud.
3. The teacher does not whisper the direct question to the student who is to ask the question nor does he whisper the direct answer. (Of course, the students are to be helped or "prompted" when necessary but if the directed drills are practiced over a long period of time, students will need little or no help at Stage III.)

Integration

(Some authors consider this a form of *Transformation Drill*)

Students are asked to derive one sentence from two sentences. For example, "I have a book. It's my English book" becomes "I have my English book." "The boy's father is ill. I'm talking to the boy" becomes "The father of the boy to whom I'm talking is ill." "You talk a lot. He talks very little" may become "You talk more than he does." "I'm late. I missed the bus" may become "I'm late because I missed the bus."

Progressive Replacement

This practice activity needs much teacher help at the beginning. It is a *multiple* substitution drill. While in the substitution drill we discussed above we changed only one element or slot filler at a time—the noun *or* the adjective *or* the verb—in this drill a new element is changed in *each* sentence. Students called upon have to remember what was said in each preceding sentence in order to form their new sentence.

Following is one example. (Incidentally, practice should also be given with the noncontracted form *would*.)

Teacher					*Student*
I'd	like	a	history	book.	I'd like a history book.
He					He'd like a history book.
				workbook	He'd like a history workbook.
Mary					Mary'd like a history workbook.
			English		Mary'd like an English workbook.
				story	Mary'd like an English story.
	prefer				Mary'd prefer an English story.

Students will find it helpful if you place lines on the board to indicate slots and if you point to the appropriate line as you say the word to be substituted.

Multiple Transformations

A brisk drill giving practice in two or more transformations lends variety and interest. For example, student 1 or group 1 will say, "He can go." Student or group 2, "He can't go." Student or group 3, "Can't he go?" Student or group 4 can say,

"Why can't he go?" Naturally, any other known, logical verb can be substituted for *go*.

Numerous other types of transformations can be combined. Following are some model sentences with possible transformations:

I'm tired.	*He's* tired *too*.
Call her.	*I'm calling* her *now*.
He'll need money.	He *always needs* money.
John is absent today.	He *was* absent *yesterday also*.
Do you do your homework every day?	*Why don't* you do your homework every day?
Here's a letter.	*What kind of* letter *is it*?
Do you know who this book belongs to?	*I think that* book is *mine*.

Question-Answer Practice

Let us examine some basic question-answer drills which can be used to good effect in teaching structure. These proceed from the simple to the more complex within affirmative and negative. (Questions which can be utilized in developing the skill of reading are discussed in the chapter on Reading.) The teacher gives explicit directions as to the response required.

1. Answer Yes. "Do you have a brother?" "Yes."
2. Answer Yes. Give a short answer. "Do you have a brother?" "Yes, I do" *or* "Yes, I have."
3. Answer Yes. Give a long answer (or a complete sentence). "Do you have a brother?" "Yes, I have a brother."
4. Answer Yes. Give a short answer and a long answer. "Do you have a brother?" "Yes, I do. I have a brother."
5. Answer No. "Do you have a brother?" "No."
6. Answer No. Give a short answer. "Do you have a brother?" "No, I don't."
7. Answer No. Give a short and a long answer. "Do you have a brother?" "No, I don't. I don't have a brother."

8. Answer No. Give a long answer and tell what you have (or what this [it] is). "Do you have a brother?" "No, I don't have a brother. I have a sister." "Is this a chair?" "No, it's not a chair. It's a desk."

9. Choose one *or* the other. "Do you have a brother or a sister?" "I have a (brother)."

10. Patterned Response: To the teacher's or another student's question or cue, the student called upon always answers with the response being practiced. For example, "Do you like playing baseball?" "Yes, very much." At more advanced levels, the patterned response drill can be used to practice changes in word form or word order. Notice: The boys are hungry. So is John (or John is too). Harry is tired. So is John.
He's thirsty. So am I. Mrs. X is sleepy. So am I.

11. Cued Response: The teacher gives the model sentence and then a word* (or words) which the student is to include in his response. For example, the teacher would say, "Where's John?" (movies). The student would say, "John's" or "He's at the movies." "What's the matter with him?" (hungry). The student would say, "He's hungry."

12. Echo Response: "Do you know where Mary's coat is?" "Her coat? It's over there."

13. Free Response: The teacher may ask a question on anything that has been practiced. It is obvious that other question-answer drills indicated above precede this one.

In addition to the many kinds of pupil participation suggested above under practice activities, question-answer drills lend themselves to chain practice drills. The direction of the "chain" should be made clear to the learners; that is, the question or statement is made to the pupil next to him or in back of him. Chain drills too have several variations:

1. Student 1 asks student 2 a question. Student 2 answers and asks the same question of Student 3.

* Some teachers prefer to give the cue word and then ask the question.

2. Student 1 asks student 2 a question. Student 2 answers. Student 3 asks the question of student 4.

3. Student 1 asks Student 2 a question; e.g., "Do you have your book?" Student 2 answers, "Yes, I do" or "Yes, I have my book." Student 3 asks student 4, "Does he (she) have his (her) book?," referring to student 2.

Chain drills should be broken frequently. After six to eight students have participated in a chain of question or statement and response at one end of the room, the teacher should begin the same chain in another part of the room. Effective, too, is to change not only the section of the room participating in the chain drill but also some element in the question, statement, or response itself. Only in this way can we keep the interest and attention of students and ensure that wide pupil activity which is basic to learning.

Some of the drills described above lend themselves better than others to specific items pupils are learning. With all items, repetition and substitution drills are essential and should *precede* all other types of drills. In teaching adjectives of color, for example, expansion and integration drills would be appropriate. In teaching verb forms, replacement and transformation drills would be effective.

It is important to vary the drill activities and to conduct them briskly. As soon as interest in one type of drill lags, the teacher should proceed to another type, or he should vary the cue from oral to picture or to real object or to written word on the blackboard or on a flashcard. The type of pupil participation should also be changed frequently: From choral repetition, we proceed to small group and then individual repetition; from the teacher questioning students, we proceed to students questioning the teacher or questioning each other.

Toward Freer Communication

Drills should lead gradually to the normal use of language in everyday communication situations. Formulas of the language, expressions such as *Of course, Not at all, How do you do?* should be practiced, as well as introductory words so common in English such as *So, Well, Then, First, Let's see.*

Practice in using appropriate courtesy expressions in the everyday situations of life should also be an important part of classroom training. Expressions such as *May I have?, Would you like?, Could you please?, Would it be possible?* should be re-entered in as many dialogue situations as possible so that students will learn to recognize the areas of communication in which each can be used most normally and logically.

In addition to dialogues in which each speaker in turn makes one statement or where one asks and the other answers a question, multiple responses and longer sustained dialogues should be learned and dramatized as soon as feasible. For example, a dialogue with younger children might show the following progressive gradations:

I

That's a nice dog.
Thanks.

II

That's a nice dog. What's his name?
Rover. I just got him.

III

That's a nice dog. What's his name?
Rover. I just got him.
Can he do tricks? (*or* Can I play with him?)
Yes, of course.

Two other techniques might be mentioned. With one, the teacher gives a model sentence and a student replaces *any* word or words using any previously learned materials. With another, the teacher describes a situation briefly and asks, "What would you say?" For example, "Jean says she's going to have a birthday party and would like you to come" or "Your father tells you he's found you a job." The learners are encouraged to say anything feasible in their linguistic repertoire.

In addition to these practice activities, such procedures as the adaptation or variation of dialogues which have been learned, the discussion of pictures or stories, role-playing, the conducting of interviews, or the summaries of materials read will give students the progressive ability to communicate more freely about gradually less controlled situations.

RECOMMENDATIONS FOR TEACHING STRUCTURES AND VOCABULARY

We wish to emphasize the following suggestions which have been implicit in everything we have said:

1. The initial sentence patterns and vocabulary to be developed should arise, if possible, from an experience—in the school, in the home, or in the community—in which the pupils themselves have participated.

2. Structures and vocabulary should be clearly interrelated and should be pertinent to a specific topic or experience. (How can we justify teaching "needle" and "apple," for example, in the same lesson?)

3. Important sentence patterns for active use should be practiced until students can understand them, internalize them, and use them in any communication situation.

4. New language forms—for example, comparisons of adjectives—should be presented and practiced with a limited known vocabulary. It is unwise to bring in, at one time, more than one new language difficulty.

5. Language should be built on patterns or forms over which pupils already have some control. For example, a teaching sequence might be:

 a. You know John.
 b. (Do) you know John?
 c. (Do) you know John'(s) (brother)?

6. Other words can and should be substituted within the same sentence pattern. Knowing most of the parts of a sentence

gives the pupils needed confidence. To illustrate: (Note that *single* slot substitutions should precede multiple slot substitutions.)

a.

Do	they	know	(Mary)?
(Do)	(you)	recognize	(Frank)?
(Does)	(she)	see	(John)?
(Does)	(Tom)	like	(Henry)?*

b.

Do	you	recognize	John's sister?
(Do)	(they)	(know)	John's aunt?
(Do)	(you)	(like)	John's father?
(Does)	(he)	(visit)	John's mother?

c.   Don't you (recognize) John's (sister)? Etc.

7. Structural patterns which are familiar to pupils should be reintroduced and practiced again and again in other situations or with other experiences. Illustrations of this principle are found throughout this book.

8. For *beginning teaching*, structures should be selected on the basis of the following criteria:

a. They are easily demonstrable in the classroom; e.g., "Open the door."

b. They are useful in a wide number of situations; e.g., "Where do you live?" "Where do you sit?" "Where do you eat?" "*What's* (this)" "*It's* a _____."

c. They are similar to structural patterns in the pupils' native tongue (whenever this is possible). This gives learners a feeling of security.

9. Vocabulary should not be restricted by word lists or other dogmatic criteria. The need for the vocabulary in a meaningful situation or in a curriculum area should always determine the selection of words to be taught for active, functional use.

10. Practice exercises should be graded. The first exercises

---

* Remember that *I, you, we,* and *they* are taught together and later *he* and *she* are introduced because of the change in verb form with *he* and *she*.

should be of the repetitive type and should not require *recall* of the words being taught.

11. Too much emphasis should not be placed on the mere acquisition of vocabulary, particularly the names of things. Too often we find pupils speaking "pidgin" English, knowing a number of nouns and very few verbs and function words, and not knowing how to put even the nouns together. It is important that vocabulary be developed and practiced in meaningful sentences. The word "butcher," for example, should be used in sentences like, "The butcher sells meat" or "The butcher is cutting the meat now" or "That butcher has good meat."

12. Vocabulary drill should be only the forerunner of important language activities such as listening, engaging in conversation, or reading with comprehension. In other words, the vocabulary should be developed and practiced in order that it may be used in a communication situation. *Vocabulary should not be taught as an end in itself.*

13. Teacher planning of lessons should allow for flexibility. If the teacher realizes that pupils already know the meanings of some of the words he has planned to teach, he should not give five or six exercises using those words. Instead, he should elicit their meanings from the pupils. He may also give practice in using the words with other known vocabulary or structural items.

14. Well-organized schematic arrangements of verbs and pronouns (called paradigms) also help to give pupils a sense of confidence and order. In teaching new verb forms or in practicing familiar verb forms, it is desirable, as we know, to insist on the sequence of pronouns: *I, you, we, you, they, he, she.* Moreover, the teaching of *I* and *you* and of questions with *you* allows for immediate conversation between two people—the essence of an act of speech.

15. Teachers will find that "boxing" or "framing" basic patterns helps pupils who can read to "see" the basic structure and to combine and manipulate vocabulary and grammatical items. An example of boxing would be the following (note how the form or pattern of the language is made clear to pupils):

a.

I	want	a	ham	sandwich
			cheese	
			chicken	
			jam	

b. Ideally, separate frames should be used for each language item or concept. However, frames such as the following are frequently and effectively used, especially for review purposes:

	I .	want	a	ham	sandwich	
	We	want	a	cheese	sandwich.	
Do	they	want	a	chicken	sandwich	on white bread?
Does	he	want	a	ham	sandwich?	

16. Frames like these above permit the practice of numerous sentences. First the sentences are said across. Then elements from each column are combined in various ways to generate other sentences on the same pattern.

17. *All* the *function words* of English (see page 37) should be taught for *active* use but in a logical sequence and in the contexts in which they are normally used. Many content words (names of things, actions, qualities) will remain part of the pupils' passive vocabulary. (See pages 130-131 for a discussion of active and passive vocabulary.)

18. Often words which would not generally be taught in the beginning stages of language learning are introduced early. Examples are "saw" and "went," which are needed to talk and write about trips or filmstrip viewing (see page 215).

19. A conscious effort must be made to enrich the vocabulary and extend the concepts of learners so that they can go from the understanding of limited speech or reading materials to a fuller comprehension of ungraded material. Whenever possible and logical, the class and school environment should be "exploited" to extend the meaning of a concept. For example, if "corner" is taught with relation to a square, the teacher will also

have the learners indicate, touch, or walk to, the corners of the room, a table, a box, a desk, etc.

Vocabulary may be enriched by giving learners practice in:

a. finding antonyms or synonyms of known words
b. finding words of the same family (the grocery, the grocer, groceries, etc.)
c. finding words under the same topic or category
d. recognizing words which create sensory images
e. studying figures of speech
f. using tools of research
g. paraphrasing words or phrases
h. adding prefixes and suffixes to known words

20. Pupils should be given extensive training in determining meanings of unfamiliar words from the context or from other clues. In addition to the vocabulary enrichment techniques indicated above, practice in guessing the meaning of a word from its position among other known words in the sentence will help to give pupils independence in listening and in reading. More will be said about this skill in the chapter on reading.

21. Although some language can be learned incidentally, particularly in an English-speaking community, it is essential that direct, consistent, and systematic practice be given to pupils in order to ensure the correct and habitual use of the basic structural arrangements of the English language.

FURTHER CONSIDERATIONS IN VOCABULARY SELECTION AND TEACHING

A word should be said about the distinction between active (functional or productive) and passive (recognitional or receptive) vocabulary and about the use of word lists. That vocabulary is *active* which is learned so intensively as to *form, meaning* and *function* that it can be used by the pupil in *any* listening, speaking, reading, or writing activity. Vocabulary is considered *passive* when students will understand its meaning in either oral or written context without, however, being able to produce it themselves. A person's receptive vocabulary will always be larger than his active vocabulary, even in his native tongue.

Some words or structures may remain part of the pupils' passive vocabulary for an indefinite length of time until the need arises for more intensive study. For example, in giving students practice in a pattern such as, "I live in," the teacher will ask, "Where do you live?," in order to elicit the response "I live in" without necessarily giving the pupils the practice needed to *formulate* the question. More detailed explanations and practice leading to habitual control of the question pattern and to active manipulation of other pronouns within that pattern—e.g., "Where does he live?"—will be deferred by the teacher for another lesson.

Other "recognitional" words may never be made part of the students' active vocabulary if the teacher feels that they are not found frequently enough in reading or that they are not needed by the pupils in communication situations in which they may find themselves.

With regard to word lists we wish to express a word of caution about their use in the English program. Research studies indicate that word lists are usually compiled as the result of a subjective selection of texts or other written materials. It is natural, therefore, that there is little or no unanimity of opinion as to what constitutes the most frequently used or needed word. The unquestioning use of word lists may be detrimental since it may prevent the teacher from developing the full English his pupils need. It must be remembered that it is the use of a word in a context which gives the word its distinctive meaning. The word "get," for example, acquires scores of meanings depending upon its relation to other words in a sentence.

Nor should the teacher confine himself to teaching the vocabulary found in one textbook alone. By doing so, pupils will acquire a vocabulary limited to the kind of situation set up by the author of the particular textbook.

It is preferable that the teacher present the vocabulary which arises naturally out of a situation or experience which has meaning for students. For example, words like "thermometer" and "doctor" may need to be taught at the very beginning of the English program, although they may be far down on a standard word list. A simple word like "museum" or "zoo," on the other hand, would be deferred if the English classes are in a rural area where such words are not within the immediate experience of the pupils.

In selecting and teaching the vocabulary which arises out of an experience that the pupils have had, the teacher will make a number of distinctions. He will select and teach *actively* those words which the pupils can use in the *greatest* number of real situations. Thus, even the word "thermometer" which is presented may be taught for recognitional purposes rather than for productive purposes. He will select for active use the general term rather than the less common, more specific word for an item. For example, he would teach the word "bread" in the beginning rather than "rolls" or "twist" or "French loaf." He would, in addition, group the words under logical headings to help pupils gain insight into their meaning through associating them with other words in a category. Names of foods, or of people performing various community services, can be taught more efficiently in this way.

SUMMARY

The teacher may find it more effective to make use of an eclectic approach in the teaching of English after consideration of such factors as his pupils' abilities, the objectives set up by the school district, and the community he is serving. We have offered several criteria for the selection of vocabulary and for the sequence of language building. Specific steps in the presentation of structures and vocabulary have been given in some detail. The importance of making speech (pronunciation, intonation, and rhythm) an integral part of language development has been stressed. Several suggestions with relation to the teaching of pronunciation have been indicated.

The interrelationships of vocabulary, sentence structure, and pronunciation cannot be overemphasized. Concomitant growth in these three aspects of language must be carefully planned and guided if pupils are to achieve effective communication.

Numerous pattern practice drills have been recommended which are necessary to help students gain habitual control of word form and word order. As quickly as feasible, however, pupils must be engaged in the kinds of learning activities which will enable them to understand and to use the knowledge gained through pattern practice in the communication situations of their everyday life in the school and in the community.

CHAPTER 4

Developing Reading
and Writing Skills

Although it is generally placed third in the hierarchy of communication abilities to be developed, an important goal of the language program is the teaching of reading. This is true not only because learning in many subject areas in the schools involves reading, but also because the ability to read all types of material with comprehension, ease, and enjoyment will contribute to the self-realization and increased personal-social adjustment of pupils.

Schools will want to organize a developmental reading program which will promote the continuous growth of pupils' reading power. Such a program, however, which should result in the pupils' turning to books for recreation and for information with a sense of pleasurable anticipation, needs to be carefully planned.

School-wide and district-wide planning will include making provision for the placement of specific reading skills at various learning levels in the curriculum, for the preparation of appropriate materials, for the individualization of instruction, for the continuous evaluation of the program, and for the training of teachers.

The teachers' planning will include evolving techniques and procedures for grouping students; for extending the pupils' experiences; for teaching word recognition skills; for developing a rich vocabulary; for ensuring comprehension; and for increasing speed in reading, while maintaining the pupils' interest in the thought behind the printed word.

Reading is a language related process. The teaching of beginning reading consists in helping pupils relate and transfer the auditory signals that they will have already learned (since initial reading is *always* based on material the students can understand and say) to new visual signals. Students will have to be guided to realize that the visual marks on paper or on the blackboard have a definite relationship to the *spoken* language. Just as in *spoken* practice exercises they were expected to utter expressions or sentences when an oral cue was given, in oral *reading* they will be expected to utter the sounds with which they are familiar when they are presented with printed or written letters. Just as our aim in the understanding-speaking phases of the program was spontaneous, habitual control of speech sounds in certain prescribed sequences, our aim in reading is to help pupils develop habitual, increasingly more fluent reponses to visual marks which represent language.

A problem in teaching reading, even to native speakers, is that in English the same written letter or letters can represent various sounds. There is still enough correspondence, however, between letter and sound on which teachers can capitalize in teaching beginning reading. Various techniques for developing letter and word recognition skills will be given below.

There are other more serious problems, though, in teaching English to speakers of other languages. And here we have to return to some of the factors within our learners that we touched on in Chapter 1. Reading is a complex process requiring the knowledge of several separate skills. Each reading skill will have to be developed in a psychologically sound, graded sequence. How can this be done? How can teachers handle various *existing* situations in their classes: one in which five- or six-year-old children enter heterogeneous classes in predominantly English-speaking communities embracing many children having a limited background of concepts; one in which ten-year-olds are literate in their native tongue but have no knowledge of English; one in which fourteen-year-olds are illiterate both in their native tongue and in English. There are, moreover, other intermediate stages with which experienced administrators and teachers are familiar but which puzzle inexperienced teachers.

Assuming, too, that the skilled teacher in the primary grades has used numerous "reading readiness" techniques before introducing the printed word, will he be able to utilize all the necessary techniques again and again for individual children who appear at the school door at any time during the semester? Will older, mature adolescents be happy for any length of time with the primers which they are often given in beginning reading classes?

There are no easy, simple answers to these and related problems. Some solutions lie in the direction of (1) training teachers in group organization and dynamics; (2) setting up materials committees on a school-wide or district-wide basis to prepare original group and individual materials or to adapt existing texts in all the curriculum areas; (3) establishing class libraries with wide ranges of reading materials; and (4), difficult as this may seem, placing—at least temporarily—language learners who could not possibly profit from instruction in regular classes, or even in language classes with their age peers, in *special classes,* with *specially trained* teachers and with *specially* designed materials for intensive instruction.

Current research also seems to indicate that there may be some advantages in teaching illiterate language learners to read in their native tongue before teaching them to read in English. The rationale appears simple. *Native* English speakers have heard and spoken English for about six years before any systematic attempt is made to transfer their aural-oral skill to reading. Since reading is language-related, native speakers of other languages can be taught more easily to read the tongue they have understood and spoken since birth. *The entire reading skill* can then be transferred to the reading of English. Problems arise, of course, when the orthography of the native tongue is not similar to English or, indeed, when the native language has no writing system. More experimentation will need to be done before this procedure can be generally recommended.

In any case, teachers of speakers of other languages should not lose sight of the fact that it will take several years for many of these pupils to catch up with their English-speaking peers. The latter came to school (and therefore to reading) with a grasp of the structure system, with a knowledge of pronunciation, and with a speaking vocabulary of varying lengths. The language learners, on the other hand, have to acquire the basic pronunciation, structure system, and vocabulary before they can begin to read.

To return to the question of how to teach reading, it is important to emphasize that language learning is a cumulative process and that reading is language-related. We cannot skip entirely or teach inadequately any of the features of pronunciation, word form, word sequence, and vocabulary which constitute the meaningful signals of English, oral or written. Reading, in addition, requires other skills which also cannot be bypassed.

What are some of these skills? Through which stages of growth should all learners have to pass? What special considerations need to be kept in mind? Our discussion now will turn to a brief overview of some of these.

It is strongly recommended that further reading be done by interested personnel in those general aspects of the topic which underlie reading programs for beginning *native* English speakers. (Consult Resources and Texts, page 457.) The terminal behavior desired, the stages of sequential growth, and many techniques are similar for native English speakers and for English learners. We will concentrate on considerations that are particularly applicable to English-language learners.

SOME CONSIDERATIONS

1. Understanding and speaking should *always* precede reading. It is only *after* students can say any material with reasonable fluency that they should be permitted to see it.

2. The length of time the teaching of reading should be de-

ferred has been a matter of some controversy among language specialists. Again, there is no one answer to suit every situation.

Language learners should hear *many* times and may be able to repeat with reasonable accuracy any material before they see it, but the number of class hours which should elapse between hearing, saying, and reading must be flexible and should depend on the factors with which we are familiar.

For example, with children who come to school at the age of six, the length of time of *possible* deferment may be two years. Depending upon their literacy in their native tongue, newcomers of ten to twelve may be given a strictly understanding-speaking period of about six months, while adolescents of thirteen or over might be shown the printed word *for words they know orally* several weeks, days, or perhaps hours after these have been taught intensively.

3. In reading, and this happens in reading our native tongue, too, we sub-vocalize; that is, we make sounds in our throat. We read faster, therefore, if we know how to make the sounds without stumbling over them and if we have learned to read in thought groups.

4. The teacher should *always* read aloud for the students any material they will be expected to read. *He should read as though he were speaking* in thought groups so that students will realize that the printed page represents spoken language.

Oral reading by the teacher is necessary at all levels. Intonation and rhythm are learned and reinforced in this way. Moreover, since English is not always written the way it sounds, it is important that he read aloud, so that: a) students do not reinforce incorrect sounds in their silent speech; b) they will comprehend words they meet in their reading which they have heard spoken and vice versa. A glance at the following words ending in *ough*: *enough, through, though, bough, dough, hiccough,* and these words containing *i*: *machine, I, pie, piece, it, ice, island* indicate some of the difficulties students will face. We could multiply the examples, but anyone who has taught English as a second or foreign language will appreciate the difficulties of students and, therefore, the necessity for oral reading by the teacher or for the pupils' listening to the material to be read on a tape or other recording.

5. Many common words in English are multi-referential. Notice *pen* or *get* or *kind,* for example. It is important to teach students the semantic range of a word by: a) reminding them of the previously learned meaning when the word is met in a new context; b) helping them to identify its particular meaning in a context by its environment or by words with which it may co-occur. The word *kind,* for example, means *type* when it co-occurs with *what* in the expression: *What kind?*; it means *generous* in front of a noun or after a form of "to be" (*He is a kind man. He was kind*).

6. Reading readiness techniques should not be used only *before* reading is introduced. Readiness for reading should be ascertained for all levels of reading growth.

7. Labored reading dulls interest and should be avoided. The teacher should clarify all difficulties of pronunciation, structure, vocabulary, or culture *before* a passage is read.

8. *Oral* reading before the entire class or a large group should be done by *able* readers only. Anything read should contain appropriate rhythm, intonation, and pauses. (The teacher may ask individuals to read aloud to him alone at his desk, however.)

9. Reading materials should include not only the basal readers for the grade or age level, but every type of supplementary reading material possible—experience charts, newspapers, magazines, catalogues, and even the better quality comic books.

10. Materials should cover a wide range of writing styles— dialogues, informal and formal narrative passages, poems, songs, short stories, plays.

11. The themes should be those, particularly with beginning readers, which appeal to students because they talk about people, situations, and incidents with which they can identify.

12. Word attack skills (see page 140) should be developed systematically but not at the expense of keeping learners from

reading interesting material, relevant to their age and interest level. Provision should be made for *both* activities in any beginning reading program; indeed in any reading "unit." Attention to the recognition of the meaningful signals of English continues through all stages of the reading program as needed.

SOME BASIC SKILLS

Pupils who already read another native language using the Roman alphabet need to be guided to understand that the same written letter in English does not always represent the same sound as it does in languages such as Spanish and Italian, for example. The letter "o" always has the same value in Spanish. In English, the value changes (go, hot, boat, of, room, etc.).

Moreover, students will need to develop skills of discriminating between letters; of associating printed or written letters with sounds and the concepts attached to those sounds; and of interpreting the meaning of the word or sequence clues in sentences in order to understand their total meaning.

In addition, young children, illiterates, or readers of languages not using letters of the alphabet and left to right writing will have to develop proper eye movements and recognition of the letters with accompanying sound correspondences.

Pupils should be given many initial exercises in which they are made to distinguish among one-syllabled words such as *fat* and *hat*, *fall* and *hall*. Some reading specialists advocate that only words containing stroke letters be taught first, followed by words combining strokes and circles, and finally by words containing circles or parts of circles alone.* Other specialists† feel that teaching can begin with series of words in which only the initial consonant is different, without respect to stroke or circle (e.g., *bat*, *cat*, *fat*, *mat*, *rat*, *sat*).

A sequence of letter recognition favored by some reading specialists is as follows:

* C. Fries, *Linguistics and Reading*, New York, Holt, Rinehart and Winston, 1963.

† L. Bloomfield and C. Barnhart, *Let's Read; A Linguistic Approach*, Detroit, Mich., Wayne State University Press, 1961.

Short vowels as in *hop, rat*
Long vowels as in *hope, rate*
Digraphs as in *see, room, train*
Silent vowels as in *boat, read*

Gradually, pupils are taught to recognize, say, and read *initial, intervocalic,* and *final* consonants and consonant blends (a list of the most common ones will be found in the chapters on materials); triple and quadruple consonant clusters; and silent letters as in *know, knit, gnat, write.* They are also taught to blend one word in an utterance into the next one *in thought groups.*

Structural clues are of prime importance. Inflections for plurality, possessions, third personal singular, the progressive (the "ing" form), and the past require instant recognition, as do verb phrases such as *He has gone* or *He may have gone* and function words (see page 37).

Recognizing the total meaning of the sequence in which words appear is also a skill to be taught through practice with numerous examples of whole utterances;* e.g., The man gave the boy the candy; The boy gave the man the candy. Among structural clues, we would also include the teaching of *contractions, prefixes, suffixes, roots, compound words,* and the division of words into syllables. In addition, homonyms require special attention and systematic practice as they are met in reading.

Furthermore, where needed, teachers should guide learners in developing a background of concepts and social situations which they can associate with words and utterances so that they can comprehend and interpret the reading material.

The rich background of experience necessary for bringing meaning to reading and getting meaning from it will result from many *non*-reading activities which the teacher will provide for his pupils.

It will result also from the sharing and group discussion of experiences which the children have had in other classes in the

---

* Carl Lefèvre, *Linguistics and the Teaching of Reading,* New York, McGraw-Hill, 1963.

school, in their homes, or in the community. Discussion of trips to other parts of the school or out into the community (a store, a park, a place of historical interest) will enable children to acquire a number of meaningful concepts and associated vocabulary.

Concepts and vocabulary can be extended, too, through the wide use of centers of activity in the classroom, through the utilization of audio-visual aids such as flat pictures, records, and films, and through encouraging pupils to thumb through and read books, other than the class or group textbook, in many fields of interest.

Word-recognition skills, in addition to those mentioned above page 140), warrant further attention in this chapter on reading. Pupils should be helped to recognize words that form part of their oral vocabulary. Even more essential, they must be guided to interpret the meanings of unfamiliar words which they meet in their reading. There are many avenues by which pupils can be aided in acquiring this skill. Among others, they can be given:

1. Many experiences in which the same word is seen on such items as labels, cards, or charts.

2. Much easy reading material in which a limited vocabulary is constantly reinforced.

3. Opportunities to see words and sentences that they themselves have said in dialogues, for example, or for inclusion on experience charts.

4. Practice in utilizing the context (that is, the situation and surrounding words) as an aid in recognizing words.

5. Techniques for detecting familiar parts in new words and for finding small words within a larger one. (This is valuable, however, only when the words *are related* in meaning.)

The ability alone to *recognize* and to sound words out is not sufficient. It is essential that *meaning* be attached to each word and that the meaning *be the one needed in the particular context* in which the word is used. Again, the teacher will find that many indirect approaches can be utilized to develop this ability.

For example, he can engage pupils in many relevant experiences; make colorful, illustrated books available to them to stimulate their desire for learning meanings; play many interesting language games with them; and encourage them to use glossaries and dictionaries—depending on their age and learning level.

Direct teaching of words, of course, is essential. Meanings of new words should be clarified and practiced in the manner suggested in the preceding chapter. Additional reinforcement of meaning can result from giving pupils practice in classifying words according to topic or group; finding synonyms and antonyms of given words; studying suffixes and prefixes of words; and where possible giving cognate words in the native tongue of the pupils, making sure, however, that they are real cognates with true correspondence in meaning.

Specific *skills in increasing comprehension* must be developed systematically even on the lowest reading level. When a child follows simple directions or draws pictures to illustrate a word or a phrase, he is being helped towards comprehension of reading material. Various reading authorities have analyzed the component factors which are included in reading comprehension. There is general agreement that, among the skills involved, are those which help pupils: (1) recognize the main idea or purpose of a paragraph; (2) see relationships among facts in their reading; (3) grasp sequence of ideas and predict outcomes; (4) draw conclusions from what they read.

Practice exercises which will foster growth in the direction of deeper comprehension of the printed page include: (1) asking pupils to answer definite questions beginning with "who," "what," "where," "when," etc.; (2) asking them to follow specific directions; e.g., "Find the word (or sentence) which tells _____"; (3) giving practice in finding the best titles of stories or paragraphs; (4) helping them to indicate sequence of ideas through such exercises as rearranging sentences which are not in correct order or numbering sentences in the order in which they appear in the reading.

When these and other comprehension skills have been developed, there still remains the problem of increasing the pupils' rate so that reading becomes more pleasurable and functional.

Very often, it is found that through the techniques cited above, increased speed or rate will come about automatically. When this is not the case and reading still remains a word-calling, halting process, the teacher may wish to try one or more of the following procedures. He may:

1. Provide activities where pupils need only to skim the material to find a particular idea or detail.

2. Discourage lip movements and pointing during reading. Encourage, through appropriate oral models, reading in thought groups.

3. Time the reading of short selections, gradually reducing the time until optimum speed is reached.

4. Formulate for pupils *specific* purposes for reading such as finding the outcome, listing the sequence of events, and obtaining some information.

5. Give extensive training in reading easy materials to get the *general idea* of the paragraph, even when meanings of individual words are not known.

Pupils should be helped to develop the increasing ability to: (1) comprehend the author's purpose; (2) apply the information and attitudes gained through reading to their own lives; (3) use tools of research such as the dictionary and the encyclopedia for information; and (4) organize and express their own thoughts and feelings.

In brief, it is evident that developing skills so that reading can eventually be done independently, with ease and enjoyment; inculcating the habit of turning to books for information and evaluation; fostering an attitude of appreciation for the wide vistas that reading can open to the individual; and supplying the information which will enable pupils to go directly to appropriate reading sources should constitute the fundamental goals of an effective reading program.

THE STAGES IN READING GROWTH

Giving pupils competency in reading for comprehension is a gradual process which calls for a step-by-step development through the following five stages:

Stage I

Students read the material they have learned to say very well or material they have memorized. The material may consist of a dialogue, a song, a poem, a series of action sentences, a simple story of an experience the class members have had and which they have discussed, or model sentences containing some of the structures taught. Words taken from utterances within these may be "isolated" for systematic teaching of letter-sound relationships and other word and structure recognition skills. The *sound* of the letter and not the *name* of the letter should be taught. Pupils become confused when they are forced to learn that "see," "ay," "tee," spells *cat*.

The teacher has the students say the known material *without* looking at it. Then he reads the material aloud as the students look at it. They can then read it in chorus after him (the number of times depending on the students' age, ability, etc.). Next, groups and individuals may be asked to read it.

Stage II

The teacher and/or a group of English teachers in the school combine the known structures and words to make a different dialogue or paragraph. The students are helped to read this newly recombined material in which all the elements are familiar to them.

Stage III

The students read material in which some of the words and structures are unfamiliar to them. A committee of teachers can write this type of material. If preferred, existing texts with a low vocabulary and structure level, but at an interest level in harmony with the age of the students, may be utilized during this stage. Experience has demonstrated that students will find little or no difficulty when one "new" word is interspersed among about thirty familiar words. Often language learning texts contain paragraphs and selections which are suitable for reading at this level and which reinforce the structures introduced or practiced in the unit. Below we will explain a detailed technique for teaching reading at this stage.

Stage IV

Some reading experts recommend the use of simplified texts in all curriculum areas and of adapted versions of classics, or magazines. There are others who object to the use of simplified or adapted texts on the grounds that they do not convey the style or spirit of the author. There are, however, excellent simplified books on the market which can be used to great advantage with students who are still not advanced enough to read the original. The technique used for teaching this simplified or adapted material will be the same as that for Stage III reading.

Stage V

Unlimited material. Students should be able to read books in any curriculum area as well as books on sports, science fiction, adventure—or love.

When do learners reach Stage V? Some may never reach it as they would not reach it in their native language. Some may reach it by the end of senior high school. All the factors in learning which we have emphasized must be considered in discussing the "mastery" of this skill as of any other.

Let us examine some aspects of the "stages" in more detail. We have already spoken of the dialogue, which has been learned and dramatized, as an excellent source of beginning reading.

The reading chart, commonly called experience chart, cooperatively prepared by teacher and pupils, has also been found effective in teaching beginning reading, since it, too, is the written representation of sentences the pupils already know how to say.

Steps in the preparation of an experience chart should include:

1. Pupil participation in an interesting experience, real or vicarious, such as going to the park, seeing a movie, listening to a story, or dramatizing a situation in the classroom.

2. Discussion of this experience in short, simple sentences in response to the teacher's questions.

3. Statement of aim: "Let's write what we did (saw) so that we can read about it later."

4. Selection of a title for the story: "What will we call our story?"

5. Dictation of short, simple sentences by pupils with the teacher's help: "What will we say first?" . . . "Then what did we see?"

6. Writing of the sentences on the blackboard by the teacher.

7. Activities based on the chart. (You will find some suggestions below and others on pages 151–152 in this chapter.)

8. Transfer of the sentences (the maximum should be five to eight to a large oaktag chart or to newsprint.

9. Copying of the chart into the pupils' notebooks, if they are capable of writing. It will be found helpful to have the pupils keep a table of contents with titles and corresponding page numbers for use in further language arts activities.

The following general recommendations may be of help in making the chart more effective for teaching:

1. There should be only one central idea or theme on each chart.

2. The sentences in the very beginning stage should preferably be short enough to fit one line.

3. A picture at the top, at the end of each line or in place of a word should be included for greater clarity and interest.

4. In general, all sentences in earlier experience charts should start with *I* or *We*.

5. In the early stages, charts might be limited to two main types, both of which emphasize *continuity* and *sequence* of action or ideas as aids to comprehension.

a. *The Action Series*
   *Every Morning**

   1) I get up at eight o'clock.
   2) I get washed.
   3) I get dressed.
   4) I eat breakfast.
   5) I go to school.

b. *The Follow-Up of an Experience:*
   Our Trip to the Market

   1) We went to the market.†
   2) We saw fruit.
   3) We saw vegetables.
   4) We saw meat.
   5) We saw groceries.

Many follow-up activities are possible with these experience charts. The class or group may use the chart for such activities as oral reading (with the teacher serving as a model of pronunciation and intonation), dramatizing, preparing picture dictionaries, developing related vocabulary and word recognition skills, extending structures (for example changing "I" to "he" or the present to the past) and writing other charts with this chart as a base.

After this initial stage, other kinds of charts which are less restricted in vocabulary and pattern will also be found helpful

* In order to teach the *present* of these verbs naturally, we must make sure that a habitual or usual action is implied. This can be done by using words like "every" or certain adjectives or adverbs which help convey the meaning of a "usual" happening.

† The use of the past tense in the early stages of learning is explained on page 216.

in developing creative expression as well as reading ability. As a matter of fact, reading or experience charts may be used even after more formal reading has begun. Some charts may include lists of responsibilities or "codes" of behavior; others may give the highlights of a story the teacher has read; still others may be imaginative creations of pupils which have been reworded to some extent by the teacher, and which have been recorded for class enjoyment.

In Stages III and IV of reading, that is, in the reading from textbooks, two types of reading lessons are recommended: *intensive* and *extensive*. In *intensive reading,* as the term indicates, each vocabulary and structural item is explained and made part of the students' *active* language; pronunciation and intonation are stressed; and each concept or allusion is clarified. In *extensive reading,* the principal aim is comprehension. Pupils are trained to get meaning primarily from the context although some common vocabulary items may be developed for active use.

When textbook reading is first begun, all reading lessons should be of the *intensive* type. Later, both kinds may be given with the material from the same text serving for either one. In general, it is recommended that the material for extensive reading be on the same or a slightly lower level of difficulty as the intensive material. In longer passages or stories some teachers prefer to use portions containing dialogue for intensive reading and longer descriptive passages for extensive or silent reading. Some teachers follow the reverse procedure. There should be no set pattern.

The length of either type of reading lesson will depend upon the age and the ability of the pupil. Only what can be accomplished without haste and with full comprehension in a 20–25 minute presentation should be attempted.

The following procedure is recommended for the *intensive reading* exercise which is, primarily, a study type of activity:

1. *Motivate the reading.* If it is a short anecdote or passage, relate it to the pupils' experiences through "you" questions. If

it is part of a longer story, have individual pupils summarize what has been read thus far and then ask questions to arouse interest or curiosity in what is to follow.

2. *State the aim.* "Today we are going to read a story about _____" or "Today we will see what happens to _____" or "Let's read this article to get this editor's point of view on the _____."

3. *Clear up difficulties in the passage.* "Before we read, let's look at (learn, study) some new words and expressions we may find in the story." This may be done in a number of ways:

    a. The teacher may prepare a list of new words, patterns, cultural items, etc., and place them (or have them placed) on the blackboard at the beginning of the period. By such means as pictures, pantomime, dramatization, synonyms, antonyms, words of the same family, and paraphrases, the meanings are made clear to the pupils. With the teacher as a model, words are repeated in chorus and/or by individuals both before and after meanings are given.

    b. The teacher may give a brief summary of the story using the new words as he tells what the reading is about. He places them on the board as he uses them. Meanings are elicited or given as above.

The number of new words or structures to be explained will depend on the age of the learners, the material to be read, etc. Even with older learners, no more than seven or eight new words should be taught at one time. When the reading contains numerous difficulties, as may be true in reading in curriculum areas such as social studies and science, the material should be divided into several logical segments with steps 3 and 4 (below) repeated for each segment.

4. *Read the passage* and ask many questions to check comprehension. With pupils' books open,* the teacher reads the

---

* In later stages, students' books may be closed as a further check of aural comprehension. The technique should be varied.

passage in sentence groups. He asks questions at the end of each sentence or short paragraph, making sure (particularly in the early stages) that the answers are contained verbatim or nearly verbatim in the text.

In the beginning stages, particularly, many kinds of questions should be asked. The first question should be an *inverted* question. Then *Wh* questions (Who, When, Where, What, How much, How many) can be asked. For example, if the sentence read is *John played baseball in the park yesterday,* the questions may be:

Did John play baseball? (Yes; Yes, he did); *or* Yes, he played baseball.
Who played in the park? (John *or* John did) *or* John played baseball in the park.
What did John play?
Where did he play?
When did he play?
What did John do yesterday?

5. *Elicit a summary of the entire passage.* One pupil may be called upon to give a brief summary. Other pupils will be asked to suggest additions. The teacher may prefer to have a number of pupils give one sentence each, maintaining, however, the sequence in which the story is written.

6. *Extend learnings.* Many follow-up activities are possible which will not only further comprehension but will also contribute to general language growth. Some of these may be done both in class (after a summary has been given) and at home as an assignment. Others, like art activities, which do not involve oral work, may be done at home by the pupils. It is assumed that the teacher will select from among the activities below those which the pupils can do profitably in the time allotted. The teacher may wish to emphasize one or two of these activities for a few sessions and then give practice in others at later times. Possible activities include:

a. Choral reading *after* the teacher
b. Individual reading (more able students only)
c. Completing sentences (multiple choice or "straight" completion)
d. Selecting true or false statements
e. Giving the correct sentence if the statement is false
f. Writing a short summary in English
g. Answering questions based on the story, either orally or in writing
h. Formulating questions to be answered by classmates
i. Writing the new words in sentences
j. Drawing or cutting out pictures to illustrate the words or the story
k. Preparing an outline of the story
l. Rewriting the story, changing the dialogue into indirect discourse
m. Preparing the passage for dramatization
n. Memorizing selected portions
o. Selecting key sentences which illustrate certain characteristics or ideas
p. Finding synonyms and antonyms of the new words
q. Using the new words in original sentences
r. Relating, orally or in writing, a similar *personal* episode
s. Finding other stories on the same theme and comparing the authors' treatments
t. Reconstructing the story orally or in writing from pictures
u. Placing sentences or pictures (particularly with younger children) in the sequence in which they have occurred

It will be noted that some of the exercises lend themselves to oral work while others are best written. If a summary is reconstructed from oral questions and then placed on the board by pupils, it is recommended that the boards be numbered and that the sentences be placed on the board *sequentially*. This will constitute still another summary of the passage and will ensure greater comprehension.

During the next recitation period and while the assignment which has been prepared is being placed on the board, class members and teacher may again engage in one or more of the aforementioned activities.

The *extensive reading* lesson differs from the intensive in a number of respects. The motivation, the statement of aim, and the clearing of difficulties are exactly the same as for an intensive reading lesson. Grammatical phenomena or words which do not further comprehension will either not be mentioned or will be glossed over. The main difference lies in the fact that the passage is read through *silently* by students for a specific purpose that the teacher will set. Since, however, there is a positive correlation between pronunciation and reading, it is desirable for the teacher to read the passage aloud at normal speed *before* the silent reading is assigned in order to make certain that pupils will read with correct pronunciation and intonation.

A time limit should be set for the silent reading. This should be decreased gradually as pupils gain in language competency.

While the students are reading, the teacher will place five or six questions, true or false statements, or other short-answer type exercises on the board to make sure that pupils have read with purpose and meaning. The pupils will be asked to follow specific directions. After placing the work on the board, the teacher should walk around the room to help pupils in the reading group or he may work with another group of pupils engaged in some other type of language activity.

After the silent reading, pupils will complete *orally* the exercise which has been placed on the board. In addition, they may do as many of the exercises listed under intensive reading (cf. pages 151–152) as are practicable.

BROADENING THE BASE OF READING

A library in the room with colorful books and magazines on various reading levels (at least a four-year span) and on various interest and maturity levels is essential in the English classroom.

The class library should also contain dictionaries and other resource materials; textbooks in the various curriculum areas; and books and magazines in the pupils' native language.

Pupils who complete their work should be permitted to take books or magazines from the class library. Provision should be made to allow a pupil to keep a book he has started until he has completed it. A chart on the bulletin board or a card file may be used to indicate titles of books or magazines which each pupil is reading, so that there will be no problem about its availability when the pupil is ready to resume the story or article.

Many educators consider it desirable to have students who are able to do so read books, newspapers, or magazines in their native tongue and summarize their reading in English for the other class members. The gain in status and the motivation for oral expression are unquestionable.

"Free" reading of a wide variety of materials should be not only permitted but encouraged. Audience situations should be created from time to time. A student can give a synopsis of a book or article he has read or answer questions put to him by fellow students. Sharing the story or experience will not only heighten the interest of the reader but may stimulate the more timid or slower students to start reading.

One answer to a question that troubles teachers and research workers in English-speaking communities—namely, "How can we make a transition from limited English to full English?"—may be found in a carefully planned reading program. If teachers of all curriculum areas will follow the steps outlined under *intensive reading* on pages 149–151, pupils will acquire the broadest range of vocabulary and concepts and will get functional practice in recognizing and using structural patterns.

If, in addition, teachers of English *anywhere* will make use of all kinds of reading material (fiction, poetry, drama, biography, etc.) as a springboard for the development of vocabulary, for the manipulation of grammatical structures found in them, or for broadening cultural appreciation, there is no reason to bemoan the fact that insufficient books have been written for the "transition"* student or for the advanced student. The whole world of books is open to them! If, moreover, books are made the basis for oral discussion and writing activities, all four aims of our English-teaching program can reach maximal development through a well-balanced reading program.

INTRODUCING WRITING

By beginning writing is meant primarily the carefully controlled marks that students will make on paper or on the board *after* they can understand and produce, reasonably well, some fundamental English materials at their maturity and learning level. How long before writing is introduced will depend on several factors: 1) The pupils' age upon entering the English language program; 2) their degree of literacy in English; 3) their literacy in their native tongue; 4) the writing system in their native language. It is reasonable to assume, for example, that the majority of pupils with little or no aural-oral facility in English entering school at the age of six and pursuing English instruction *without* interruption will be on a par with their English-speaking classmates by the fourth or fifth grade. Some children who have heard and spoken English before entering school, because they have lived in a predominantly English-speaking community or because they have been enrolled in Head Start or similar programs, may be able to make the same progress as their classmates in writing. On the other hand, pupils who have to learn a completely different writing system or who are adolescents and yet illiterate in their native tongue and English will need systematic guidance for several additional years.

It is unrealistic to expect that many of the language learners entering a school for the first time after the ages of ten or above will be able to make great strides toward original or creative writing unless they are particularly gifted. This, however, is also

* This term is used to refer to students who have a fair command of English but who are still not considered "ready" to enter the regular subject area stream of a school.

true of native English speakers. It is not a question of the teacher's lowering his expectation for students but of recognizing that not all of us are innately capable of using the nuances of the language to write beautiful prose or poetry. Students who seem to have creative talent should be encouraged and guided individually. *All* students can be helped toward writing for practical or functional purposes (letters, outlines, notes, summaries) and for creative self-expression to the best of their ability.

Whether writing and reading should be taught concurrently and whether writing should precede reading are the subjects of current research. My own observation based on informal experimentation favors a Hear, Say, See, Do (Write) method. The writing step may be introduced soon after the reading step. In some situations, the teacher will find it possible to have students copy an utterance or a brief experience chart soon after it is heard, said, and read. In others, learners may need to learn to write individual letters of the alphabet and many monosyllabic words in which the same letters are repeated many times before they can be asked to copy materials.

SOME GENERAL CONSIDERATIONS

1. Children in the primary grades, illiterates, and students who use a different writing system should learn to print capital letters first and then small letters before they are taught *cursive* writing. Language learners in the primary grades will transfer to cursive writing when their classmates do. (This transfer usually takes place in the third grade.) The other language learners will transfer as soon as the teacher judges that they are able to.

2. The sequence in which the letters are taught need not be in alphabetical order. The sequence may depend on the strokes or curves which the printed letter includes. For example, capital A, E, F, H, I, K, L, etc., might be taught in one group over several lessons, whereas letters containing curves, such as B, C, D, G, etc., would be introduced and practiced in separate lessons.

3. It would be desirable to prepare duplicated material on which these students are asked to make letters of the alphabet by closing broken lines, by copying over letters, or by writing one letter, one word, or one utterance numerous times based *always on a teacher model and not on their previous model.*

4. Beyond the primary grades, little writing should be done in class except by students who cannot write or who have a different writing system. Class time should be devoted primarily to listening and speaking and later to listening, speaking, and reading.

5. Written pattern practices can be started in class, structural frames can be copied into notebooks, dictations and aural comprehension exercises can be given occasionally, but, in general, little writing should take place. When writing is done, it should preferably be toward the end of the hour so as not to interrupt the rhythm of the lesson.

6. Writing activities should be designed to reinforce listening, speaking, and reading abilities and to give practice in the structural and lexical items which have been introduced.

7. Students have to be taught to write legibly. Writers of other languages have problems in making many English numbers and also in distinguishing and producing loops, strokes and curves. The spacing of letters will also require attention and guidance.

8. The use of punctuation marks will have to be taught directly—one or two at a time, however. Two different ways of reinforcing their use are (a) to give dictations in which the punctuation marks are dictated during the second and third readings (see page 176 for the procedure); (b) to write paragraphs (either on the blackboard or to be flashed on the opaque or overhead projector) for "proofreading" by the teacher and students.

9. Spelling principles have to be introduced gradually, practiced intensively, and examples of them reintroduced whenever feasible. Students should learn, for example, that (a) there are some recurring patterns (*hat, fat; hate, fate*); (b) meaning is

changed by inflections and marks (*boys, boy's, boys'*; *it, it's, its*); (c) *y* usually changes to *i* before a suffix (*happy, happily, happier*); (d) *i* usually comes before *e* except after *c*. (In Chapter 21 will be found a list of vowel sounds and their most common spelling correspondences.)

Oral spelling should be practiced only in the normal situations in which such spelling is required; e.g., spelling one's name, the names of family members, one's street. Occasional spelling "bees" are also interesting to students.

The letters of the alphabet should be taught and practiced in normal activities such as looking up names of people and places in a telephone book, finding words in the dictionary, filing materials, creating individual dictionaries, or playing games in which the order of letters is important.

10. Through intensive oral practice, writing activities, and the use of such devices as colored chalk or markers (for cards), students should learn in subsequent stages that the *same sound* may be represented by different spellings; e.g., give, *gu*ess; red, *re*ad; coat, tic*k*, *k*ite; and that *different sounds* may be represented alike; e.g., *th*ick, *th*ere; re*a*d (base verb) re*a*d (past tense).

11. All writing, whether done by students in class or at home, should be corrected as quickly as possible.

12. Some reading specialists feel that initial reading is best taught by having students print or write the words and *then* read them. They insist that the kinesthetic will reinforce the visual. As yet, this is a moot question. It might be interesting to conduct or to read about further experimentation in this area to note whether such positive correlation does in fact exist.

GUIDING THE STUDENTS' WRITING

Students should be asked, after they have developed a reasonable listening and speaking facility with them and after they have learned to write capital and small letters, to (1) *copy* sentences, dialogues or charts; (2) *write out in full* pattern practice sentences; (3) *combine* elements from two or three columns to make new sentences; (4) *transform* or *convert* sentences (used in *dialogues, experience charts* or *pattern practices*) by changing *singulars* to *plurals, present* to *past* or *future* time, *statements* to *interrogatives* (either inverted or *Wh* questions); (5) *add* new elements or longer structures to sentences, to dialogues, to charts, or to other appropriate passages.

For example, in (3) above the teacher may ask students to write ten sentences combining words or expressions from each column:

John		to the store	yesterday
Mrs. Jones	went	to the hospital	last week
The boys	drove	to school	a week ago
Mr. and Mrs. Smith	rode	to the library	an hour ago

In addition, students may be asked to complete sentences, to take dictation, to proofread, to add details, to answer sequential questions, to summarize, to outline, to take minutes, to write reports, and to do other types of guided written work we have described throughout this book.

Toward Freer Writing

With students who have had several years of continuous English instruction, one of our goals should be to help them acquire the power to do expressional and creative writing in accordance with their ability. All the listening, speaking, reading, and writing done in class; all the vocabulary enrichment work; all the experiences in which learners have been engaged will contribute automatically, but only incidentally, to the ability to write original "compositions." Some systematic teaching is essential to help pupils acquire expressional writing ability after they have gained a modicum of language competency.

Beginning composition work may be developed in a number of ways. In addition to the experience charts which are a form of teacher-pupil prepared composition, a few other types are suggested here for adaptation or implementation.

1. The teacher gives a list of words within one social or cultural situation and asks the student to use them, in the sequence presented, in short dialogues, paragraphs or letters.

2. The teacher may write a short composition on a topic close to the children's interest. After study of the composition by the class (reading, answering of questions, etc.), the pupils may be asked to write a similar composition changing the name of the character or animal which the teacher may have used to, let us say, "My Friend" or "My Dog."

3. The teacher may ask pupils to answer a series of specific questions about an experience they have had. For example, after a school holiday, the pupils may be asked to answer questions such as:

What time did you get up yesterday?
Did you eat a special (breakfast)?
Where did you go?
With whom did you (play)?

4. The teacher may ask pupils to answer a series of *sequential* questions on a story they have read in class.

5. After extensive training in finding answers to a series of *sequential* questions, pupils may be asked to write a summary or résumé of a page or chapter which has been read.

It will be noted that when we use experience charts, "controlled" compositions, and questions based on an experience, the structural patterns can be limited or restricted. On the other hand, responses to a series of sequential questions based on a story and the writing of a résumé involve the use of a combination of structural patterns, a broader vocabulary range, and the use of introductory words (*then, since, although*).

From this transitional stage in composition work pupils should be ready for a more creative type of writing. Even "creativity," however, will have to be brought about through systematic procedures which the teacher will plan.

At regular intervals, a theme should be selected for composition work. The theme may be suggested by a student or by the teacher as the result of some reading, movie-going, or other shared experience. After appropriate motivation and statement of aim three columns can be drawn on the board. The teacher and students together should evolve an outline of the major ideas which should be included under the topic in Column I. Vocabulary and idioms needed to develop each idea will also be suggested by students and/or by the instructor (Column II). (If necessary, words and idioms should be practiced in sentences so that there is no doubt as to their meaning.) The ideas should then be organized into an outline with main ideas and subordinate ideas listed in the *proper* sequence (Column III). (The development of reading comprehension skills should facilitate this type of outlining. It should be remembered, however, that "transfer" of method, idea, or learning is usually the result of the teacher's *pointing out* the similarity in the process or idea. If pupils are helped to see analogies and if learning is made a functional, integrated process, they will eventually be able to transfer a skill from one language art activity to another—in this case, from outlining in reading to outlining in writing.)

If time permits, the students may be asked to start writing in class so that the teacher can answer questions or give other help as needed. In general, it is advisable to assign compositions or creative writing exercises as out-of-class work.

Examples of pupils' expressional writing ability should be collected, read by the teacher, and returned with comments and corrections. Occasionally, paragraphs from one or two of the more successful pupil attempts may be read to the class either by the teacher or by the writer himself. Students should be encouraged to keep compositions in folders for purposes of noting their own growth in writing. Where necessary, pupils should be asked to rewrite the same composition making the corrections suggested.

This writing stage for pupils should be limited only by the bounds of their own imaginations, the richness of their vocabulary, and their ability to use a variey of sentence structures. Although any language arts experience will further pupils' growth toward this kind of imaginative writing, specific appreciations and skills can be developed which are particularly conducive to the development of "freer" or expressional writing.

Systematic guidance may be given to pupils in finding words which: (1) Express ideas more vividly (instead of *say*, we may use *utter, exclaim, cry*, etc.); (2) Convey the *smell, sound, color*, or *feeling* of an object or a sensation. Pupils should be given extensive practice in using idioms and in paraphrasing them. They should be given many experiences of an artistic nature such as looking at paintings and listening to music which will enrich their background and sensitize them to the need for finding the "right" word to convey an idea or an image. Oral discussion should always be part of the experience.

Creative activities of this type need not be deferred until students are older but should be an important part of the program for pupils of any age.

Summary

The reading process is extremely complex and demands the knowledge of many related word recognition and comprehension skills. Although the teacher may find indirect approaches, such as taking pupils on trips, effective in contributing to the development of some skills, a direct attack on each of the skills needed for reading with comprehension is essential in the language program.

Reading, particularly in the beginning stages of learning, should not be from textbooks. Nor is it imperative that reading for more advanced students be from formal texts. Teacher-prepared materials, particularly suited to the pupils for whom they are written, may be used for as long as needed. Such materials are essential when no others are available.

Pupil-teacher prepared reading materials commonly called experience charts are recommended for a beginning reading program. They can also be used with profit to pupils at any stage in the English program.

In this chapter we have suggested the methodology of conducting both the intensive and extensive reading lesson; we have emphasized the necessity for providing opportunities in the classroom for "free" reading; we have highlighted one way in which teachers can help bridge the gap between a pupil's limited knowledge of English and a broad comprehension of the language.

There is no doubt that a classroom library with well-illustrated books and magazines on many subjects of interest, and on many ability levels, will contribute to the development of a love for reading—the fundamental prerequisite for further language growth.

It is hoped that wide reading in many fields of personal concern will also bring about the cultural appreciations necessary in a world in which mutual understanding has become more important than ever.

Writing both practical and creative should emerge as the end product of many guided language activities and of numerous experiences including those of art and music which will heighten the pupil's appreciation of sounds, shapes, colors, words, and feelings. The teacher has a dual responsibility: (1) to develop the students' skill in using the English language correctly; and (2) to provide the students with many experiences which will enrich their lives and thus enlarge the fund of ideas they will be enabled to express.

CHAPTER 5

Activities Fostering Language Learning

Questions often arise among teachers with relation to the planning of varied language activities which will contribute to the development of communication skills and at the same time fit into the time allotted to the English session. Some beginning teachers find that time hangs heavily on their hands. One of the questions often asked is, "What can I do for an hour or more with these people whose language I don't understand?" Other teachers find it difficult to allocate time for drilling pronunciation, for fostering sociocultural concepts, for developing language competency, for creating and maintaining interest, and, since this is vitally important, for helping pupils retain a pride in their own cultural heritage.

Let us consider the type and placement of some possible language learning activities which may help answer these questions in teachers' minds.

SELECTING THE ACTIVITIES

The primary criterion for the selection of pupil activities (including creative and game activities) should be the contribution the activity will make to the growth of one or more phases of language development. If we are agreed that habitual control of vocabulary and language patterns is essential for communication and that pupil activity is fundamental to learning, the instructor must make provision for a well-rounded, varied, stimulating series of activities which will help pupils towards language mastery. Another criterion would be the utility of the activity in the widest range of communication situations.

No specific grade placement for the activities listed below will be recommended since the placement will vary from one class to another. The instructor will select those activities which he knows—by observation, experience, testing, and study of pupils' records—the pupils will find profitable. For example, an activity such as attending a lecture will be deferred until pupils have attained a fair level of achievement in language unless the lecture has been planned with due regard to age and English ability of the students.

It is essential to remember that language activities—listening, speaking, reading, and writing—are *integrated* in actual communication. Inasmuch as it is often more desirable and more efficient to give practice in each skill separately, the activities below are listed under the abilities to which each makes the greatest contribution, although overlapping will be inevitable.

Since classroom directions such as "Open your books," "Say," "Repeat," "Read," "Write" should always be presented in the English language from the very beginning of the semester, we will not make special mention of these obvious language activities centered about everyday classroom routines.*

Aural Activities

1. Listening to the English teacher during all phases of the English period (model sentences for practice; cues for practice drills; story telling; oral reading, etc.)

2. Listening to other pupils give directions or ask questions

---

* As noted above, it is desirable, however, that teachers learn to say, "Look," "Listen," "Say," "Repeat," "Ask," "Answer" in the native language of the learners and that they use the native language *and* English equivalents for the first few days.

3. Engaging in a conversation or in a role-playing activity

4. Listening to outside speakers or to other school personnel

5. Distinguishing between contrasting sounds in lists of words or sentences

6. Listening to phonograph records of language lessons, songs, plays, poems, speeches

7. Listening to tape recordings of pronunciation, structure or vocabulary drills; dictations; comprehension exercises; poems; songs; lectures; plays

8. Listening to sound films—those especially prepared for language learners or short clips of longer general ones—and selected radio and television programs

9. Taking dictations given orally by the teacher or through a tape

10. Interviewing people

11. Attending lectures, conferences, and meetings

12. Participating in discussion groups and panel discussions

13. Going to the movies and to the theatre

14. Playing language games

Oral Activities

1. Choral repetition of word, phrase, or sentence (class, group, row)

2. Individual repetition of word, phrase, or sentence

3. Responding to directions given by the teacher or by another pupil

4. Formulating directions for other pupils; for example, "Show me (Show us) the _____."

5. Answering questions based on any class or out-of-class experience (clubs, TV programs, movies, work)

6. Framing questions based on reading or on an experience to ask the teacher or other pupils

7. Preparing original sentences based on language patterns or vocabulary being learned

8. Engaging in oral drill activities (see page 115)

9. Combining elements from various slots to make new sentences

10. Telling what appears in a picture or on a chart

11. Engaging in conversion or transformation exercises such as changing singulars to plurals, nouns to pronouns, indicative to interrogative, affirmative to negative, etc.

12. Telling a favorite tale or experience in the pupils' own words

13. Giving reports on a prepared topic

14. Summarizing a paragraph, an article, or a book

15. Setting up stores, libraries and other agencies and simulating realistic conversations for each. (These can be made increasingly longer and more complex as learners grow in language ability.)

16. Conducting a discussion, a forum, or some other oral group activity

17. Making tape recordings or records

18. Engaging in telephone conversations and in role-playing activities

19. Reading a book in the native language and giving an English report on it

20. Dramatizing a dialogue, a situation or a play

READING ACTIVITIES

1. Reading any of the above materials which have been written down

2. Reading from experience charts or later from texts

3. Reading materials such as arithmetic problems, maps, charts, experiments, from other curriculum areas

4. Practicing any of the word or comprehension skills suggested in the chapter on Reading

5. Classifying words or concepts under categories

6. Placing sentences in the sequence in which they occur in the reading

7. Reading signs and interpreting them; e.g., *Wet Paint*

(*Don't touch this or sit on this. The paint isn't dry.* Or *It was just painted*). Signs the students should be able to read as quickly as possible include *Bus Stop*; *Danger*; *Keep Out*; *Stop*; *Walk*; *Go*; *No Smoking*; *Ladies*; *Gentlemen*; *No Trespassing*; *Poison*; *Entrance*; *Exit*; *Up*; *Down*; *Keep to the Right*; *Stairs*.

8. Reading abbreviations, hours, dates

9. Indicating stressed syllables in words

10. Crossing out vowels of unstressed syllables

11. Reading aloud a paragraph containing no punctuation marks and supplying the correct stress, phrasing, and intonation

12. Using all tools of research (dictionaries, encyclopedias, maps, charts, index, table of contents)

13. Reading newspapers and magazines

14. Reading American and English literary masterpieces

Writing Activities

1. Copying letters, words, utterances, experience charts from the blackboard into notebooks

2. Completing sentences where a choice of words is given

3. Filling in blanks with the subject word, verb, complement, or other

4. Placing sentences in correct order and writing them

5. Choosing the unrelated word from a group of words

6. Completing phrases from one column with related phrases from another column

7. Completing words with the correct endings; e.g., stud*ent*, merch*ant,* par*ent*; alphabet*ize,* critic*ize,* anal*yze*

8. Inserting punctuation marks in sentences or paragraphs (commas, periods, question marks, capital letters, quotation marks, etc.)

9. Classifying words under appropriate categories: food, recreation, etc., or by stress on the first or second syllable; e.g., *ap*ple, *ne*ver, be*gin*, *fa*ther

10. Writing words that begin or end with certain sounds as the teacher says them

11. Addressing envelopes

12. Writing an experience chart

13. Writing expanded sentences when these require a change in word order or form; e.g., Who is he? *I don't know* who he is.

14. Writing out in full any of the practice drills which have been done orally

15. Making several short words out of a long one

16. Separating the word root or stem and the affix (prefix or suffix)

17. Supplying the missing letters in known words and checking the spelling in a dictionary

18. Alphabetizing lists of words

19. Engaging in conversion or transformation exercises such as changing nouns to pronouns, declaratives to interrogatives, etc.

20. Answering questions based on reading or other experiences

21. Writing dialogues and narrative passages from dialogues

22. Preparing reports on individual research activities

23. Writing carefully guided compositions (see page 158)

24. Filling out business and official forms

25. Writing carefully structured, practical or social letters

26. Preparing labels, captions or titles on pictures, stories, etc.

27. Engaging in an aural comprehension exercise, in which answers are written (see page 178)

28. Assisting in the preparation of instructional materials such as flashcards, board slips, worksheets

29. Taking dictation (see 176)

30. Writing "freer" compositions

31. Writing a telegram

32. Taking notes on a lecture

MISCELLANEOUS ACTIVITIES (*All* leading to oral language development)

1. Cutting out and labeling pictures

2. Preparing scrapbooks (transportation, clothing, other)

3. Drawing pictures to illustrate some theme or concept

4. Playing charades

5. Preparing displays (books, artwork)

6. Memorizing songs, proverbs, documents or portions of documents

7. Preparing and giving a daily, brief news broadcast

8. Giving lists of words which describe nouns or action words

9. Naming and describing the objects seen in a large situational picture

10. Giving the steps in a sequence for making something (scientific, artistic, culinary, etc.)

11. Making a "short" sound long by adding an "e" and using the new words orally and in writing; e.g., *hat, hate*; *rat, rate*

12. Planning future activities and discussing past activities

13. Preparing pictures to be inserted into experience charts (in a word slot [as a substitute for the word] or at the end of the sentence)

14. Locating places of interest in the community and country on original or commercial maps

15. Setting up bulletin boards (weather, current events, realia)

16. Arranging pictures or objects on a flannel or magnetic board to conform to a story sequence, to furniture placement, etc.

17. Playing games—making sure, however, that they lead to language growth

18. Constructing dioramas

19. Making puppets or other articles of papier-mâché

20. Engaging in any form of creative activity

21. Going on trips to English-speaking places

22. Visiting homes of English-speaking people

23. Giving more specific words for a general term; e.g., dog: mongrel, pup, boxer, bulldog, poodle, terrier

24. Preparing lists of words related to touch, smell, sound, feeling; e.g., re *touch:* soft, hard, rough, sticky, damp, icy, wet

25. Finding the origins of words in dictionaries

26. Drawing up lists of *false* cognates in their native language and English; e.g., (Spanish) *asistir* means *to be present* and not *to help*

27. Studying pictures of various items and telling where these could be found; e.g., *at the butcher's, at the library,* etc.

28. Learning parliamentary procedure in voting for class or club officers

29. Taking pictures on trips and writing commentaries on them

30. Preparing a monthly newsletter of the class members' activities (school or home)

Relating the Activities

In actual classroom practice, as has been noted, more than one of the language activities may be engaged in during the study of a unit of work. Below you will find one way in which a number of related activities are grouped under a specific topic.

Possible Learning Activities in a Unit of Study

Let us assume that you wish to develop the concept of food (names, uses, values, necessary consumer education facts, preparation). You may wish to include one or more of the approaches below for the entire class, for groups of children, or for individuals. Each activity, however, should be made to give practice in pronunciation, in structural patterns, and in vocabulary. To illustrate, suggested activity 1 below may afford practice in learning names of foods (with correct pronunciation) and pattern variations such as:

What do you have?	I have a _____.
What does he have?	He has a _____.
What did you bring?	I brought a _____.
What did he bring?	He brought _____.
Show us the _____.	Here's the _____ *or*
	Here it is.

Who has the _____?	I have the _____ *or* I have it.
	He has the _____ *or* He has it.
Do we cook the _____?	Yes, we do.
	No, we don't.
How do we cook the _____?	We boil it—roast it—fry it.

The activities suggested here may be utilized with some adaptation in the teaching of *any* topic or in the presentation of *any* unit of work. Teacher and/or pupils:

1. Bring in samples of real food; taste them; talk about them
2. Cut out pictures of food from magazines, newspapers; label them; tell the class about them
3. Make picture dictionaries
4. Group pictures of foods under various categories such as vegetables, breakfast foods, party foods, foods to illustrate a balanced diet
5. Make food items of papier-mâché
6. Place pictures of foods in groups on the flannel board (for example, *Foods for Breakfast* or *Dairy Foods*)
7. Write lists of foods at the blackboard under specific categories
8. Prepare flashcards with names of foods to:

   a. Match the word on the board with the word on the flashcard
   b. Identify the real food or picture from the word on the card
   c. Play games; e.g., "Who has the name of a breakfast food?"

9. Group names of foods under various categories (where to buy, for what meal used)
10. Prepare experience charts re: names, recipes, shopping, nutrition

11. Read stories (either commercial or teacher-prepared) and engage in various follow-up activities such as sentence completion and preparation and answering of questions which test comprehension

12. Make up songs containing names of foods (using a familiar tune), such as:

Save, save, save your health
Eat the proper food
Corn and potatoes and rice and tomatoes
Are excellent for you.

13. Visit a food market

14. Set up a mock food market in the class (include prices, etc.) and dramatize a food-buying situation

15. Prepare dialogues in which food is ordered by telephone

16. Individual pupils may:

   a. draw some items of food
   b. color drawings of fruits, vegetables, etc.
   c. find pictures to fit the experience chart
   d. tell how their parents prepare certain foods
   e. make up a shopping list for a week
   f. prepare some simple food in class
   g. write sample menus

17. Learn to read recipes

18. Learn the formulas used at meals

Again the possibilities for practice are endless, depending upon the factors of which all teachers are aware: limitations in the English ability of pupils and limitations of time to explore any one topic fully, particularly with older students who may need to be prepared as quickly as possible either to enter a regular school or community program or to find gainful employment.

Some Basic Procedures

Because of their value in developing language ability, we have considered it desirable to treat a number of specific language activities in greater detail.

The Learning of Dialogues

The dramatization of dialogues is particularly well suited for developing linguistic competence and social insight in students of all ages. Pupils gain control not only of pronunciation, structure, and vocabulary but also of the cultural situations in which various features of language are used by native English-speakers. Well-prepared dialogues and their dramatizations duplicate the communication situations in which individuals use English normally in their everyday lives.

Dialogues may be used to *introduce* features of pronunciation and grammar or to *reinforce* them. Their primary value lies, however, in showing pupils how the elements of language they are learning fit together in actual use.

The dialogues prepared for beginning teaching should be short—two or three utterances perhaps. At intermediate or advanced levels they may be longer—eight to twelve utterances—but these need not be learned in one lesson. The teacher may introduce the entire dialogue the first time it is presented but have students *learn* only the first two or three lines during that lesson.

Following are some suggestions for presenting and practicing the entire dialogue or the portion of it to be taught in the lesson for the day. (Samples of dialogues will be found in the chapter on "Teacher-Prepared Materials.") The teacher:

1. Gives the situation in simple English, pointing to each of the figures of the speakers (which have been placed on the black—or flannel—board) as he tells about what each one is

saying. (Hand puppets may also be used effectively to indicate the person speaking the particular line of dialogue.)

2. Teaches new expressions and concepts in the dialogue through dramatization, pictures, etc.

3. Says the part of the dialogue he is going to present intensively three or four times. The first two times he stands at the board and points to each figure as he or she speaks (or he has the puppet nod). The next time or two, the teacher walks to various parts of the room so that his mouth and gestures will be visible to all the class members.

4. Says each utterance several times and engages the *entire* class in choral repetition.

5. Takes one role and has the class take the other. He then reverses the roles.

6. Divides the class in half and helps each group take a role. He then reverses the roles. (This procedure is repeated several times.)

7. Dramatizes the dialogue with one of his more able students, and then reverses the roles as above.

8. Has pairs of students dramatize the dialogue either from their seats or at the front of the room.

It is important to keep the *dialogues* alive and to keep adding to them. They can be dramatized during warm-up, review, or summary segments of the lesson. When introducing some feature of grammar or pronunciation for *intensive* study, the teacher will remind the students that they have previously met it in a dialogue. As the students learn new features of English, they can be helped to extend or change a whole utterance in a previously learned dialogue by adding new phrases or sentences where these fit logically. In addition to being dramatized, dialogues may be read, written, summarized into a narrative paragraph, varied—to talk of different people, places, or times—adapted to talk about oneself, and used, naturally, as the basis for many oral practice activities.

Dictation

Dictation is a teaching technique which has proved extremely effective at all levels of instruction from the primary grade in the elementary school through the senior high school. It has positive values when used to reinforce the many phases of language arts activities. It ensures attentive listening; it trains pupils to distinguish sounds; it helps fix concepts of punctuation; it enables pupils to learn to transfer oral sounds to written symbols; it helps to develop aural comprehension; and it assists in self-evaluation.

In the early stages of learning, the material should be familiar to the pupils. Its source may be: notes for the class diary; an experience chart that has been cooperatively prepared; a Gouin (action) series that has been practiced and acted out; a short poem or paragraph that has been used for choral reading; a simple song that is sung in class, in the assembly, or in the community; a dialogue that has been dramatized.

In the intermediate and later stages the teacher may use any selection of about ten lines, such as an anecdote, a short poem, a passage from a reader, or an original passage prepared by the teacher to illustrate a structural item or some cultural concept. The material should be slightly more difficult than that which has been used in the early stages. Samples of dictation materials will be found in Chapter 22.

The following procedure is recommended at *all* stages of learning (except with isolated words):

1. The teacher *motivates* the dictation by relating the material to an experience with which the pupils are familiar—a trip they have taken, a story they have read, a picture they have seen, or a song they have sung.

2. He *gives a short summary* of the material to be dictated.

3. He *explains any difficulties* in vocabulary, concept, structure or punctuation which may appear in the passage. These explanations should follow the general principles of methodology

which have been given already. It is also desirable in the early dictations to review the terms used for punctuation marks which students will need for the day's exercise.

4. The teacher now *reads* the passage at normal speed. The pupils listen attentively but *do not* write during this first reading.

5. The teacher *reads* the passage again in thought groups, *including punctuation*. The pupils at their seats write what they hear while two pupils may be asked to write the same material on the back or side board. (Pupils selected to go to the board should be among the pupils with better than average ability so that other pupils will not see too many errors during the correction.)

6. The instructor *rereads* the passage at normal speed, at which time pupils insert words or punctuation marks they may have missed during the second reading. Pupils should be trained to leave a space for words they have not understood during the second reading. There should be *no* repetition of words or questions at any time during the three readings.

7. *The material is now corrected* in the following manner:

   a. The pupils may keep their own papers or exchange papers with a neighbor. It is desirable, however, for the teacher to collect the papers at regular intervals to note individual errors and to check growth of ability in proofreading.

   b. A pupil (*other* than one of those who did the original writing) is sent to the board to make corrections. The correct forms are given, where possible, by class members as the pupil leader asks such questions as, "Who sees the mistake in line 1?" or "Can you find an error in line 1?" or underlining the word himself, "How do we write _____?" (Notice that this is another activity in which *oral* spelling becomes *functional*.)

   c. Pupils at their seats correct their own or their neighbor's paper. The teacher or an able student may walk around the room to ascertain that correct forms are being substituted for incorrect ones.

d. Pupils record the number of errors they have made into their notebooks. The teacher may also keep a class-wide tally of types of errors made.

After the work has been corrected, one or more of the following related activities will help to reinforce correct intonation and/or structural patterns:

1. The teacher reads the passage in thought groups and asks pupils to repeat in unison *after* him.

2. Individual pupils are called upon to read one or two sentences.

3. The teacher asks pupils questions based on the material.

4. Pupils ask each other questions.

5. Pupils give summaries of the passage in their own words.

6. Pupils dramatize the passage if it lends itself to such an activity.

7. The class or group engages in word study exercises—synonyms, antonyms, and words of the same family.

8. Pupils tell or write about a similar experience they have had.

These same procedures are used when "spot" dictations are given. The teacher will distribute duplicated material on which certain language items are missing. The learners will write in the missing words on the same paper or on a separate paper.

Aural Comprehension

This type of language exercise is also valuable in developing all the communications arts skills. As with the dictation, the material to be used should be carefully selected. In the early stages of learning, the material should be familiar to the pupils. Passages from the textbook or from magazines, cooperatively prepared experience charts, and oft-told stories and anecdotes will be most effective. Later the material selected may be taken from any source—a magazine article, an unfamiliar text, or a newspaper.

It is recommended that short anecdotes or passages which constitute an entity in themselves and in which a *sequential* situation is presented serve as the basic material. The teacher should also choose a passage or an anecdote which lends itself to the formulation of four or five questions, the answers to which can be found almost verbatim in the text.

At all stages of learning, the following technique is recommended:

1. The teacher *motivates* the reading by giving a one- or two-sentence explanation of the story or anecdote.

2. The teacher *explains any difficulties* in either vocabulary, structure, or idea which appear in the selection. (It is desirable to leave on the board the names of persons or any difficult words in the story in order that the pupils may refer to them.)

3. The teacher *reads the entire passage* through at normal speed *two times.*

4. The teacher sends two pupils to the side or back board.

5. *Pupils at seats (and the two at the board) write answers* to the questions based on the passage which the teacher gives orally.

6. The teacher *repeats* the questions.

7. The teacher *rereads* the passage at normal speed.

8. The teacher *repeats* the questions.

The procedure used in correcting dictations will be found satisfactory in correcting aural comprehension exercises.

As with the dictation exercise, the aural comprehension material may serve as the basis for varied oral, written, or creative activities. Any one of the activities found in the list on page 166 which the teacher considers appropriate may be used to extend or enrich learnings.

A word of caution is in order. If this exercise is to be effective, pupils should be taught to write the answers to the questions *without* copying the questions. If they are unable to write the answer at the first or second reading of the question, they should be trained to write key words or phrases *omitting* the question word. For example, if the question is "Who went to the store?," the pupils should write "_____ went to the store."

Continuous practice will be needed to help pupils acquire this skill. The following suggestions may be of help:

1. Review *question words* before each aural comprehension exercise.

2. Give pupils practice in *formulating* questions and in *answering* them in connection with all types of oral activities.

3. Prepare short reading passages with written *questions* and *answers* which the pupils will *copy, repeat in unison* and *individually,* and which they will ask each other.

4. Prepare *questions* and *specific directions* for intensive and extensive reading exercises which give pupils training in looking for answers.

5. With more advanced pupils, give practice in *answering* "*why*" questions.

Memorization

Occasionally the teacher may feel that certain sentence series, dialogues, or passages are valuable enough to be committed to memory. The Gouin or action series which lend themselves to pupil activity and which have "built in" continuity of action so that they leave no doubt as to meaning are excellent in the beginning stages. A series of sentences relating to an everyday class activity may be:

Every Day

1. I get up.
2. I go to the board.
3. I take a piece of chalk.
4. I write my name.
5. I write a sentence.
6. I return to my seat.

Memorization of this and similar series will come about naturally through constant repetition, by as many pupils as possible, while each is performing the actions.

Any song, poem, short document, or passage may be memorized. It is important, however, that the teacher *motivate, state the aim,* and *clear up any difficulties* before asking students to commit the passage to memory. If students have not learned how to memorize, the teacher should spend some time training them to do so. Authorities have found that the reading of the entire passage a number of times *followed* by memorization of single lines is the most effective method for memorization.

Translation

The problem of translation deserves some mention, if only because there is so much confusion about its value and the extent to which it should be used—if at all.

In English-speaking communities where the teacher does not know the native language of his pupils; where no capable, truly bilingual "informant" may be available; where pupils may not be grouped homogeneously with relation to native language background, translation should be used sparingly—if at all. The reasons are obvious.

This recommendation should not prevent a student "buddy," teacher aid, or a teacher who knows a few words of the pupil's native tongue from giving equivalent words or phrases occasionally if the equivalent will clarify a meaning or a concept for a pupil. What is to be avoided is an inaccurate translation by pupils who supposedly know both languages. Inexperienced teachers often make the further mistake of having the word or phrase (sometimes incorrectly spelled in the native language, unfortunately) placed on the board.

With older pupils, who are literate in their native tongue, carefully planned *brief* "translation" exercises of *limited* structures may be used by the bilingual teacher since they have certain advantages: (1) They help focus attention on important contrasts between the students' native tongue and English; and

(2) they give the teacher an added measure for judging the students' comprehension of structures or vocabulary.

It is important, however, that the teacher say the sentences in the students' native language and that the students give them *in English*. Following are some examples in Spanish:

Teacher	Pupil
¿Sabe Ud?	Do you know?
¿Ve Ud?	Do you see?
¿Lee Ud?	Do you read?
¿Conoce Ud a Juan?	Do you know John?
¿Sabe Ud el cuento?	Do you know the story?

Again, no generalization can be made. The literacy of the pupils, the knowledge of the teacher, the value of the translation for the entire class or group will determine the extent to which translation should be used as an *additional* medium for developing and reinforcing language learning.

SUMMARY

There are numerous language learning activities which will contribute to the growth of the four basic communication skills of understanding, speaking, reading, and writing. Some of the activities are designed to take the pupils from the confines of the classroom into the wider community of the English-speaking world. Others simply give needed practice in blending sounds into meaningful wholes, in making sound and word arrangements habitual, and in increasing the breadth of vocabulary.

Dictations, aural comprehension exercises, well-chosen memory selections and dialogue dramatization will be found useful in developing all the communication arts skills and in giving pupils knowledge about the social and cultural situations in which language items function. The judicious use of all the language activities at different times in the English program will not only contribute to the pupils' growth but will also add needed interest and variety to the instructional program.

CHAPTER 6

Vitalizing Learning

We are all cognizant of the fact that inherent factors within the pupils, the school, and the community will affect interest and achievement in the learning of English. Extensive research in the field of foreign languages has demonstrated that motivation and interest are two factors of crucial importance in language study. Where intrinsic motivation is lacking in the students for any reason and where the classroom situation cannot fan out to the home and to the community for further stimulation, the teacher will have to use all the knowledge and skill at his command, in addition to his personal qualities, to engender interest and to sustain it throughout the program. Apathetic students, poor results, and numerous requests for "dropping out" should make us ask ourselves, "What can I do to make my subject come alive?"

In subsequent chapters we will discuss the importance of establishing rapport, of providing a desirable classroom atmosphere, and of enlisting active pupil participation in planning and carrying out lessons. These guiding principles are fundamental. There are, however, a number of techniques or procedures which will be found particularly valuable in vitalizing English-language learning. A few of these are given now for your consideration and adaptation.

The Trip

Class visits to places of interest in the school and in the community (even if it is not a predominantly English-speaking community) are excellent media for clarifying vocabulary and concepts and for functionalizing learning. In the case of younger children, the teacher should always accompany the class. Older students can be encouraged to visit places on their own after school. Provision should then be made to have them report their reactions or to share their experiences with other pupils in some way.

The places to visit are those which will, concomitantly, further an understanding of the cultural-social patterns of the English-speaking community and help build language. In the non-English community the places to visit are those which will help to clarify language and those which are either similar to or different from places that might be found in an English-speaking community.

The possibilities for developing language skills through trip experiences are inexhaustible. Let us examine a few. In preparing for the trip, the teacher and pupils will engage in some or all of the following activities. We cannot repeat too often that as much English as possible should be used in all phases of this preparation period if the activities are to serve more than one purpose.

1. Discussing practices of social behavior on the trip
2. Discussing safety precautions
3. Planning expenditures for fare, meals, and admission fees
4. Setting time for departure and arrival
5. Arranging meeting places
6. Making inquiries about the route to be taken
7. Writing letters to parents asking for consent
8. Calling the place to be visited in advance to ask about such things as special features, hours, fees, and eating facilities
9. Arranging for a special speaker or conference
10. Planning questions which will be asked of personnel
11. Writing out some of the information and facts above

12. Planning for notes or outlines to be taken while on the trip

For language activities during the trip and as a follow-up of the trip, suggestions will be found under Language Learning Activities on pages 165–171 and in the Suggested Time Schedule on pages 213–220.

Some communities have prepared lists of suitable resources to be visited by student groups. Various school systems have also compiled lists especially appropriate for student groups and in harmony with the curriculum in such areas as social studies. It is recommended, however, that the first trips taken be to various places in the school and that there be a gradual branching out into the community.

THE PICTURE FILE*

A picture file should be an integral part of every classroom where there are pupils learning a second language. The organization of the file may be a cooperative activity of the teacher and all the pupils in each class or may be a group project for those pupils who will derive the greatest benefit from finding, sorting, and mounting pictures. The very selection and mounting of pictures can be used as teaching lessons which will help pupils acquire language. Sentence patterns such as "Can you find _____?"; "We need (glue)."; "Let's look for _____." will be practiced naturally during these lessons.

If teachers find it difficult to organize a complete file, the director of the learning center or school may set up a central file in the general office, in the teachers' workroom, or in the library. School service squads or civic-minded community members may be trained to mount, file, and distribute pictures. As the teacher approaches a special unit, he should plan to borrow the folder containing pictures related to the unit so that it will

* Lists of appropriate pictures will be found in Chapter 24.

be available for the entire lesson development, from motivation through culmination.

A file of flat pictures will be found invaluable in:

1. Ensuring motivation and stimulation
2. Providing for economical learning
3. Vitalizing any of the steps in teaching
4. Providing uniformity of concepts among pupils
5. Presenting initial concepts which are correct, real, complete, and clear
6. Overcoming the limitations of restricted personal experiences of the pupils
7. Clarifying words and concepts which permit pupils to get ideas of proper perspective and proportion. For example, a picture showing the *relative* size of an elephant and a dog is much more valuable than plastic or clay models of a dog and an elephant
8. Overcoming the narrow limits of the classroom
9. Providing for the direct interaction of the pupils with the realities of the social and physical environment
10. Reducing learning and teaching time by attracting the immediate attention of the pupils and by making possible fewer and shorter explanations of words and concepts
11. Furnishing varied practice for making automatic the structural arrangements of English

A picture file assumes even greater importance in the class in which pupils are enrolled at any time during the term. The most conscientious teacher will not have time to go back over all the units of work the class has covered with each incoming pupil. A pupil helper, "buddy," or teacher aide can be guided in the use of the pictures and the accompanying worksheets (samples of which will be found at the end of this section) so that the newcomer can be brought up to the conceptual level of the class.

Pictures should be of two principal types. Every picture file should contain both individual pictures and situational pictures. An individual picture is one in which the item to be taught is found alone or is highlighted in some fashion. In the situational picture, many items which have been taught are included.

In teaching the word *shoe* for example, in addition to utilizing the fact that *he and the pupils are wearing shoes,* the teacher would have *several individual* pictures of various kinds of shoes. The *variety* of pictures is important to avoid confusion of concept that often arises with people who are learning a second language. If in teaching *shoe,* for example, the teacher inadvertently points to the heel or to the lace, pupils may associate the word *lace* or *heel* with the concept of *shoe.* Many different pictures of various types of shoes would ensure the proper association of word and idea.

The individual pictures containing persons or objects which appear in the situational picture should be reviewed with pupils before the latter is studied intensively.

In order to obtain optimum results, it is suggested that pictures be arranged according to Sociocultural Topics found in Chapter 2. Pictures should *not* bear titles or numbers in front. The number should be placed on the back; e.g., a kitchen may be numbered 4 C1, the 4 corresponding to the Family, the letter C to the sub-topic Home, and the 1 to Kitchen.

A flashcard (3″ by 14″) in manuscript containing the title of the corresponding individual picture should bear the same number on the back. These cards should also be arranged in categories and filed in a separate box near the picture file.

The system of numbering rather than of having the word under the picture* enables the teacher and/or the "buddy" not only to give practice in numbers and letters of the alphabet but also to ensure comprehension and to reinforce association of words, symbols, and ideas. The teacher or "buddy" would direct the learner to:

1. "Find Picture 1A."
2. "Look for another _____."

---

* Situational pictures should never be labeled so that they can be used at different times as needed to illustrate a variety of concepts possible with each of them.

3. "Find the picture of the _____."
4. "Look at all the pictures in 3B. What does each one show?," etc.
5. "Match this picture with a word."

With relation to the picture file, certain considerations will be found helpful:

1. Mounting should be neat and artistic.

2. Colored pictures, if possible, are to be preferred to black and white ones, not only for their attractive appearance but for the language learning that is possible with them; for example, "What color is the _____?" "How many red _____ do you see?" "Who's wearing the blue _____?"

3. Pictures for use with the entire class as a group should be large enough to be seen by all the pupils.

4. Oral explanations should be used *in conjunction with* pictures, so that pupils can associate sounds and concept.

5. The showing of an object in the classroom or on the person of the teacher or a pupil should *precede* the picture when possible.

6. Pictures should be supplemented by blackboard sketches or other illustrations.

In addition to the mounted pictures, it is desirable to have sets of smaller cut-out pictures for use on the flannelograph (explained more fully below) and for use on experience charts. For example, in teaching structures and words relating to table settings or room arrangements, the teacher may ask a pupil or pupils to arrange the pictures on the flannelograph to illustrate place settings or room arrangements. In preparing an experience chart on a trip to the zoo and on various animals found there, pictures may follow each sentence to clarify it and to make the chart more attractive.

It is expected also that pupils will have sets of smaller pictures for their picture dictionaries or for illustrations in their individual notebooks. Units of study such as "Transportation," "Pets in the Home," or a "Good Breakfast" will acquire more

meaning if they are colorfully illustrated. The picture dictionaries need not all follow an alphabetical arrangement. In order
to teach related words and ideas, the picture dictionaries may
contain sections such as "Things That Go," "Foods We Eat,"
or "Resources in Our Community."

The method that will be used in teaching vocabulary or sentence structures through pictures is similar to the method already
given on page 111. It is reviewed here because we consider it a
fundamental teaching procedure.

1. *Show the picture* that represents the word you wish to teach.
2. *Say the word* that is represented *in a sentence,* "This is a
_____." Model the sentence as many times as necessary. Ask
the *class to repeat* the sentence, saying, however, "*That's* a
_____." Call on *groups* and then on *individual pupils to re-
peat* the sentence.
3. Have some pupils remain at their seats, saying, "*That's* a
_____." Ask other pupils to come up to the picture and touch
it, saying, "This is a _____."
4. *Write the word* in a sentence on the blackboard, *say* it
again, and *ask the entire class to repeat* the word or sentence.
Ask individual pupils to repeat. (This step is done only *after*
reading has been introduced.)
5. *Practice using the new words.* For example, with the picture of an object, the teacher may ask, "Show us the _____."
A pupil will request the teacher first and then another pupil,
"Show us the _____." The same procedure may be followed
with "Give me the _____" or "Where's the _____?" This
initial drill would be one in which the word being taught is
used. Later, "What's this?" with the answer required, "*It is* or
It's _____" will require recall of the word.

It is not expected that all these practice activities will be used
with each picture. As has been indicated, the number of exercises
will depend upon the age, the ability, and the maturity level of
the pupils. It will also depend upon the use (active or merely
recognitional) to be made of the word or concept.

There is an intermediate step in sentence practice which is

possible with well-arranged pictures. Between the pupils' learning to say "That's a boy" and their *discussing* a boy's activities as illustrated in a situational or in an action picture, two pictures, such as those of a person and a means of transportation, can give practice* in sentences such as:

Picture (boy)   *Picture* (vehicle)
The *boy* takes a *bus* every day.
The *boy* takes a *train* every day.
The *boy* takes a *boat* every day.

   or

The *boy* always goes there *by bus.*
                    by train.
                    by boat.

   or

The *boy* took *a train* yesterday.
         went *by train.*

   or

How did the boy go?
Who took a train? (The boy did)
Did the boy take a train or a bus?
What did the boy take?

Three pictures can be combined to teach statement, question, and response patterns such as

Person		Place	Vehicle
The boy	is going	to school	by bicycle.
	went		
The girl		to the clinic	by train.
		to the store	by bus.
		to the post office	by car.

How's *the boy* going *to school?* (By car, by bus, by train, by bicycle.) Is *the girl* going to the *post office by car?* Etc. (Yes, she is; no, she isn't.)

---

* The same technique can be used by combining any two pictures whose relationship can be made to produce common useful structural arrangements in English. It is especially helpful in practicing prepositions; e.g., He writes *with* (a pencil); The (book) is (on) the table.

In teaching patterns such as those above, it is desirable to stack pictures of people, places, and means of transportation on the blackboard ledge and to vary one or more pictures at one time in order to produce the *same* pattern but with different words in the sentence slots. Two students can be asked to change either of the end pictures, the middle ones, or two sets of pictures simultaneously.

Below are illustrations of worksheets for use with individual and situational pictures which the teacher or a central curriculum committee may wish to prepare. Others will be found in the chapter on "Individualizing Instruction."

It is assumed that the teacher, a teacher aide or a "buddy" will guide the learner in following directions for "coloring," "repeating," "completing," etc.

A SUGGESTED WORKSHEET FOR USE WITH AN INDIVIDUAL PICTURE
(based on a "book") *

Oral Exercises

Teacher or Assistant	Pupil
1. Say, "This is a book."	1. "This is a book."
2. What's this?	2. "This is a book." ("This" is used when the object is close to speaker.)
3. Show me a book.	3. "This is a book."
4. Show me another book.	4. "This is a book," or "This is another book."†
5. Is this a book?	5. "Yes, it is."
6. Is this a book or a pencil?	6. "This is a book. This is not a pencil," or "It's a book," etc.
7. Do you have a book?	7. "Yes, I have a book," or (if the negative has been taught), "No, I don't have a book," or "Yes, I do." ("No, I don't.")

* Recommended for use with younger pupils or beginning learners.

† Many variations may be given to and required of pupils depending upon what has been previously taught. For example, in answer 4, we may wish to practice, *Here's a book* or *Here's another book.* In answer 5, we may wish to give practice in *Yes, it is a book* or *Yes, it's a book.* In answer 6, we may wish to stress, *It's a book, It's not a pencil.* In answer 7, another possibility may be *No, I haven't a book.*

Written Exercises

1. Write the word *book*.
2. Put a line under the word *book*. (black, back, book, boy)
3. Complete the sentence: This is a _____.
4. Draw a picture of a *book*.
5. Color the *book* red.
6. Complete the word B_____K.
7. Underline a word that begins with the same letter as *book*. (boy, bark, dark, duck)
8. Write as I read: *book; This is a book; I have a book; It's a book.*
9. Write a sentence with the word *book*.

A WORKSHEET FOR USE WITH A SITUATIONAL PICTURE

A number of the following oral and written exercises may be used in connection with situational pictures. It is expected that teachers will adapt these to language abilities and needs of pupils and will supplement them with materials from their own experiences.

This worksheet is based on a picture showing a family in a living room. The father is playing the piano, the son is singing, and the mother is sewing.

Oral Exercises

1. If necessary, give practice in "father," etc., using individual pictures.

2. Introduce each person or object in the picture; for example, "This is the father."

3. Question and answer technique:

Teacher or "Buddy"	Pupil
Who's this?	The father *or* This (*or* that)* is the (father); *or* It's the father.†
What's this?	This (or that) is the piano, etc. *or* It's the piano.
Who's singing?	The son. *or* The son is. *or* The son is singing.

* Please remember that if the learner is holding the picture or is close to it, he says, "This is," whereas the form "That is" or "That's" should be required if he is at any distance from the picture or object being studied. "It's" may also be used.

† Notice the sequence of possible answers. This sequence may be used throughout.

Teacher or "Buddy"	Pupil
Who's playing the piano?	The father is playing the piano. *or* The father.
Who's sewing?	The mother is sewing. *or* The mother.
Where's the father sitting?	The father is sitting at the piano. *or* He's sitting at the piano.
Where's the mother sitting?	The mother is sitting at the table. *or* She's sitting at the table.
Where's the son standing?	The son is standing near the piano. *or* He's standing near the piano.
What's the father doing?	The father is playing the piano. *or* He's playing the piano.
What's the mother doing?	The mother is sewing. *or* She's sewing.
What's the son doing?	The son is singing. *or* He's singing.
Is the son singing?	Yes, he is. Etc.

4. Substitute *man* for *father,* then for the name of someone, Mr. Smith, for example.

5. Substitute other words for *son* and *mother,* for example, John and Mrs. Smith.

Written Exercises (to be supplemented by other examples)

1. Copy these sentences. Then put a line under the *name of the person:*

The mother is sewing. The father is sitting at the piano.

2. Put a line under the words which tell what is in the picture:

pencil, table, piano, bench, chalk, desk

3. Complete these sentences.

a. The _____ is playing.

b. The son is _____.

4. Match the words that correspond:

Column 1	Column 2
mother	playing
father	singing
son	sewing

5. Make sentences with the words in 4.
6. Answer these questions in complete sentences:
   a. Who's playing?
   b. What's the mother doing?
7. Write five sentences telling what you see in the picture.
8. Make *ten* sentences using the words from these columns.

The son	is singing	with John.
The mother	is sitting	near the window.
The father	is playing	the piano.

A PICTURE SERIES

A series of related pictures—about six to eight—on one chart will be found invaluable. The picture charts may illustrate contrasting sounds, e.g., chip, cheep; dip, deep; hip, heap; lip, leap; ship, sheep; *countable* objects in the classroom (pen, pencil, ruler, book, etc.) ; items of food which *cannot be counted,* such as milk, butter, meat, bread; or work activities being performed by a carpenter, butcher, policeman, doctor, etc.

Such charts will permit the teacher to give extensive practice in numerous structures and intonation patterns without unnecessarily increasing the vocabulary load for students. Students will not be bored by the repeated use of the same group of pictures. In fact, they experience a certain sense of security from "knowing" the words. Their knowing the word permits them to concentrate their attention on the pattern being practiced.

When *mass nouns* are taught, that is, names of items which *cannot be counted,* the same series may be used in many lessons to practice patterns such as:

What's this? It's milk.
Is this butter? No, it's milk.
Is this butter or milk? It's milk.
Where's the milk?
Do you have any milk?
May I have some milk?

How much milk do you want?
I'd like a bottle of milk, please.
How much does a container of milk cost?
Please get the milk from the refrigerator.
Drink a glass of milk.
Where do you buy milk?
Why are you going to the store? To buy milk.
Did you buy the milk? Yes, I did.
Did you buy the milk? No, I didn't. There wasn't any.
I don't think this milk is fresh.
Thank you for buying the milk.
Etc.

By dint of choral or individual repetition as the teacher or a student touches each picture in the series—first in the order in which it appears and later out of sequence—the students will internalize the recurring pattern, e.g., Where do you buy milk? Where do you buy butter? Where do you buy meat? Where do you buy bread?

Later, individual students may be asked to point to the pictures in the series either in or out of sequence and to ask their classmates questions about each of them.

THE FLANNEL BOARD

This is a most effective device for helping students visualize concepts, story sequences, and grammatical changes. It can be constructed easily and inexpensively by tacking a square of white or green flannel to a board about 24″ by 24″. A one-inch square of sandpaper (rough side out) or of flannel glued to two corners of the picture or of the cut-out to be displayed is sufficient to keep the picture on the board.

The flannelograph is a useful teaching adjunct during any step of the lesson development. For example, in presenting the story of Cinderella, the teacher might place the appropriate cut-out as he tells about it in the story. He may, however, place all the cut-outs on the board at one time before beginning to tell the story, and point to each one as he comes to it. Later, the cut-outs may be placed out of sequence and students can be asked to put them in the proper sequence using appropriate sentences as they do so, e.g., First we see Cinderella in the kitchen. Then her stepmother scolds her, etc. Such an activity helps children to develop sequence and paragraph sense.

Another effective use of the flannel board involves learning names of children; number; concepts of younger, older, same, etc. Names of students and numbers from 1 to 20 may be placed on flannel-backed oaktag. Four or five names with numbers next to them can elicit practice such as *Mary is eight. John is eleven. Is Mary eight? Yes, she is. Is Harry ten or twelve? He's ten. Is John ten? No, he's not. He's not ten. He's eleven. Who's younger, Mary or Harry? Mary is. Is Mary older than Harry? No, she isn't. Etc.*

A flannel board can serve a multitude of purposes. Stick figures of the speakers in the dialogue being learned can be placed on the board and constantly referred to as they "speak." Articles of clothing, pieces of furniture, food, in short, anything which can be pictured, can be placed on the flannel and manipulated to give practice in pronunciation, structure, and vocabulary, and to develop comprehension.

At the beginning level, a large X (to indicate the negative) and a question mark made of flannel can help give practice in patterns such as Where's (John)? or Where did (John) go? (using a cut-out of a boy and the question mark); Is (John) in the (living room)? or Did (John) go into the (living room)? (using the question mark, the cut-out of a boy and a couch as a symbol for the living room). To practice John's not in the living room, or He didn't go into the living room, the teacher would use the boy, the couch and the X. People and places can be changed to extend practice in the patterns being learned.

By removing the X quickly and placing another symbol on the flannel board, sentences such as (He) didn't go into the (living room), I think (he's) in the (kitchen) could be practiced. With two figures of people, plural forms could also be practiced.

The flannel board, as we have mentioned, can be used in any step of the lesson development. Let us assume that you plan to teach a unit on food. The pictures needed will be a picture of someone waking up, of a person having breakfast, many pictures of breakfast foods, a cardboard clock, and an oaktag card labeled, *A Good Breakfast.*

In the *motivation* step, the clock is used to convey the idea of time for meals. The picture of the person waking up and eating breakfast helps associate the idea of time with the fact that this is a breakfast rather than any other meal during the day.

During the *development,* the picture of each item of food is placed on the flannel board after its name has been practiced orally. The display is now labeled. We would recommend that only a few foods be displayed at one time, not only because of the confusion which may arise from attempting to teach too many new words at once but also because we would not want to give our learners the impression that any one breakfast need contain more than the few foods to which most people are accustomed.

During the *practice* period, individual pupils may select from the pictures on the teacher's desk the foods eaten for breakfast that day. He places them on the flannel board while saying, "I drank milk" or "I ate bread" or "I drink milk every morning" or "I eat bread every morning" as the response to questions such as "What do you drink every morning?" Another pupil may ask, "What did he (she) eat this morning?," eliciting the answer, "He (she) ate _____" from still other class members, or "What does he eat every morning?" eliciting the appropriate answer. This type of activity can be extended indefinitely. To illustrate, if family members have been studied, the teacher or pupils may ask, "Show us what father eats (or ate)" or "Show us what baby eats (or ate)."

REAL OBJECTS

It is important to have readily available a collection of everyday objects which can be used to clarify concepts; to make practice in punctuation, structure, and vocabulary more meaningful; or to play games. Some of the objects related to the unit to be studied may be on display on a table; others may be stored in a box or in a closet and used when needed. The collection should be added to and freshened whenever feasible.

Toys; stuffed animals; dolls of various colors, shapes, and sizes; wedgie figures of community helpers and family members; bottles; cans; containers; flags; toy money; plastic flowers; papier-mâché foods; pieces of different kinds of cloth; bus, train and movie tickets—all have a place in the object box. Where possible, *more than one* item related to a concept should be available so that students can understand that the objects, although individually different in some respects, still illustrate the basic concept. For example, a fish store, candy store, hardware store, etc., are all "stores."

When feasible, real food items, real flowers, and fabrics should be brought into class so that students can taste, smell or touch.

Creative or Play Activities

Any form of dramatic play, any type of game, any audiovisual experience *leading to language growth* may be used to stimulate learning. These activities, of course, will differ for various age groups.

With younger children, such activities as finger plays, block building, finger painting, housekeeping, dancing, playing in the rhythm band, making puppets, and setting up various stores can be made to lead to language development. For example, in making puppets the teacher may ask questions such as the following:

1. "What color is the paper (cloth, paint, etc.) ?"
2. "What do we call this?" (pointing to various parts of the puppet)
3. "How many eyes does the puppet have?"

4. "How do we make the mouth?"
5. "What are we going to call him?"

In setting up a food store, for example, language related to the names of the articles found there, to prices (consumer education), to formulas of courtesy in purchasing and selling, to cleanliness, to weights and measures, and to nutritional facts will naturally be developed.

With older students, creative or play activities may run the entire gamut from working out crossword puzzles and playing Scrabble games with the aid of a dictionary to writing and producing a play for an audience.

The language growth and the emotional and social gains resulting from creative or play activities make experiences of this nature a "must" in the language classroom.

LANGUAGE GAMES*

Games which reinforce vocabulary and language patterns can be bought or can be made with pictures taken from discarded magazines. Here is one example which may be adapted in many ways. Individual pictures related to one topic—the home, for example—can be mounted on cardboard. The teacher can give one or more pictures to each child and then ask questions or give directions such as:

"Who has a lamp (or the picture of a lamp)?"
> A pupil answers: "I have a lamp," or "I have," depending upon the language emphasis for that period.

"Show us the lamp."
> A pupil answers: "Here's the lamp," or "Here it is."

"What color is the lamp?"
> A pupil answers: "The lamp is red," or "It's red."

"What do you have,—?" (naming a child)
"What does he have?" Etc.

---

* Other games are suggested in the chapter on Materials for Vitalizing Learning and are listed in texts found in Resources and Texts.

After the pupils gain some proficiency in manipulating question forms, pupil leaders may ask the questions or give the directions, calling upon the teacher or other pupils to supply the answers.

THE TAPE RECORDER AND LANGUAGE LABORATORY

Tape recorders and language laboratories warrant special mention at this point because of the growing interest in their use. Where money is available, the school or center will find that tape recorders are invaluable. The recorder serves many purposes, not the least important of which is the fact that it enables pupils to evaluate their own progress in the language. The following procedure has been found successful in measuring growth in pronunciation, for example:

A pupil will record a paragraph on tape *at the beginning* of the semester, stating his name for later identification. A space is left on the tape for a subsequent recording by the same student of the same paragraph. In addition to the time needed to record the paragraph, it is wise to allow another 20–30 seconds. The space on the tape for each student is marked off either by the built-in counter on the more modern machines; by accurate stop-watch timing; or by pasting a tiny piece of red tape marking the ending of the pupil's recording (plus his reserved space) and the beginning of the next pupil's.

Later on in the semester, in the space that has been reserved for him, that is, next to his original recording, the pupil will again record the same selection. In this manner it will be comparatively simple for teacher and student to compare the first and second recordings and to judge progress in such matters as the pronunciation of sounds, the blending of sounds and words, and melody. Of course, phonograph records can be used for the same purpose but these are more costly.

The tape recorder may serve many additional purposes in the class and in the language laboratory. A few are mentioned here:

1. The teacher or informant records language items which individual or small groups of pupils can practice by means of earphones. An excellent idea is to leave enough space after each so that pupils will have time to repeat; the space should be followed by the teacher's or informant's repetition of the same item again. Thus pupils will *hear, say,* and *rehear.* Even more effective is the four-phase drill explained below.

2. The teacher or an informant can record paragraphs for dictation or aural comprehension.

3. Special radio or television programs can be transcribed for future class or group activities.

4. Fairy tales, anecdotes, or short stories can be taped for listening by small groups while the teacher may be working with other groups.

5. Dialogues or entire plays (original or otherwise) can be transcribed.

6. Any pattern practice exercise can be done.

It is important that two model examples be given before students are asked to respond to cues or to make required changes of word form or word sequence. The ideal situation is one in which the teacher prepares the tapes based on his more expert knowledge of the students' needs. There are, however, many excellent tapes on the commercial market, some of which are designed to accompany specific textbooks and others which give practice in some of the fundamental grammatical structures of English.

Many tapes are three-phase tapes; that is, the students (1) *listen to the cue;* (2) *make the desired response;* (3) *hear the correct model response.* Even more effective, however, are the four-phase tapes in which students (1) *listen to the cue;* (2) *make the desired response;* (3) *hear the correct model;* (4) *repeat the correct model.*

Several other thoughts come to mind in any discussion of tape recorders:

A single tape recorder placed in the center of the classroom can be heard by an entire class of thirty to thirty-five students. Materials appropriate for group listening are stories, dialogues, poems, speeches, songs, dictations, and aural comprehension exercises.

Pattern practice exercises are best done by individual students either with one tape recorder to which six to eight listening jacks can be attached or with individual tape recorders in a larger laboratory installation.

To be effective, students should be asked to practice a minimum of eight examples of the same structural item.

Playback facilities for students are not absolutely necessary. In fact, until such time as the students can *hear* and *distinguish* sounds (as ascertained by classroom practice), they cannot note how their responses differ from the model response. Often, their errors are reinforced by listening to their own voices. Where playback facilities are available and where students are at the stage of learning where they can hear distinctions, occasional playback creates interest and may serve as a spur to learning.

Whenever possible, the first presentation of material should be *live* by the teacher. In this way, students can see both the shape of the mouth as sounds are produced and any accompanying gestures.

Passive listening should be avoided. Pupils should be encouraged to engage in some activity while listening such as repeating silently, looking at pictures or other related materials, or answering questions.

Integration of taped material and classroom work is vitally important. The tape should reinforce and further classroom learning. It should not generally introduce new learnings. Moreover, students who have used the language tapes should be given the opportunity in class to "show off" the results of their practice.

THE RECORD PLAYER

Songs, dances, finger plays, stories, speeches—all of which can be found on records—are invaluable in language teaching and should be used extensively.

THE TELETRAINER

Two telephones permit pupils at opposite ends of the room to engage in conversation as the rest of the class (or group) listens.

FILMS, FILMSTRIPS, TELEVISION, AND OTHER PROJECTED MATERIALS

Filmstrips and *slides* can be used to considerable effect in the teaching of English. They help take pupils out of the narrow confines of the classroom and community while affording them the opportunity to practice pronunciation, grammatical structure, and vocabulary. A filmstrip can be stopped at each frame and a slide can be held as long as necessary in the machine, thus enabling teacher and students to take as much time as needed to make statements or to ask questions.

The fact that there is no sound track and that, even in filmstrips with accompanying tapes, the recorder can be operated separately, makes it possible to practice language at the students' ability level. As students grow in their knowledge of language, the slides or filmstrips can be repeated and the accompanying language made more complex.

Films, and especially sound films, have several disadvantages in the beginning stages of learning. It is difficult to stop them to concentrate on a scene, and the language used may not be simple enough. Of course, there are numerous films of fairy or folk tales and cultural situations which can be shown to pupils. These can be shown repeatedly with oral explanations, the explanations becoming more complex each time the films are shown. Silent films or film clips, illustrating cultural situations, can be used effectively at any time.

Television programs, unless specifically designed to teach English, share the disadvantages of the sound film for beginning learners. The language may be too advanced; the program cannot be stopped or viewed again unless kinescopes of the programs are prepared for later playback. On the other hand, many television programs would be invaluable in helping students visualize the social or cultural situations in which communication takes place. Moreover, teachers should capitalize on the fact that the majority of children watch television programs nearly every night and on weekends. The wise teacher will familiarize himself with these programs and use his knowledge of them to motivate many learning situations.

Teacher training television or film programs in many curriculum areas can suggest numerous ideas for vitalizing learning.

Opaque projectors are excellent for showing pictures, pages of a book, or duplicated materials. For example, passages from which words have been omitted can be inserted in the projector. The teacher can then dictate the passage, including the missing words, and students can write those words on their papers for later correction. Such spot dictations should be alternated with dictations of entire passages.

In the same way, reading passages or dialogues which have been learned intensively can be projected on the screen with some words omitted. Students would be expected to say the dialogue or passage recalling all the words. More and more words can be omitted in later lessons, gradually requiring the students to reconstruct the entire passage.

Overhead projectors are also effective since they permit teachers to write while facing the class—the material written being projected on a screen for all students to see. Moreover, through the use of overlays, the addition or deletion of material is made possible with a flip of the hand. Students can see at a glance how language elements are added, deleted, or substituted in sentences. The fact that the overlays come in different colors can dramatize the grammatical constructions which fit into different slots—for nouns, verbs, adjectives, or adverbs—if different colors are used for each part of speech.

The movement of the tongue from one position in the mouth to another in the production of sounds can also be made visible through the use of overlays. Fairy and folk tales come alive as overlays are added to existing scenes.

The brochures which accompany the projectors and the teacher's increased creativity as he uses the machine will suggest numerous other techniques.

TEACHING MACHINES AND PROGRAMED LEARNING

A comparatively new aid in language learning is the misnamed "teaching machine." The "machine" may be as simple as a cardboard box with a slot into which a program (the course content) is inserted and with a knob which the student turns as he completes one "line" or, as it is called, one "frame." On the other hand, it can be a highly complex, electronically controlled device into which the program is inserted.

The program is the important element in the teaching machine. A good program is one that is carefully graded with each language item subdivided into its smallest possible components. In addition to the fact that the material is presented in the smallest possible steps, or increments, as they are called, and that their sequence is carefully planned, the great advantage of the "teaching machine" is that the student learns immediately whether he has answered satisfactorily. He finds this out as he turns the knob uncovering the correct response or, in the electronically controlled machine, when a light flashes or he hears a buzz or some other signal. The student who has made an error will be directed to study the material again or, in the more complex machine, he may be given more practice exercises subdivided even more simply or presented in another way.

More and more programed textbooks are appearing on the market. The problem of synchronizing sound and structure—

so important in language learning—has not been entirely solved as yet. But a good programed text is extremely useful when older students already know the sound system of English reasonably well or when the teacher or a "buddy" can go over the material orally with them *before* they start studying it.

Programed texts are excellent for individualizing instruction. Not only can students work at their own pace but they receive immediate confirmation of the correctness of their response. Both these features incorporated in programed materials follow, as we know, accepted principles of psychology.

THE RADIO

In many school systems in English-speaking countries, provision has been made to teach language through radio broadcasts. In some cases, the language material to be heard on the radio also appears in one or two community newspapers.

General radio programs, except at advanced levels, share the disadvantages of films and television. It is simple for the teacher, however, to tape unusual and interesting radio programs for later repeated listening at spaced intervals.

OTHER DEVICES OR TECHNIQUES

1. The *Pocket Chart,* of great value, is made very simply by stapling four or five narrow strips of oaktag to a larger sheet of oaktag to form pockets. Clearly labeled folders or envelopes containing cards with the words necessary to form language patterns centered around one cultural unit or language feature should also be prepared and stored in a convenient place. Folders are attached to the bottom of the chart as needed. Sentences which have been part of experience charts and of action series may also be cut into strips and used effectively in the pocket chart.

This pocket device can be used in various ways to practice language items. For example, the teacher or a pupil will suggest a title or a word which will be placed in the top pocket. Other pupils will form patterns from the words or phrases in the envelope which are related to the title or key word. These are placed in the pockets. Reading and other oral activities follow.

The pocket chart enables students to see dramatically changes in word form and in word order. For example, in teaching the *negative form of suggestions,* the teacher might place the pattern *Let's run* in the chart pocket. He then would push apart *Let's* and *run* and insert *not.* The position of frequency words *always, never, usually,* etc., before the verb can easily be dramatized in the same way as can the troublesome *Do* and *Does* which begin some inverted questions in English.

Pattern practice drills can be briskly and pleasurably done if the teacher stacks appropriate cards in various slots. At beginning levels, *we, you, they* can be placed under *I* in the subject slot. As a student (or the teacher) removes a card and the new card is revealed, the new sentence can be practiced.

It is advisable to have the children make smaller individual pocket charts of paper or oaktag. These can be used by them to duplicate the manipulation of sentences being shown on the large class pocket chart or to create sentences of their own during language practice periods or other individual or group activity periods.

It is strongly recommended that pupils *not* be given scrambled sentences to unscramble. There is no reason to have incorrect sentences on display. In some cases the incorrect sentence is the one which sticks in the learner's memory. Moreover, the time spent in unscrambling a sentence like "to basket park the take of I eggs a" will be spent more profitably in imitating the teacher's correct speech or in practicing a correct pattern.

2. *The Vocabulary Wheel* is another interesting and inexpensive device. A large circle is made of oaktag or other stiff paper. At regular intervals on this circle are placed pictures of uniform size, either related to a central theme or, for review purposes, without any specific relationship. On the circle is placed a sec-

ond circle with a small window, the size of a picture. In the center is a long paper fastener which permits the second circle to spin around so that a picture will appear in the window.

The wheel may be used for identification of objects, for forming original sentences based on the pictures, for building up stories around the picture, and for many other types of practice exercises; for example, "What do you see?" "Who can find _____?" "Tell us something about the _____." "What is _____ doing?"

3. *The Sliding Selection Chart* is an excellent device for developing habitual control of language patterns by permitting substitution of language items within one frame or sentence.

The materials needed are a strip of oaktag about eight inches wide and about twenty-four inches long and one narrower strip which is slightly longer. The wide strip will contain a pattern which the pupils know well; e.g., "Give him the large book." Slits will be made on both sides of *him* and *large* to permit insertion and easy sliding of the narrower strip. The latter strip will contain words which we will want the students to substitute for *him* and *large;* for example, *me, them, her, English, red, small.* These should be carefully spaced so that the new language combinations will appear clearly as the strip is moved. By sliding the narrow strip through the slots, combinations such as *Give me the English book,* or *Give them the red book* are formed. These combinations can be practiced in oral and written activities.

Any number of language patterns can be practiced and mastered in this manner while providing pleasurable activity. Similar strips can be prepared which will furnish practice in the negative; for example, "Don't give him (them) the book"; in interrogatives, "Did you give?," "Why did you give?"; in using the past, "Did you give him the book yesterday?"; and in numerour other language combinations.

4. *Individual Notebooks and Folders.* All students, young and old alike, should be made to keep a well-organized note-

book. The pages of the notebook should be numbered and a table of contents kept in the front of the notebook with page references for each unit or experience chart. This will enable the teacher and pupils to use the same situation or "cultural" experience in building new sentences or in reviewing familiar ones. It is also an excellent means of providing meaningful practice for newcomers to the class or for brighter pupils who have completed an assignment. Let us take, as an example, a simple, beginning chart which has been built around a mealtime experience:

> *Every Evening*
> I go to the dining room.
> I sit at the table.
> I place my napkin on my lap.
> I pick up my knife and fork.
> I eat my dinner.

The same chart will be used to develop and practice other language items. For example, pupils may be asked to:

1. Change *I* to *You, We, They, He, She, Mr. Smith, The family, The boys, Who?*
2. Change *Every Evening* to *Yesterday,* to *Tomorrow,* to *This Evening.*
3. Make any of the above combinations *negative* or *interrogative.*

One can readily see that there are enough combinations of exercises to fill more than one class period and to maintain the interest of pupils of varied abilities.

It may be helpful to ask pupils to divide their notebooks into various sections such as *Pronunciation Helps, Sentence Patterns, Vocabulary, Dialogues, Assignments* so that they can turn easily to these sections when asked to copy materials into their notebooks and so that they can study more systematically.

As has been mentioned, younger pupils will also enjoy making and keeping picture dictionaries or sets of pictures under certain specific areas such as "Things That Grow" or "Things We Eat."

UTILIZATION OF COMMUNITY RESOURCES

In addition to the trips that may be taken into the community, the people and places in it may be utilized in numerous ways to help us attain the dual objectives of our language program.

Speakers may be invited to give short talks on topics of interest to the class. The pupil-teacher planning and language work for such an event will include the invitation to the speaker; a discussion of social amenities; questions to be asked of the speaker; an outline of suggestions listing material the class wishes pinpointed to be given to the speaker before the meeting; a letter of thanks after the talk; a discussion of how this talk or conference fits into the total program, and of the further use that will be made of it.

Agencies in the community and in government services often prepare simple and excellent literature to explain their programs or their functions. Materials from health centers, hospitals, community centers, banks, travel agencies, employment bureaus, governmental agencies, and other schools are gold mines of information and excellent sources of reading and discussion. If, instead of procuring the material himself, the teacher will make the sending for the material a discussion and writing activity, the materials will be made to serve a multiple purpose.

With older pupils, visits to homes of English-speaking persons can often be arranged. A teacher will find that many of his colleagues are willing to cooperate by inviting students for coffee and discussion during week-ends or on holiday occasions. Visits of this kind provide true tests of the functional use of language in a sociocultural context.

The cooperation of many community members should be sought to vitalize classroom teaching. The librarian, for example, can be invited to arrange a book exhibit in the library or to prepare a display in the English classroom. Centers in larger cities often arrange conferences both for students and for teachers in which reciprocal understanding is developed of cultural patterns and of teaching techniques. Many schools set up "language centers" where language learners are pledged to speak English only and where they can participate in varied programs designed to increase language ability. Bibliographies of source materials useful both to the teacher and to students are often compiled by these language centers or by the community librarian.

To illustrate further, a local printing concern or newspaper will often contribute materials, services, and techniques as a community service. These and all other sources of enrichment and of vitalization offered by the community should be used by the teacher in creating and maintaining a stimulating learning situation.

SUMMARY

In planning for the enrichment or vitalization of any lesson there is one fundamental question that should guide the teacher's thinking, "Does this bring the pupils nearer to the attainment of fundamental language and cultural objectives?" Any device or technique should be used which gives pupils a sense of achievement and mastery and which helps them towards more habitual control of language features while providing pleasurable, purposeful activity in the classroom. The source may be the wide world of other school experiences, of games, of national songs; in short, anything which contributes to the growth of the knowledge, skills, interests, and attitudes which are the desired outcomes of our teaching program.

CHAPTER 7

Planning a Balanced Program

Unless careful planning is made for a definite allotment of time to the various facets of language work and to related curricular activities, some important aspects of learning may be neglected. It is essential that a proper balance be maintained among the various activities in order to sustain the interest and attention of the language learners. Periods of intensive language practice should be preceded or followed by activities calling for a different type of pupil participation. Lessons devoted to the acquisition of structure and vocabulary should be followed by dialogues, reading, or controlled writing sessions in which the vocabulary and structures are put to functional use.

Some representative schedules which illustrate planning for a week and for one language session alone are given below. It must be remembered, however, that no single time schedule will operate in every situation. Scheduling will vary in accordance with the number of hours in the day devoted to the study of English. It will be guided also by the type of class organization for which it is intended. A class in which English is taught exclusively to a homogeneous group of language learners will require one type of planning. A class in which English is one of several areas being taught to a small group within a heterogeneous group will require another.

With all classes, integrative activities—in which all pupils can participate—should precede differentiated, individualized activities. This is important for several reasons: (1) All pupils will acquire a feeling of belonging to a group; (2) the teacher will be able to present certain segments of material—from which all can profit—more efficiently; (3) the language learners will hear English spoken by teachers and/or their native English peers in authentic, normal situations.

It is hoped, however, that the material contained in the "schedules" will suggest ideas for "balancing" a program to our colleagues who may find it impossible to adopt the recommendations as stated.

A Suggested Time Schedule for Younger Pupils: Beginning Level

The suggestions contained here are intended primarily for those teachers who give instruction in English as a second language for about an hour each day. The activities and techniques recommended can be used, however, in language-orientation classes where language learners remain for the greater part of the day. They are also useful in "regular" classes where the pupils whose native language is not English form one group within a larger class group of native English speakers.

In the language-orientation class, for example, the teacher will make provision for additional activities, for wider use of audio-visual materials, and for more extensive language practice. In a "regular" class, where English is taught to a small group within a class of English-speaking pupils, the teacher will set aside definite periods of the day when other groups are engaged in worthwhile activities to work with language learners. He may also ask a capable assistant or a "buddy" to present and give practice in the simpler language material through pictures, flashcards, and individualized worksheets. Many of the worksheets suggested throughout this book are designed for independent practice by language learners. It is important, however, that the teacher or a capable assistant present the new material *orally first* so that the learner will practice the correct pronunciation and intonation while working out the exercises.

Learning in the classroom should revolve about these main activities or experiences:

1. Preparation for and follow-up of trips in the school building and in the community, especially if the community is English-speaking and such trips are feasible.

2. Systematic practice in the communication arts, discussion of experiences, extensive language practice drills, and the use of a wide variety of audio-visual materials.

An intensive session may be divided in the following manner to provide these activities (exclusive of longer trips into the community, of course). (The length of the session will vary depending on the age of the pupils. Children of 6–8 generally become restless after about 20 minutes. When more than 20 minutes is needed, children may be asked to return later in the day for an additional block of time. Older learners can be programed for forty minutes or more if different kinds of activities are provided during the session to vary the pace and maintain interest.)

First few minutes—Warm-up (the entire group): Recital of previously learned material (such as, day, date, dialogues, chain drills, songs, proverbs, stories) ; taking of attendance; correction of assignment (if given). (Some pupils may place the assignment on the blackboard while the teacher provides oral drill on related work for pupils at their seats. The board work is then corrected by class members with teacher guidance.)

Next few minutes (the entire group): Intensive systematic practice of English sounds and of intonation patterns.

Next block of time (the entire group): Study of a unit of work.

Next segment of time: Division of pupils into two or three groups depending upon their ability to speak, understand, read or write English. Each group will be assigned a leader from among the more proficient pupils in the class who will report to the teacher. The teacher will work intensively with one group at a time or with one individual. Where a teacher aid is available, he may be given the responsibility of working with a group or individuals.

Last few minutes (*the entire group*): Coming together of groups for such activities as summaries of group work; summary of the lesson; preparation for the next day's assignment; recital of materials learned through the tape recorder or in the language laboratory.

The *week* may be divided in the following manner:

Monday—The Trip*

1. Trips around the school building—to the principal's office, the nurse's office, the gymnasium, the library, the shops, etc.

2. Trips in the community—to the various food shops (it is best to take only one type of food store each week), to the drug store, to the bank, to the health center, the community house, the movies, the library, the park.

    a. While on the trip, the teacher will point out various items; for example, in a fruit store, "This is an apple" or in a drug store, "This is a toothbrush." Pupils may be asked to repeat a word or a sentence in a low voice at that time or later in some quiet spot for which the teacher has arranged.

    b. As an assignment, younger pupils may be asked to bring in pictures showing the type of store, building, or room visited that day. These pictures may be taken from a newspaper or magazine or created by the pupils themselves.

Tuesday—Follow-up of the Trip

Pupils, with the help of the teacher, talk about what they have seen on the trip. (The entire class should take part in this activity, even the students with little previous English training.) Following is a brief outline of the *method* using, as you will note, the effective *hear, say, see, do* pattern of development.

* As soon as pupils are able, the teacher may select one to conduct the tour or to ask the questions. The teacher should assist by suggesting statements, questions, or possible responses. These might be given to the "conductor" in writing.

1. Pupils are given the opportunity to:
   Hear and *Say:*
   a. After simple questioning; e.g., "Where did we go on Monday?" "Whom did we see?," the teacher helps individual pupils say, "On Monday, we went on a trip." "We visited the drug store." "I saw the druggist."
   b. The class in chorus, in small groups, and then individual pupils repeat each sentence immediately *after it is composed.* (The teacher always serves as the model for pronunciation.)
2. Pupils are given the opportunity to:
   See and *Say:*
   The teacher writes the sentence on the board, says each sentence, and asks the class to repeat it in chorus.
3. Pupils *do,* that is, they practice the new words or forms:
   a. Individual pupils repeat the sentences.
   b. The teacher asks simple questions requiring only the answers listed on the board; for example, "Where did we go?" (The teacher indicates the correct sentence on the blackboard if this type of extra help is necessary.)
   c. Pupils ask each other the same questions. (It will help in the beginning stages to place the question on the board.)

With the aid of pictures the teacher then elicits from the pupils the names of the articles they have seen. These utterances are added to the list at the board. (The material based on the trip is usually in the simple past and in the first person singular because subsequent grammatical forms—other subject pronouns, plurals, other tenses—will be based on these original sentences.)

Although it is true that we are using regular and irregular verbs in the past tense in these questions, pupils will learn them as simple vocabulary items at this time through their repeated use after each trip experience. Moreover, since in English-speaking communities, particularly, pupils will hear words like "went" and "saw" all around them, it is desirable that we help them to recognize their meaning and use as quickly as possible.

In the early experience charts, the teacher may prefer to structure questions and answers in the present tense only; for example, "What's this?" (showing a picture of a fruit store) and "What do you see in a fruit store?" The answers and the resultant experience chart will contain sentences such as, "I see fruit," "I see apples," "I see pears," etc.

Varied practice will also follow this stage of the recalled experience. For example, after choral and individual repetition of the names of the objects they have seen in the stores, pupils will show pictures which they or the teacher have prepared and ask other pupils to identify the articles. A situational picture, showing a complete interior, may also be projected on the wall by means of an inexpensive opaque projector or displayed in some other way. Practice, of course, is followed by a summary and by the copying of the chart into notebooks—if pupils are capable of writing—so that the chart can be used at some future date for additional language work.

Wednesday and Thursday

The class works together for several minutes and then separates into groups.

The plan may consist of the following:

1. After giving attention to routines of classroom management, the teacher may check the assignment by correcting notebooks or by sending pupils to the board to write out portions of the assignment while he works with pupils at their seats. This seat work may consist of a more detailed check of the assignment, an oral practice exercise similar to that being placed on the board, and/or informal questions related to the pupils' in-and-out-of-school life, or any of the warm-up activities above.

2. The teacher may conduct a five-minute drill on sounds and intonation patterns.

3. The next few minutes may be devoted to any one of the Sociocultural Topics listed in Chapter 2 and to related lan-

guage patterns or to topics for older learners, such as the following (the content will be determined by the age and ability level of the group):

    a. Happenings of interest in the school or community
    b. Good books to read
    c. Places of interest for leisure-time activities
    d. Good radio and television programs
    e. How to get working papers
    f. How to find a job
    g. Good grooming for job hunting
    h. Neighborhood employment opportunities
    i. Telephone conversations based on various situations
    j. Hobbies
    k. Any special areas of student interest

The method of development of each topic should follow the simple procedures outlined above in discussing the trip. To illustrate further, let us assume that the topic for the day is *The House I Live In.**

The teacher or a student will show mounted pictures of a house illustrating the exterior and various rooms. Vocabulary and sentence patterns such as the following are developed:

I live in this house,
It's on _____ Street.
This is the door,
This is a window.
There are four windows.

Many practice activities will follow. Choral and individual repetition, pattern practice, questions by teacher to pupils and later by pupil to pupil, should always be included among the basic language activities. Dictations and Aural Comprehension exercises should also be planned. If the unit is studied later in the semester, it can be integrated with vocabulary about various

* The house shown should be similar to houses with which the learners can identify.

family members; for example, "Who's in the kitchen?" or with different verb forms; for example, "We eat breakfast in the kitchen." "My sister always sets the table."

After the sentences are practiced orally, the pupils may be asked to copy them into a notebook. It is essential that notebooks contain a *table of contents* so that the stories or experience charts can be easily referred to for future use to build additional structural patterns or vocabulary.

The class may now be divided into two or more groups. Individuals in one group may be asked to read aloud to the teacher while another group reads silently and completes exercises designed to test comprehension. Another group may spend this time in fixing language patterns by changing sentences from singular to plural, from present to future, or from declarative to negative or interrogative. Group numbers with assignments should be placed clearly on the board. A group leader should be made responsible for checking the work of his group while the teacher concentrates on new arrivals or on others in need of special help or guidance.

Friday

This day may be devoted to a recapitulation of the language items taught during the week and to emphasize the cultural phase of the English teaching program. Although cultural appreciation is interwoven in all the learning activities, it is desirable to focus the attention of pupils on this important aspect of our program during definite periods since cultural appreciation and understanding help to create rapport between pupils and teacher, and, often, between home and school.

During the first few minutes of the period the assignment is checked as usual. Then the class may engage in a number of activities which will extend and deepen interest in the cultural facet of the program.

Through such means as the studying of pictures, reading by the teacher, and listening to a speaker or to a recording, concepts related to the geography, history, and social customs of the English-speaking communities can be presented. These should be so developed that older pupils, especially, gain insight into the interrelationships of geography and history on the social customs or mores of a nation and into the differences that may exist between their country of origin and the English-speaking country because of differences in geography or history. Naturally, the age of the pupils will determine the extent to which these cause-effect relationships will be pursued in the English program.

Music, too, is an excellent medium for heightening interest in the language as well as for extending sociocultural concepts. It is recommended that words of songs to be learned by pupils be thoroughly explained so that the singing acquires meaning and purpose. Recordings of popular songs, folk songs, national hymns, and simple concerts will help also to awaken a love for music while stimulating language and cultural learnings.

A Time Schedule for More Advanced Pupils

A good plan to follow in order to achieve balance is to devote approximately two sessions per week to the presentation and practice of structural items, two sessions to intensive or extensive reading, and one day to area study (direct teaching of culture), to singing, to dictations, to aural comprehension exercises, or to written composition.

The day set aside for area study (which may be Friday or any other day) should be divided into two sections, the second half of which can be devoted to a longer dictation (reviewing the vocabulary and structural patterns of the week), to an aural comprehension exercise, or to the preparation for a more creative writing activity. As a matter of fact, the concepts presented within the "area" period may be woven into a simple dictation or aural comprehension exercise, or may be made the basis for the composition.

Naturally, the arrangement suggested above is flexible. If pupils have shown tremendous enthusiasm for a story they are reading, the emphasis on a grammatical item should be postponed. Sometimes, particularly with untrained students, the preparation for a composition may take more than one period. If a dictation practice exercise has led to disappointing results on one day, the teacher may prefer to follow up with a dictation on the next day.

In another type of plan, the teacher may prefer to spend one week or more on a topic of general interest. He will naturally provide for a number of *related* aural, oral, reading, and writing activities within the center of interest which he, or he and the class, have selected. Such a plan, which has been used successfully in a number of schools, is outlined in the chapter on Planning a Balanced Program (see p. 218).

Summary

The systematic planning of a balanced program will result in wider pupil participation, greater availability of materials, and fewer gaps in the presentation of the varied activities necessary to build competency in English. Planning should provide for both integrative and differentiated individual activities.

Pupils by and large prefer the teachers whose classes are characterized by orderliness, by a definite sequence on which they can depend, and by some degree of formal planning. Even very young children sense and appreciate the difference between a sequential, systematic, familiar approach and a confused, disorganized one. Psychological principles of learning are violated if pupils, who are mentally prepared for a trip on Monday, come to class to find that the schedule has been changed.

The importance of maintaining a balance between unrelieved skill training and creative or play activities which call for the use of different senses or muscles cannot be overstressed. This is particularly essential for younger children.

If we accept the two fundamental objectives of our program, it is imperative that the teacher provide a program of language and sociocultural activities which will result in the parallel growth of the four communication arts while fostering the personal-social integration of each individual pupil.

CHAPTER **8**

Individualizing Instruction

Individualization of instruction is a commonly accepted principle of current education. In a program of teaching English as a second language the principle of individualization has not only gained general acceptance but is considered a practical necessity for effective instruction.

A wide range of abilities and interests is common in any classroom. In the language class there will be found, in addition, wide variations among pupils in the basic language abilities. Some pupils may be able to say short utterances, but haltingly and with poor pronunciation; others may have a fair pronunciation but will be unable to get meaning from a paragraph; others may not be able to make the substitutions within the sentence patterns which are necessary for "freer" expression.

When these situations exist, the teacher will find it more efficient and effective to work with individual pupils (or to have "buddies" or assistants work with them) in order to reteach the specific skills in which weakness is noted or in order to reinforce newly learned but poorly acquired skills. Individual pupils can thus receive help as needed, while other class members can engage in language or concomitant activities for which they are already prepared.

Individualization of instruction does not necessarily mean that each child must be helped singly. There is no reason why pupils needing the same type of help cannot be grouped together to learn one skill or to practice one language item or concept. The length of time this help will be offered to a pupil or to a small group will depend upon the progress made in acquiring the skill or learning in which help is needed. Mastery of the skill may not be required. The individual may need only to be brought up to a level commensurate with that of a larger group so that he can participate in language learning activities with that group, both with profit to himself and to the other group members.

In English-speaking communities, where pupils are obliged to develop a level of English competency to enable them to sustain themselves in the total school program, individualized instruction may be the only practical and feasible means of teaching. This is particularly important if pupils do not enter school at the beginning of a semester.

When in such communities there exists the additional problem of pupils with little or no previous schooling being assigned to an upper grade because of the policy of placing children with their age peers, individualization of instruction becomes a professional and moral obligation of school and teachers.

Only by training student helpers, parents serving as teacher aides, or teacher interns and by preparing appropriate materials for developing language as well as for teaching concepts in the various curriculum areas, can the teacher hope to give all pupils, including the late arrivals, a basic, common program of learnings.

Individualization of instruction may take many forms. However, because of their suitability for independent study and for group work, and because of their widespread use in classrooms, major emphasis in this chapter is placed upon *worksheets* as a means of helping individual pupils. It is recommended that graded worksheets based on all units of work in the curriculum (as indicated in Chapter 2) be prepared by a committee of teachers. It is urged, too, that worksheets providing varied language practice also be made part of the file of materials in every classroom.

The worksheets should be so prepared that either the teacher will be able to use them with the entire class or with a small group; or that the assistant or "buddy" will be able to use them with a group or with an individual; or that a more able pupil can use them by himself.

The independent study of these worksheets by the learner should be preceded by 1) the oral development by the teacher or by an able assistant of the new sentence patterns, vocabulary, and concepts involved, and 2) the study of the individual worksheets which accompany the picture file as indicated on page 191. Preparation is particularly necessary for younger or less able students.

Instead of preparing separate sheets for varying ability levels, it has been found desirable in actual practice (cf. I Go Shopping, p. 234) to place graded exercises on the same page. It is hoped that less able pupils will thus be stimulated and challenged to complete all the exercises.

The same worksheets may be used to practice language items other than those indicated. In the worksheet on health, for example, *he*, *she*, *his*, or *her* may be substituted for *I* and *my*; questions based on the short reading selection may be added for the more able students; a short dialogue may be prepared between doctor and patient. Again the possibilities for giving practice and for extending learnings, with a minimal amount of preparation by the teacher, are limitless.

The worksheets can be prepared on inexpensive paper by any duplicating process. Although mimeographing is clearer and permits one to run off many more copies at one time, most teachers will find the spirit duplicator or hexograph machines simpler to use. The master sheets of the latter two can be written in pencil, in manuscript, or cursive writing (depending on the policy of the school and the age group of the pupils), or typed, as the teacher prefers.

Worksheets may include many types of materials. There should be entire sheets devoted to the *repetitive practice of one item alone*. There should be some in which pupils will have to *make a conscious choice between two items they have learned*. There should be others in which related items are indicated and pupils are asked to *select the correct item*. Others, like the work-sheets on health and shopping, will start with an *experience* as the core and will permit *review* of varied, perhaps unrelated language items.

Because of limitation of space, we will give only one or two illustrations of possible types of exercises, including the directions to students. (The directions should be given *orally* by the teacher or his assistant.) The teacher can then expand the list of exercises to include others he feels are necessary to give his pupils adequate practice. He will utilize, of course, the specific vocabulary area that he has developed with his pupils.

It is desirable to develop as many sentences as possible orally, before asking pupils to work independently with the sheets. When writing is required, a written example should also be given.

The representative exercises given here are not grouped together for any specific grade or age level. Some of them are on various developmental levels. Others assume a minimal level of reading ability. Often a teacher will find that exercises which he considered "immature" at first glance are done with enjoyment and profit by older pupils.

The basic principle to observe in working with these sheets is that pupils—even older ones—should not be expected to work on them for more than about fifteen minutes at one time. In this activity, as in any other, the teacher should vary procedures frequently enough to prevent boredom and diminishing return.

SAMPLE WORKSHEETS FOR DEVELOPING LANGUAGE SKILLS

A. To Develop Pronunciation. (It is expected that the learner will work with the teacher or a teacher aide who will guide him toward understanding the directions.)

1. Say these words. (All of them contain the same sound.)

   f*oo*d   r*oo*m   s*oo*n   n*oo*n   sp*oo*n   sch*oo*l

2. Say these words. (All of them contain the same sound.)

   *ch*oose   *ch*eck   *ch*ew   *ch*ild   *ch*ildren

3. Practice saying these words. First, practice all the words in *column 1*. Then practice all the words in *column 2*.

	1	2
a)	*Th*ere	*da*re
b)	*Th*ey	*da*y

4. In exercise 3, *say* the *word* in column 1 and then the word in column 2.

5. When I (or your friend) read these words to you, *underline each word* that is pronounced like the word *I*.

buy	my
fill	time
dinner	him

6. *Practice* these sentences. Pay careful attention to the words beginning with *b* and *v*.

   a) Go *b*y *b*oat.
   b) *B*uy the *v*egetables.
   c) *B*ob *b*urned the mo*v*ie film.

7. *Repeat* the following words.

| wanted | waited | needed |
| tested | ended | shouted |

8. *Practice* saying the following words.

| helped | talked |
| walked | worked |

9. As I (or your friend) read these words, *underline* the *part* that I (or he) *stress* (or that is loudest).

| mother | father | visited |
| paper | baseball | piano |

10. *Underline* the part of the *word* in the sentence which I (or your friend) *accent* or (*stress*).

   He's eating his dinner.
   I'm studying English.
   Let's have lunch.

B. To Develop Habitual Control of Language Patterns. (Any writing should be preceded by extensive oral practice.)

   1. Use *he* instead of the name in all the sentences. Change *is* to *'s*.

      John is here.
      Mr. Smith is our teacher.
      Harry goes there every day.

   2. Use *Let's* in front of each word.

read	learn
listen	see

   3. Use *Don't* in front of each word or expression.

shout	open the door
cry	sit down

C. To Give Practice in Choosing among Two or More Items.

   1. Use *is* or *are* in these sentences.

      a) The man _____ here.
      b) The girls _____ pretty.
      c) The book _____ red.
      d) The money _____ in my pocket.

   2. Use *in* or *on* in these sentences.

      a) The boys are _____ the room.
      b) The picture is _____ the wall.

   3. *Choose* the correct word in *parentheses*.

      a) The boys (plays, play) _____ together.
      b) The men (speak, speaks) _____ English.

   4. Use *whose, which* or *what* in these sentences.

      a) _____ time is it?
      b) _____ color are you using?
      c) _____ brother are you?
      d) _____ of the desserts do you like?
      e) _____ pen is this? It isn't mine.

D. To Develop Letter Recognition.

1. *Draw a line* to the words that begin with a *c*.

come	can
did	hat
for	baby

2. *Copy* all words that begin with *g*.

girl	green
you	go
jelly	garden

3. *Copy* the words in each line that *end* alike.

a)	can	man	get
b)	dog	cat	hat
c)	fall	bed	hall

4. *Draw* a line under the word that is the *same* as the *first* word.

a)	fun	fan	fun	fan
b)	flow	slow	blow	flow

E. To Develop Concepts and Vocabulary.

1. *Use* the word which makes the sentence correct.

   a) The boy wears a
      1) bat 2) fat 3) hat
   b) We sit at the table to
      1) eat 2) sleep 3) seat

2. Cross out the word that *does not belong* in the group.

a)	milk	eggs	butter	bed
b)	nickel	penny	dollar	inch

3. Write the correct words under each title.

Animals		*Ways of Traveling*	
boat	train	lion	cat
zebra	car	bear	dog

4. Find the word in the line that means *the same* as the *first* word.

   a)   pretty   ugly   rough   beautiful
   b)   easy   fine   simple   sunny

5. Find the word in the line that means the *opposite* of the *first* word.

   a)   dark   sad   light   angry
   b)   wrong   easy   rapid   right

6. *Add* a word that is in the *same group* as the other two.

   a)   Sunday   Monday   _____
   b)   four   five   _____
   c)   red   yellow   _____

7. *Cross* out the word that *does not belong* to the same family.

   a)   bake   back   baker   baking
   b)   garden   gardener   guard   gardening

F. To Develop Paragraph Comprehension.

Read each letter. Tell what kind of letter it is by putting the right number next to it.

1. A birthday letter.
2. A get-well letter.
3. A letter asking a friend to come somewhere.
4. A thank you letter.

Dear Uncle John,

I want to tell you that I like the new game you got me. I played with it last night.

Thank you very much. It's a nice game.

                                 Mary

Dear Henry,

Next Saturday, Father and I are going to see Grandfather on the farm. Can you come with us?

We can play games and ride on the pony.

Please let me know if you can come. You will make us very happy.

                                Tommy

Dear Sal,

I miss you. I wish that you were here at school. I began to read a new book this morning. Tomorrow we're going to visit the fire-house. I hope you can come back to school soon.

Please get well.

Richard

Dear Rosemary,

You are really a big girl now. Soon you will go to school with other children. I made this doll for you on your birthday. I hope you like it.

Have a happy, happy day.

Aunt Fay

G. Language Activities for Younger Children.

The teacher may wish to prepare language games involving art or play activities. Pupils may be asked:

1. *Draw* what you read.

   Two red balls
   A green tree

2. *Find* articles which have been hidden. *Tell* what you found.

   I found a green ball.

3. *Guess* who has done something.

   Was it Mary—No, it wasn't.

4. Pin the part on the doll (or on the animal) if you have it.

   (The teacher will have distributed cardboard cutouts of arms, eyes, etc. Pupils will be expected to say—"I have the _____. It belongs here.")

5. *Match the word and the picture.*

   (The teacher will cut rectangular cards from oaktag. He will cut a crooked line down the middle of the card. On one side he will draw or paste a picture. On the other side, he will print a word.)

ANOTHER SUGGESTED WORKSHEET FOR USE WITH AN INDIVIDUAL PICTURE

(Based on the word "shoe")

The pupil would engage in the following activities by himself *after* oral presentation of the word by the teacher or pupil assistant.

A. The young *beginning* pupil would:

1. Match the picture with the word on the flashcard.
2. Match the picture with the number on back of the picture.
3. Match the word with the number.
4. Find a picture of a *shoe.*
5. Cut out and paste the picture in his picture dictionary.
6. Draw a picture of a *shoe.*
7. Color the *shoes* black (brown, red, blue).
8. Circle the picture of a *shoe* (when three unrelated pictures are given).
9. Write the word *shoe* into his notebook.
10. Label the *shoe* in his picture dictionary.
11. Complete the word SH__E.
12. Use the word *shoe* or *shoes* in these sentences. Copy the sentences.
    a) I wear _____.
    b) I need _____.
    c) My _____ are brown.
    d) I wear a size 7 _____.
13. Underline the word *shoe*:
    hat, gloves, shoe, coat, boy, shoe
14. Use *the* in front of shoes: _____ shoes are new.
15. Label the parts of a shoe.

B. The more *advanced* pupils would:

1. Complete these sentences using the correct word:

    a) A shoe is part of (clothing, food, people).
    b) We wear shoes (during the day, at night).
    c) We wear shoes over our (socks, pants, underwear).
    d) We put our shoes in (the window, the clothing closet).
    e) We (keep on, take off) our shoes in the classroom.

2. Answer these questions:

   a) What are the parts of a man's *shoe*?
   b) What are the parts of a lady's *shoe*?
   c) Can you describe the *shoes* you are wearing?

WORKSHEETS WHICH DEVELOP LANGUAGE AS WELL AS SOCIOCULTURAL CONCEPTS
Good Health Is Important

A. Label the parts of the body.* Start each sentence with

   This is a (an) or *These are*

B. Label all parts of the head. Start each sentence with

   This is the or *These are the*

C. Label all parts of the body and head. Use *my* instead of *the*.

   Example: This is *my* head.

D. Read this story to your teacher or to your group leader.

1. My head hurts.
2. My ear hurts.
3. My throat is sore.
4. I have a temperature.
5. The doctor examined me.
6. He said that I have a bad cold.
7. He says I need medicine.

E. Write the numbers from 98 to 104.

   Example: *ninety-eight*

F. Fill in the blanks with the correct word.

1. This is _____ hair.
2. These _____ the teeth.
3. _____ are the legs.
4. This _____ the throat.

* Simple duplicated pictures should be included.

G. Use the correct word in each blank.

1. My head _____.   3. The _____ examined me.
2. My _____ is sore. 4. He _____ I need medicine.

I'M LEARNING TO READ THE NEWSPAPER

A. Tell in what section of the newspaper we would find each of the pictures:*

1. (Ex) We may find picture 1 in the sports section.
2. _____.
3. _____.
4. _____.
5. _____.

B. Read this story to your teacher or to your group leader:

1. I read the newspaper every evening.
2. I look at the list of contents to find the page I want.
3. I like to look at the comics.
4. I read the sports page to find the names of the winning ball teams.
5. I read the HELP WANTED section to find a job.
6. I read the APARTMENT FOR RENT section to find an apartment.
7. I read the RADIO AND TELEVISION PROGRAM section to find the names and the hours of programs I like.

C. Fill in the blanks with the correct word:

1. I look at the _____ to find the page I want.
2. I read the HELP WANTED section to _____ a job.
3. I read the APARTMENT FOR RENT section to find _____.
4. I like to look at the _____.

D. Complete each expression in Column A with the correct expression in Column B.

A	B
1. I read the newspaper	1. to find the page.
2. I look at the list of contents	2. to find the names of the programs.
3. I read the sports page	3. every evening.
4. I read the radio program section	4. to find the names of the winning teams.

* Pictures should be geared to the learner's interests.

E. Change *I* to *he* in sentences 1–7 in B.

F. Write the complete word for the abbreviations:

1. apt.   4. H.S.
2. E.   5. rm.
3. St.

I GO SHOPPING

A. Tell your teacher or your leader what you see in each of the pictures:

    e.g.   milk   eggs

1. In picture 1, I see _____.
2. In picture 2, I see _____.

B. Read the following conversation to your teacher or to your group leader.

    Storekeeper: Good morning, Mrs. Williams.

    Customer: Good morning. I need a bottle of milk, a dozen eggs, and a pound of butter.

    Storekeeper: Here's the milk. Here are the eggs. Would you like sweet or salt butter?

    Customer: Sweet butter, please. How much are eggs today?

    Storekeeper: Here's the sweet butter. Eggs are 73 cents a dozen. Do you need cereal today?

    Customer: No, thank you. How much is my bill?

    Storekeeper: $1.83, please.

    Customer: Here's $5.00.

    Storekeeper: Here's your change. Thank you. Good morning.

C. Fill in the blanks with the correct word.

1. Good _____, Mrs. Williams.
2. I _____ a bottle of _____.
3. I need a _____ eggs.
4. Would you like _____ or _____ butter?
5. Sweet _____, please.

6. Eggs are _____ three _____ a dozen.
7. How much is my _____ ?

D. Write out in full:

45¢   25¢ $1.00 $4.65   19¢ $3.99   50¢

E. When you complete Exercises A through D, answer these questions in complete sentences:

1. What does the storekeeper say when the customer enters the store?
2. What does the customer need?
3. Would the customer like sweet butter or salt butter?
4. How much are eggs today?
5. Does the customer need cereal?
6. How much is the bill?

F. When you complete Exercises A through E, find the answers to the following problems:

1. If the bill is $1.83, how much change does the storekeeper give the customer?
2. If one dozen eggs are 73¢, how much are two dozen eggs?
3. If I buy a pound of sugar at 29¢, a box of cereal at 28¢, and a bottle of milk at 28¢, what is my bill?

G. Make a list of things you may buy at the grocery store for breakfast.

UNIT III

GENERAL METHODS
OF TEACHING

CHAPTER 9

Fundamentals of Lesson Development

Although this book is devoted primarily to the teaching of English as a second language, we have considered it desirable to examine many of the elements which are component parts of any teaching act. There are many "constants" in the teaching process. The teacher's personality, his judicious use of materials, his skill in questioning, his ability to develop a lesson clearly, and his techniques for vitalizing learning and for securing the broadest kind of pupil participation are fundamental factors in teaching and not the special province of any subject area.

It is not expected that any teacher will attempt to include all the steps or processes which will be discussed in this unit in planning his daily lessons. The beginning teacher, in particular, will find, however, that careful thought to one or more of the items each day will be rewarded by increasingly excellent teaching results.

STEPS IN DAILY PLANNING

The new portion of each daily lesson, to whichever aspect of learning it may be devoted, will contain in general:

1. *The Preparation* or *Introduction* (not to be confused with teacher planning)—which may be divided into two sections:

    a. *Motivation* or *Approach* based on interests and experiences of children.

b. *Apperceptive Basis:* that is, *review of previously learned material* which bears a definite relationship to the material which will be developed.

2. *The Statement of Aim:* which should follow naturally from the motivation.

3. *The Development* or *Presentation:* by the teacher of the new material.

4. *Repetition:* by the students of the new material.

5. *The Generalization* or *Statement of Rule:* especially important for older pupils in a lesson on structure.

6. *The Practice:* divided into *Drill* and *Application.*

7. *The Summary:* stated ideally in terms of the initial motivation.

8. *The Assignment:* the natural outgrowth of the lesson.

Let us analyze these basic lesson steps in more detail. Let us also take a close look at other items such as teacher planning, use of blackboards, and techniques of questioning. Careful attention to these lesson elements will help make teaching more efficient and rewarding. Since language learning includes the development of *aural-oral, reading,* and *writing* skills, the examples we have chosen to illustrate concepts of methodology are taken from one or the other of these skills.

TEACHER PREPARATION OR PLANNING

Provision should be made for materials (commercial or pupil-teacher prepared) to be used in connection with each step of the lesson. These may include: real objects to arouse interest; pictures to clarify pronunciation, structures, concepts and vocabulary; boardslips based on the previous day's assignment or on practice exercises needed for the lesson; word cards (often called cue cards) to give practice in vocabulary or sentence patterns; materials to be used by students, such as pencils and worksheets; material needed for groups or individuals.

The number of minutes to be allocated to each step in the

lesson should be carefully planned. For example, with young children or with slow learners, the lesson should not be longer than approximately 20 to 25 minutes because of the pupils' shorter attention and interest span. With *any* group the time usually spent on *Introduction* and *Statement of Aim* should be about five minutes, with about seven minutes for *Development of the New Item*. The longest period of time should naturally be assigned to *Practice*, both aural-oral and, later, reading and writing. Time must be allowed for an adequate *Summary* and for the copying by pupils who can write of important new learnings into notebooks. (Copying should be done at the end of the hour, however.)

The use to be made of the available board space should be planned in advance. Since, ideally, we should be able to reconstruct any lesson from the materials on the blackboard, the sequence of the writing on the board (review, statement of aim, new work, and practice exercises) assumes importance.

METHOD

The techniques and method to be used will be determined by the type of lesson being presented; for example, structure, dialogue, reading, pronunciation, dictation, or vocabulary building. The questions the teacher should ask himself in general are:

a. Is this method suitable for this age and ability group? For example, should more visual materials be used in the development?

b. Could I *elicit* much of the material that I am presenting?

c. Am I trying to elicit material that I have not as yet presented? (This is a common fallacy among inexperienced teachers.)

d. Am I providing adequate examples so that the form, recurring pattern, and meaning become clear?

e. Is the majority of the class at the stage where it can profit from this lesson; in other words, do the learners know the materials on which this lesson is being built?

f. Have I made adequate provision for the slower or more advanced pupils?

g. Have I included an interesting approach, a statement of aim, a clear and systematic development, varied practice activities, a summary, and an assignment?

h. Is *this* method the most appropriate to lead to the pupil's acquisition of the linguistic items and to an appreciation of cultural patterns?

CONTENT

The type and amount of material in any one lesson will depend upon the age and ability levels of the students. To illustrate, whereas in the lower grades in the elementary schools only two new words might be taught in one lesson, between five and eight new words may be presented to the intermediate grades. With our young adult students, only their motivation, their intelligence, and our skill will limit the number of structural patterns, words, or idioms* to be presented in one session.

Current experimentation indicates, however, that with the normal young adult learner no more than eight words can be learned effectively at any one time. In other words, if in a reading lesson, for example, there are twenty new words, the teacher might present seven words toward the beginning of the session with the appropriate segment of the reading lesson; the next seven after several minutes; and six toward the end of the hour.

All the essential aspects of one topic should be included in the lesson without undue emphasis on irrelevant or comparatively unimportant items. For example, in a lesson on structure the important material to be taught should be developed carefully through review, many illustrations, class and individual repetition, practice activities, and a summary.

The content of the lesson should have relevance to the stu-

* The term *idioms* is used to indicate a group of words which acquire a special or unexpected meaning having no relation to the meaning of each individual word in the group; for example, *to put up with* meaning *to tolerate* or *endure*.

dents' own experiences, lives, and aspirations. Even though the teacher's aim may be to give his students some cultural orientation to the English-speaking country, the point of departure for the lesson should be something familiar to the pupils and within their own immediate experience. In a language lesson each step should give the pupils practice in hearing and saying material which has meaning for them because they feel they can use it immediately in a communication activity.

MOTIVATION OR APPROACH

Unless the teacher makes a definite attempt to arouse and sustain interest throughout the session, the best planned lesson will not produce the outcomes sought. Motivation should be planned for *each* phase of the lesson as well as for the beginning of the lesson. Every step of the lesson should be introduced by brief statements such as: "Now that we have learned the meanings of these words, let's see how we use them in sentences."

In going from the development phase of the lesson to the practice phase or from the practice activities to the summary, a statement which will "ready" the students for the activity and which will link what *has just been said* to what *is about to be said or done* will give the entire lesson a sense of cohesion, of balance, and of unity.

The term "intrinsic" is frequently used in discussing motivation. Ideally, the motivation should be based primarily on the interests and needs of the learners. This is not always easy or possible. In the first place, learners may not be fully aware of their language or social needs; in the second place, a teacher with a new group may not know their individual interests. The skillful, alert teacher, however, will know how to set up a classroom environment or how to create an emotional tone which will make the students feel that the lesson to be presented is of importance and of interest to them. In other words, an extrinsic motivation should be, and can be, made intrinsic.

This can be done in a number of ways, depending upon the type of lesson and other relevant factors. Colorful pictures related to the unit can be displayed on the bulletin board or placed around the blackboard ledge or shown to the pupils in some other manner. A visitor may be invited to the classroom to initiate the topic. The class may take a trip. The teacher can elicit some sentences about a current radio program or movie. The teacher may tell or dramatize an incident which may have happened to him, or he may elicit some sentences about an experience that he knows the students have had.

In a reading lesson, when the passage is part of a longer unit, the motivation may consist of a brief overview by the students of what has been read already. This summary should be followed by a question or statement by the teacher designed to arouse the curiosity of the learners in the story sequence.

With older pupils the best motivation is their awareness of their improved communication skill. *With all pupils,* success is the best motivation.

The Statement of Aim

When interest has been aroused, the teacher should state the aim of the lesson himself or attempt to elicit it from the students: "What do you think we need to learn today?" or "What do you think we're going to talk about?" The aim, which has been made clear to the class, can be placed on the front board where it can remain for the entire lesson.

We wish to emphasize the fact that the aim should be an outgrowth of the motivation. To illustrate, if the motivating sentence has been: "How did you travel to _____?," the statement of the aim might be (after some questions and answers or discussion, naturally), "Today we're going to learn about many ways of traveling from one place to another." The *written* aim may be: *Traveling* or *Ways of Traveling* or *Means of Transportation* (depending as always upon age, etc.). The same principle should guide us in presenting a language pattern lesson which does *not* result from an experience or from a unit topic. In teaching comparisons, for example, the teacher might review patterns such as *John is tall*; *Henry is tall*; *The book is large,* then ask the pupils to observe carefully the two pupils or the objects which have been placed next to each other. Then the teacher, with many gestures indicating height or width, might state, "Today we are going to learn how to compare (the two boys, or books, or chairs)."

There should be little or no digression from the stated aim throughout the lesson. All language and concomitant drills and activities should be related clearly to each other and should lead to the achievement of the initial aim.

The final summary (and evaluation by the teacher as to whether students have learned the important parts of the lesson) should be in terms of the aim. For example, in the unit on traveling, the summary might begin: "We learned that there are four ways of traveling. Who can tell us what they are?"

RELATING LEARNINGS TO PREVIOUS EXPERIENCES

This phase of the lesson development, which will serve to link the old or familiar with the new, may take a number of forms, depending upon the type of lesson. The review may come either *before* or *after* the statement of aim. To illustrate, if you wish to teach the *plural of nouns*, you will want to review the singular forms and either write them or have them written by a capable student on the front left board. This review will take place *after* the statement of aim, and naturally *after* the motivation. The teacher may introduce the review with a sentence such as, "Before learning how to talk about *more than one thing*, let's see if we remember the words we use when we're talking about *one thing*."

On the other hand, in a reading lesson based on a continued story, a summary of a page or a chapter already studied will *precede* the statement of aim. The summary thus takes the place of some other kind of motivation and includes the review.

Eliciting personal experiences of students lends interest to the lesson and makes the work more meaningful to them. The experiences should be related to the story to be read or to the language lesson to be presented. For example, in studying about food stores in the community (or the language pattern *I go shopping*), the teacher may ask, "Is there a grocery store near your home? What do you buy in the grocery store?" It is important to remember that, in letting pupils talk about incidents in their own lives, language errors remain uncorrected at this point unless they impede understanding. The teacher, however, will make a mental note of the errors and use them as the basis for a lesson with the pupil or, if they are of sufficient general interest, with the entire group.

The personal experience or "you" approach should be used throughout the period and not only for purposes of initial motivation. For example, after reading a story or dictating a passage, the teacher may ask, "Have you ever _____? Tell us about it."

It is essential that pupils, young and old, be given the feeling that the language or facts they are learning will function in their own lives. This can be done by making a conscious effort to relate new language learnings to the kinds of things that pupils of that age would ordinarily say in conversation. In this way they will appreciate the fact that the language patterns or vocabulary items being learned are used in communication situations.

THE DEVELOPMENT

The actual oral development or presentation of the new lesson should follow logically from the motivation and the review. Detailed steps in developing several types of lessons used in teaching English as a second language have been indicated on page 99. In any lesson, the following recommendations will be found helpful in planning the development:

a. Provide for smooth transitions from one step of the development to the other by introducing each lesson step with a brief statement.

b. Give as many concrete illustrations and examples in normal, everyday English as possible both in the related review and in the new material.

c. Lead the pupils by questioning designed to point up *comparisons* and *contrasts* with review material to see the general pattern or "rule." Help them to get more immediate insight by underlining or circling key letters or words. Use colored chalk if possible. To illustrate:

In teaching plurals, the teacher would elicit the *singular* forms (which the pupils already know). These are placed on the *left side of the front board*. The word "the" is underlined. The word "one" is placed by the teacher or a pupil above the singular forms. The new work (the plurals) is placed to the right of the review material. The word "the" is underlined; the letter "s" is underlined or circled. The teacher elicits, "We're talking of more than one book," and writes *more than one* above the plurals. She elicits the facts that "the" remains the same in *more than one and one* and that to say *more than one* we add an "s" sound to the word. The board would look like this:

One	*More Than One*
the book	*the* books
the notebook	*the* notebooks

In teaching the simple past of *come,* for example, the blackboard outline might look like this:

Every Day	*Yesterday*
I *come* to school.	I *came* to school.
You *come* to school.	You *came* to school.
He *comes* to school.	He *came* to school.

d. With young students, the written material on the board and the actual statement of rule or generalization should be omitted. Our primary purposes are to have pupils understand the structures, to have them use them correctly, and eventually to have them use these forms or patterns habitually in any language situation.

e. If a rule or generalization is elicited from older students, it should be expressed in the students' own words and should be a description of the sounds, form, position, or function of the item or structure being learned.

f. No *exceptions* to the basic structure or pattern should be taught or practiced unless there is complete understanding of the regular, recurring pattern based on numerous language drills and activities. For example, the plural of "man" or "knife" should be deferred until the concept of plurals with the three "s" sounds has been firmly fixed, that is, after plural words in [s], [z], and [iz] had been presented and drilled separately.

g. There should be little digression from the topic during the development. All pupil and teacher activities should aim toward fuller comprehension and functional use of the material being presented.

h. There should be provision for many varied practice activities and medial summaries throughout the lesson to check on understanding. In reading, for example, such questions or clinching statements as "Who can tell us what we've read so far?" or "Let's make sure we understand the story or the article" may be made.

i. Nothing that has been said under *Development* should be interpreted to mean that opportunities for enriching or vitalizing the lesson by interpolating pertinent pupil or teacher experiences should not be used. A plan should not be followed so rigidly that worthwhile contributions or questions of pupils are not utilized or that a pertinent anecdote of the teacher or of a pupil is not allowed to enliven the lesson.

THE PRACTICE

We have already indicated several basic pattern practice activities (p. 114) such as substitution, replacement, transformation, question and answer which will be found effective in developing comprehension, speaking, reading, and writing skills. Here we will limit ourselves, therefore, to additional general suggestions and illustrations which the teacher may find helpful in giving practice.

Many authorities divide practice into *drill* and *application*. In language teaching, the terms *habituation* or *manipulation* are often used to indicate the drill phase, while *communication* indicates *application*.

The term *drill* is used to mean repetitive practice of the one item being studied; *application*, as the term implies, means the use of that item with other language items or in other language situations. For example, in studying the names of animals, the *drill* on different animals may take the following form:

(After the teacher has shown the pictures of many cats and has said, "This is a cat.")

a. Class, and later, group, repeat *in chorus* "That's a cat."*

b. Individuals repeat "That's a cat."

c. *Teacher* asks *pupil,* "Show us a cat." Pupil answers, "This is a cat" or "That's a cat."

d. *Pupil* asks *teacher,* "Show us a cat." Teacher answers, "This is a cat."

e. *Pupil* asks *pupil,* "Show us a cat." Pupil answers, "This is a cat" or "That's a cat."

f. *Teacher* asks *pupil,* "What's this?" Pupil answers, "That's a cat."

In drilling *items of structure*, the teacher would vary the names of the animals but *keep constant* the structural item. For example, in teaching the position of "big" before the noun, the drill may consist of (1) unison and individual repetition of the sentences below after the teacher, substitution drills (see page 116); (2) teacher to pupil, pupil to teacher, and pupil to pupil questions such as "What's this?" or "What's that?" which would stimulate the responses:

* Pupils are trained to use "that" when the object or picture is at any distance from them.

That's a *big cat.*   That's a *big lion.*
That's a *big dog.*   That's a *big bird.*

The *application* will consist of the functional use of the words that have been drilled individually *in addition to* or *in conjunction with* other known vocabulary such as, "Do you have a cat?," or "Does your cat like milk?"

In practice, particularly in the drill phase, the following general recommendations will prove helpful:

1. Try to remember the mnemonic "Fan." There should be *focalization of attention, attentive repetition, and no exception.*

2. Drill only one item at a time.

3. Present the first type of practice exercise in the form of choral repetition in order to give pupils the feeling of security which comes from concert responses.

4. Call first on the more able students for individual repetition.

5. Make sure the drills are *graded* and *sequential.* Notice that above in drilling the word "cat," the first five drill exercises *contained* the word "cat."

6. Vary the drill procedures, emphasizing pupil activity at all times. Have pupils ask you questions or allow them to ask each other questions. For example, choral and individual repetition of items such as "Open your coats," "Close your coats," or "Show him the book" should be followed by pupils *asking the questions or giving the directions* and other pupils supplying the correct answer or action. Use flashcards and pictures to add interest.

7. Drill the form as it will be used by students. For example, it is not desirable to drill oral spelling unless a spelling "bee" or "tournament" is arranged which makes oral spelling natural.

8. Make provision for both *oral* and *written* activities if pupils are capable of writing.

Practice activities to be used in connection with reading lessons or as a follow-up of dictation or other language work have been discussed as we considered each of the language activities (see p. 152). A long but by no means exhaustive list of additional practice possibilities is given in the chapter on Activities Fostering Language Learning.

THE SUMMARY

Every lesson should end with a summary, preferably expressed in the students' own words. A question such as "What have we learned today?" is still a basically good one for pupils with some language competency. If the boardwork has been neatly organized, the teacher may help elicit the summary by pointing to each item of importance on the board and asking one or more questions about it. During the development of a reading lesson, if answers to questions have been placed on the board sequentially, the rereading of the answers (*after* they have been corrected) may well constitute the summary.

If the summary is short, more than one student may be called upon to give it in its entirety. A longer summary may be given cooperatively by a number of students, each one contributing a sentence or an idea. One pupil may then be asked to restate the highlights.

The summary should be in terms of the initial statement of aim. If the aim was *Words which describe,* the summary may start with a statement such as: "We learned to use 'pretty,' 'tall,' 'red,' etc." (The wording of the statement and the grammatical nomenclature used will naturally depend upon age and literacy levels of the pupils.)

It is essential that time be provided (particularly with older pupils) for copying or writing in their own words the major elements of the lesson. This is best done at the *end of the lesson.* Since our students may range from the nearly illiterate to the highly literate, they will undoubtedly write at different rates of speed. Writing or copying during the lesson will cause confusion and will interrupt the smooth development of the lesson.

THE ASSIGNMENT

To ensure carryover and to give further needed practice, an appropriate assignment should be given after each lesson. The assignment should be an outgrowth of the lesson which has been presented.

Although, as an outgrowth of the lesson, the assignment should *follow* the presentation, teachers will find it more practical and efficient to place the assignment for the lesson on the front board, upper left-hand corner, at the beginning of the lesson. In this way, everyone will copy the assignment into his notebook routinely at the beginning of the hour. This avoids forgetting or copying after the bell has rung when students are going to the next class or to their homes. Time should be provided after the presentation and practice, however, to sample one or two of the language exercises or the questions on the reading which have been assigned.* Some teachers like to use exercises in the textbook as class practice exercises. These may be done orally in class and then written at home.

Assignments should be differentiated according to pupils' ability, stage of literacy, or age, particularly when the age range in a class of younger children is over two to three years. Whereas near-illiterates may be asked to trace words or sentences or to find pictures, more able students may be asked to complete sentences, and superior students may be asked to do some original writing such as a short dialogue.

All assignments should be corrected. When the assignment being corrected is *undifferentiated,* a few pupils may be sent to the side board, either with or without their notebooks, to place portions of the assignment on the board. Only more able students should be sent to the board. This prevents the correction from taking an inordinate amount of class time. It also safeguards other class members from seeing too many errors.

* When home conditions make the preparation of assignments difficult, time should be allowed in class for supervised study and "doing homework." Nor should teachers take it for granted that parents are going to "help" pupils.

The correction of the boardwork should be a cooperative activity of teacher and pupils. Students, *other than those who did the original writing,* should be trained to go to the board, to ask class members to find the errors, to cross out the incorrect word, and to write the correct word over it. Students at seats should be trained not only to participate actively in the general correction, but also to make changes in their own work and to ask questions for clarification.

When the assignment is *differentiated,* the following correction procedures may be applied: The teacher may use the board technique described above in correcting the work of one group; he may assign more able assistants to check group work by means of a check list or model; he may write a key on the board and have students correct their own work; or he may collect the assignment of one group for more careful grading at home.

No work on the board should be read aloud until after it has been corrected.

Summary

In this chapter we have discussed the preparation the teacher should make before presenting a new lesson to his classes; the relationship of various phases of planning to the lesson whole; and the importance of following a systematic development in presenting any lesson.

Suggestions were offered with relation to such fundamental steps of lesson planning as the integration of the new learnings with the previous knowledge or experiences of the pupils and the practice activities to ensure language growth.

Needless to say, careful planning based on clearcut daily and long-term goals will bring order and sequence to our teaching, while enabling us to guide pupils towards "fuller" communication in the new language.

CHAPTER 10

Other Essential Elements in Lesson Planning

Let us turn our attention now to other elements in the teaching process, which are of equal—and in some cases, of even greater—importance. No lengthy discussion will be necessary, since these are recognized universally as essential features of teaching. Practical brief suggestions will be given under each topic. Wherever necessary for clarification, the suggestions will be specifically related to some phase or activity in the English teaching program. Of course, it will be necessary to make adaptations to meet individual situations and local conditions.

QUESTIONING (DISTRIBUTION, FORM, TYPE)

a. Call on each person in the group at least once. If the size of the group makes this impossible, secure total pupil participation by engaging in much choral repetition of questions and answers.

b. Call on both volunteers and nonvolunteers, but don't force timid pupils to answer.

c. Gear your questions to the abilities of your individual students. For example, address the simpler questions, to which only one new word may be required in answer, to the slower pupils.

d. In the beginning stages, use only fact-type questions or

those in which most words required in the answer are contained in the question; for example, "Who went to the store?"; "Where's John?"

e. Help students to begin answers by suggesting the first word or two. This is especially important when a change of verb form or sound is required in the answer; for example, "When *did* you *read* the book?" "I *read* the book on _____."

f. Ask the same or similar questions of many students so that correct responses will become automatic.

g. Have many questions of the same type so that the form of the question will also become automatic; for example, "*When did you buy* the suit?," "*When did you buy* the coat?"

h. Have students ask each other questions so that they can learn how to manipulate question patterns.

i. Place the question on the board occasionally and keep pointing to it to help the slower pupils.

j. Place the beginning of the answer pattern on the board for reference by pupils.

k. In reading lessons (particularly in the early stages of instruction), where questions are asked at the end of each sentence to check comprehension, word your questions so that students will be able to find the answer in the written sentence. Start with inverted questions beginning with "Is," "Are," "Do," "Does," "Can," etc.

l. The short, more natural form of response such as "Yes, he did" or "No, he didn't" should be practiced extensively and accepted unless pupils are specifically directed to give the long response. For example, "Did he go to the movies last night?" is generally answered by "Yes, he did" or "No, he didn't."

It is important that the question be worded to elicit the response desired for the particular practice purpose. For example, in order to elicit the *complete* sentence using the simple past ("He went to the movies"), the question should be "*Where* did he go last night?" rather than "Did he go to the movies?" which would normally elicit "Yes, he did."

m. Although in other curriculum areas a question eliciting simply a "yes" or "no" is usually frowned upon, this type of question is used profitably in English classes since it affords pupils excellent opportunities to listen to questions and to give the authentic responses used by the majority of native English speakers.

n. Keep your questions short and word them clearly. Double questions such as "Where did he go and at what time?" cause confusion.

o. *Ask the question first,* allow a brief pause for thinking, *then* call on a pupil by name.

p. Ask questions at random and not by row or by alphabetical order. These two cautions are necessary to ensure attention and to maintain interest. In chain drills, however, a pre-established sequence is more desirable. (See page 123.)

q. Plan your pivotal questions in advance. Carefully word those questions that help to clinch comprehension of a language item, of a concept, or of a story. It is always desirable to include pivotal questions in the written plan; for example, the motivating questions, the one that will lead pupils to understand the basic generalization in a language lesson, and the summary question.

r. Put your question to the entire group but allow only one person to answer. Choral answers to questions that may elicit varied responses create disorder unless the response has been practiced extensively immediately before.

   If you wish to practice choral questions and answers, divide the class in half. Prompt one half of the class to ask the question by modeling it several times yourself, and the other half to answer it. Then reverse the roles of the students.

s. If a pupil called upon cannot answer the question, call

upon someone else to answer or answer the question your-self and then *ask the first person to repeat the answer correctly.*

t. If pupil responses are not satisfactory, direct a student to ask you the question. This will enable you to give the model response and, if advisable, to engage all the pupils in additional repetitive practice.

u. If repetition of a question is necessary, *ask a student* to repeat it or repeat it yourself.

v. If you wish to reinforce a point by having an answer repeated, *have another student repeat it* unless you wish to model the answer.

w. Encourage students to ask questions to clear up lesson difficulties.

x. Praise correct answers.

Use of Objective Aids

Contrary to general belief, objective aids include the blackboard and chalk and not only such items as films, film strips, and tape recorders, which may still be beyond the reach of many teachers.

With relation to the blackboard, please note the following in addition to what has been said in the preceding chapter:

a. The blackboard should be free of all extraneous matter *before* the lesson begins.

b. After appropriate motivation, the statement of aim can be placed on the center board.

c. The presentation of the new work should be neatly and schematically arranged on the center board *after it has been developed orally.*

d. The related review work should be on another board immediately to the left of the new work for easy comparison and contrast.

e. Practice exercises should be placed to the right of the new work or on a side board if one is available.

f. The writing should be clear and legible from all parts of the room.

g. Writing may be in manuscript or cursive depending upon school policy, age of pupils, or literacy of pupils. Older illiterates, for example, may find manuscript writing easier at the beginning, since it resembles printed material.

h. Colored chalk may be used to point up verb or noun endings, to underline "irregular" spelling, or to emphasize contrasts or comparisons in pronunciation.

i. Stick figures on the board add interest and may take the place of more elaborate illustrations.

j. Any visitor coming into the room at any time during the lesson should be able to reconstruct the lesson to that point from an examination of the material on the board.

k. In general, the more able students should be sent to the board to avoid overlong corrections. If the teacher feels, however, that skills in *proofreading* or skill in explaining incorrectly written items need practice, he may wish to send less able students to the board occasionally in order to give class members opportunities for such practice.

l. Reading of any material which has been written by students at the board should be deferred until *after* it has been corrected.

The category of objective aids is very comprehensive. It may include flashcards or cue cards (with letters, words, or sentences), thinking cards for mathematics, experience charts, flat pictures, books, magazines, maps, globes, dioramas (three-dimensional sets similar to stage sets), puppets, miniature furniture, menus, bill forms, application blanks, bank checks and stubs, film strips, slides, films, and other items too numerous to mention. Any of them may be used to clarify, to give practice, to enrich the lesson or to vitalize learning.

Phonographs, records, tape recorders, and the audio items of language laboratories such as earphones for individual listening are excellent devices for enriching the lesson, for permitting pupils to hear voices other than that of the teacher, and for affording varied practice. In a few years it may even be possible to have television sets in all classrooms as another important tool for learning. Many of these audio-visual aids are too costly to be used generally. Although we know that the proper use of some of these would create interest and enthusiasm among our students, we wish to reaffirm that their absence should be no bar to effective teaching.

In using any aid, the following suggestions may be helpful:

a. The aid is intended to *supplement* the teacher and not to *supplant* him.

b. In the early stages of language learning, the best objective aids are *the students and teacher themselves.* For example, in teaching the names of articles of clothing, their materials or their sizes, the most effective technique is to point to the items which the *teacher* or the *students are wearing.* Pictures or other devices should *follow* and not precede the "live" examples.

c. In general, only one aid (the one best suited to the development of that particular item) should be used at any *one time.*

d. Material such as a film that may have been shown for pure enjoyment or recreation should also lead to discussion and to other language activities.

e. Equipment to be used in a lesson should be made ready *before* the lesson.

f. The simplest aid—a flat picture, for example—is often the most effective.

g. More elaborate aids, such as films, should be carefully previewed by the teacher or by a committee of teachers, not only to ensure their suitability, but also to prepare pertinent lesson materials around them.

h. Regular routines should be established at the beginning

of the semester for the distribution, use, and storing of aids. Mechanical equipment should be inspected regularly so that it will be available when needed.

i. Standards of neatness, cleanliness, and attractiveness in preparing and storing materials should be maintained.

j. Those aids not in use at the time should be carefully labeled and filed in manila envelopes or boxes and stored in closets.

GROUPING AND INDIVIDUALIZATION

Although some facets of these two topics have been discussed under other categories, a few additional remarks are necessary at this point. Primarily, we wish to re-emphasize that, however homogeneously students have been grouped with relation to language ability, they will differ in such factors as motivation, native intelligence, interests, time for study, time of arrival into the class, and many others. Grouping of pupils and individualization of instruction, therefore, will be found indispensable.

Some teachers find it difficult to manage more than one group, while many enthusiastic theorists insist that four groups can easily be managed. There is a happy medium. More than one group *can* be managed, but teacher training, including observation of teachers who have learned how to organize groups, is necessary. The following suggestions may be helpful:

a. If possible, try to present a lesson to the entire class as a group, even if it is only the vocabulary phase of the lesson. Then divide the group into smaller groups.

b. Limit your groups to two or three at the most.

c. Start working with one group of your better pupils. Let the remaining pupils watch as you develop routines and mechanics with this pilot group.

d. Train the second group only *after* routines with the first group have been so well established that it can work independently.

e. Assign and train group leaders who will be responsible to you.

f. Place the assignments for each group clearly on the board or on charts.

g. Provide individual and group worksheets. (Samples of these will be found in Chapter 8.)

h. Prepare, cooperatively with students, charts clearly outlining group and individual responsibilities.

i. Ask for secretary volunteers to keep a log of group assignments and of individual assignments within the groups.

j. Organize groups for specific needs and purposes. For example, more than one group will be needed for reading activities if the age or the reading span among class members is too wide. Illiterates will have to be grouped separately for writing and reading activities.

k. Train pupils to engage in other activities when they have completed a group assignment if you are not ready to work with them. They may read, do research, or continue working on an art project they have started.

l. Assign a "buddy" or assistant, to help the new arrival or the very slow pupil. (A student assistant should not be asked to work with these pupils except for brief intervals during the session and only *after* he has completed his own assignment.)

m. Have *individual* pupils read aloud to you alone. You may, however, wish to create an audience situation occasionally by having more able students read to the class or to a group. Even these pupils should read alone to you first, so that you can be sure that pronunciation, stress, and intonation are correct.

n. Arrange, if possible, to have an English-speaking student from another class or section, or a community member, give supplementary practice to individuals or groups in the classroom.

o. Have exchanges of oral reports among groups from time to time to stimulate interest.

TEMPO OF THE LESSON

a. A well-planned lesson should begin and end on time. This does not mean that the teacher should not spend the first few minutes of the language period establishing and maintaining rapport by asking students questions about their other in-or-out-of-school activities and about English materials previously learned.

b. The tempo should be brisk, particularly during practice periods.

c. Sufficient time should be allowed, however, for students to ask questions or for the teacher to introduce interesting sidelights that are pertinent to the lesson.

d. Long, personal digressions on the part of the students or teacher should not be encouraged during the lesson.

e. Lengthy explanations that are of interest and value to only one student should not be made except when the class is profitably occupied or when the lesson is over.

f. Normal speech and intonation patterns must be used by the teacher at all times. It is unwise to speak slowly or in short breath groups in the mistaken notion that such speech will aid pupils in understanding. Not only will it not do so, but it will actually retard comprehension. The pupils will rarely have occasion to hear slow, halting speech among native English speakers or in any recording of English speech.

SOCIALIZATION

a. Since pupil activity is basic to learning, many opportunities should be provided that will ensure pupil participation in all phases of planning and lesson development.

b. The teacher should be alert to discourage domination of the lesson by a few of the pupils.

   c. The arrow of recitation should not always go from teacher to pupil and from pupil to teacher. Pupils should be encouraged to ask the teacher and each other questions and to answer each other's questions.

   d. The teacher should avoid the expression "Tell *me*" or "Show *me*." He should substitute "Show *us*" or "Tell *us*" in order to include all class members in all classroom proceedings.

   e. Many opportunities for creative expression should be provided. There should be a free discussion period at the beginning of the lesson (for example, things pupils have done the evening before, a movie they have seen, a news item) or after the summary when pupils are encouraged to express themselves to the best of their ability. We wish to repeat that during this discussion period, errors (except for very glaring ones, which limit understanding) should remain temporarily uncorrected.

TEACHER EVALUATION OF PUPIL GROWTH

Every lesson should make a contribution to pupil growth in habits, attitudes, knowledge, and skills. The teacher should ask himself, after the lesson has been presented, whether or not the new learnings have furthered the aims of the program of English teaching. Among the questions he should consider are:

   a. Have I inculcated *habits* of using the correct word form or word order, of copying material into notebooks, of using dictionaries and other reference books to check information, of asking questions for clarification of facts, of preparing assignments, of bringing reports in on time, of working independently when I am busy, and of using English when the occasion arises outside of the classroom?

   b. What new *knowledge*—either linguistic or cultural—have the pupils acquired today?

c. Have I made adequate provision for integrating this new knowledge into existing language or cultural knowledge?

d. Have I related all the new facts to real situations, so that students will recognize their functional value for listening, speaking, reading, or writing purposes?

e. Did the new material confuse old learnings, or was it presented in such a manner that relationships between the new and the old became apparent to the pupils?

f. Did I stress comparatively unimportant bits of information which did not contribute to the primary aim of the lesson?

g. Was there sufficient emphasis on the growth of language *skills,* such as in framing questions, answering questions, summarizing, outlining, increasing speed in reading and learning to get the sense of a passage from the context?

h. Did I promote an *appreciation* of important social and cultural values?

i. Did I encourage *a desire for further knowledge,* either linguistic or cultural?

j. Did I take every opportunity to stress socially desirable *attitudes,* or was I overly concerned with imparting knowledge and developing skills?

Writing the Lesson Plan

All that has been said in this section about lesson planning should not lead the inexperienced teacher to believe that preparation for teaching a lesson need take hours of time. After a number of lessons in each area of language development are thought through carefully, lesson plans will fall automatically into certain well-defined patterns.

It is strongly recommended that lesson plans be prepared in advance even by the most experienced teachers. The written lesson plan need not be elaborate. The kind of lesson plan prepared is often determined by school policy.

The plan for each lesson may include the following data:

1. Date and class designation
2. Aim (for various groups if necessary), including new sounds, structures, and words to be taught
3. Motivating question
4. Review items
5. Model sentences (containing the item[s] to be taught)
6. Pivotal questions leading to generalization
7. Practice activities
8. Assignment
9. Material needed

It will be helpful to keep daily plans in a special notebook for easy reference by the teacher and/or the substitute and to devise some personal scheme to indicate whether all the material planned for the lesson has been covered and mastered.

SUMMARY

We have indicated some additional basic factors in lesson development. The use of questions that are challenging and stimulating, objective aids that clarify and enrich concepts, group procedures that make learning more effective, a brisk tempo in a cordial atmosphere in which pupils learn English while learning to live together—all these are important facets of the teaching-learning process. Their inclusion can help make language learning a pleasurable activity for both teacher and pupil.

CHAPTER 11

Creating a Desirable Classroom Climate

Whereas systematic lesson development is of paramount importance, of equal value is the creation of a class climate in which learning is encouraged. A pleasant, colorful classroom in which the acquisition of knowledge is made a friendly cooperative venture between teacher and students is something for which all of us should strive. Unless motivation within the students is at an extremely high level, it is difficult for them to maintain interest in an atmosphere of rigid formality in which the teacher dominates every phase and activity of the lesson. It is only by participating in varied activities in an atmosphere that is conducive to learning that the students will be enabled to acquire those habits or skills needed for language competency.

All teachers can create a cheerful atmosphere, even those who teach in the oldest building in the most underprivileged community. What is needed, primarily, is a sympathetic appreciation on the part of the teacher that language learning thrives in a pleasant, cheerful, but workmanlike atmosphere. Certain principles and techniques will favor the creation and maintenance of such a classroom.

Our discussion of classroom climate will include four such principles that we have found particularly significant: (1) rapport between teachers and pupils; (2) teacher-pupil planning; (3) centers of activity in the room; and (4) classroom management.

RAPPORT BETWEEN TEACHERS AND PUPILS

Perhaps the greatest single principle that distinguishes "traditional" education from our current practices is the underlying mental-health, or "success," approach in teaching. Good "traditional" teachers, however, have always instinctively used the mental-health approach without labeling it as such. The difference today is that the voluminous literature in the field has made *all* teachers more aware of the implications of the "success" theory in teaching so that increasing numbers apply its principles in their classrooms.

We shall not enter into needless and controversial discussions of difficulties in articulation among teachers and schools when all do not subscribe to the success principle; nor shall we discuss the danger that undeserved success in school may bring to students, since (it is argued) they will not always meet with success in other walks of life.

In teaching English to speakers of other languages we may state categorically that it is imperative that all students—young or old, literate or illiterate—be given a sense of success and achievement. It is also important that the students feel secure in the teacher's liking and respect for them as individuals. How can this be done? The concrete suggestions below relating to the actual teaching of English, added to the teacher's personality —which made him choose teaching as a vocation in the first place—should help to provide the friendly atmosphere which will further learning.

1. Use the "you" approach in your teaching. Try always to relate the various phases of the lesson to personal experiences of the pupils. Make frequent use of statements such as, "Have you ever gone shopping? Tell us about it," or "Would you have acted like _____ in the story? Why not?," or "How do you do this in _____?" (naming a pupil's community or country of origin).

2. Permit judicious freedom of movement in the classroom. For example, when students have completed their assignment,

allow them to use the library or other centers of activity in the classroom according to their personal interests. Ask students to go to the board frequently to write words or sentences that you might ordinarily write. Create opportunities for wide pupil participation.

3. Encourage students to ask questions. Students should be made to feel that you will answer their questions either during the lesson (if they are of general interest) or after class. New arrivals should feel free to ask questions quietly of their "buddies" or of other class members if they need help during the lesson.

4. Use praise lavishly but judiciously. Find something favorable to say when a student has recited accurately or has shown *any* improvement. This is particularly important in the case of students who have been timid or "late starters."

5. If classwork is put on display, make sure that each child in the class has his work exhibited at one time or another. This is essential with younger children especially.

6. Give students a feeling of security. Always provide choral repetition *before* individual repetition. Call on volunteers before calling on nonvolunteers. Help the more timid students along by pointing to pertinent phrases on the board to get them started or by suggesting the beginning words of answers to questions. Try not to force a very timid child to speak in the beginning sessions if he appears very reluctant to do so. (If after a few weeks of concerted effort on your part, the student still refuses to speak, confer with a guidance worker or with a parent or, in the case of an older student, have a private talk with the student himself.)

7. Do not embarrass students. If errors are to be corrected in front of others, do it casually and softly. In many cases it is more desirable to allow errors to go by (particularly during a "free" discussion period) but to make a mental note of them for later individual or classwide correction.

8. In asking questions, give pupils time to think. Allow some time for the student to answer a question. Reword it if necessary

or have another student repeat it. If after a reasonable amount of time the student either cannot answer or answers incorrectly, ask another student to give the correct answer. *Then ask the first student to repeat what he has just heard.*

9. Individualize your instruction. Gear your presentation, your questions, your assignments to the abilities and aspirations of your students. For example, your superior students may be capable of doing some creative writing, whereas other students may only be capable of filling in blanks or of completing sentences.

10. Make as few demands as possible for expensive materials or assignments that are overlong or that necessitate frequent trips to libraries or other places. With older students, particularly, consider home and work responsibilities.

11. Plan a reasonable testing program. Except in unusual circumstances, do not spring tests on pupils. Tell them what the test is going to be about. After all, you are interested in their studying and in finding out what they have been able to learn. Provide adequate time for answering questions. If possible, go over the test items immediately after the test. Within reason, excuse pupils from taking tests after an absence or if they indicate that they were unable to prepare for the examination. *If most pupils do badly, reteach the lesson.*

12. Utilize the abilities of your students. Those with superior ability may act as "buddies" or assistants, correct test papers, act as group leaders, or be assigned to do research. The less able students may prepare audio-visual materials, print charts, or take charge of bulletin boards.

13. Show an interest in your students' out-of-school life. Ask questions (which you are sure won't embarrass them) about their families, other classes they may be attending, and their work and interests.

14. In your teaching, build on what your students know. Go from the *known* in their native language or in English to the *unknown* and from the *concrete* to the more *abstract*. Plan for a warm-up session and for a short *pertinent* review at the be-

ginning of *each* lesson. Provide for frequent sequential drills.

15. Make provision for sufficient class activity and practice. It is only through attentive repetition that students can hope to achieve any degree of mastery. Let your students do the talking. Remember always that *they* are the language learners.

16. Provide a socialized setting. If possible, have pupils' seats arranged in a semicircle. Try not to sit or stand in one central place alone but move to other parts of the room occasionally.

17. Create audience situations when possible. Plan for group dramatic activities. Encourage individuals to give reports and to read stories or their own original compositions in front of the class or to a group.

18. Do *nothing* yourself that students can do as well. For example, under your guidance, allow them to correct board work or test papers, to write on the board, to set up room centers or exhibits, to prepare questions on reading assignments.

19. Allow pupils to cooperate in planning. (This is discussed at some length later, page 271.)

20. Make your role that of friendly guide and leader. Do not dominate the classroom scene. With older pupils particularly, the role of the teacher should be that of a more experienced group or committee member.

21. Allow students to speak their native language if they wish during certain clearly designated minutes during the school day in elementary schools, or during some portion of the English lesson in secondary schools. It is perfectly normal for students to revert to their native language when they want to say something and are not ready to do so in English.

22. Keep some books in the students' native language in the classroom. Let students who are able to do so read them either after they have completed their assignment or *instead* of reading something in English. Let them, however, give an English summary of what they have read to the entire class.

23. Where only one or two languages are involved, learn to say one or two formulas of welcome or concern. Use these whenever feasible.

24. Learn to say also (for beginning learners only) the requests *Look, Listen, Repeat, Say, Answer,* and *Ask* in the students' native language (when only one or two languages are involved).

25. Make them feel pride in their cultural heritage by asking them to bring in recipes for food, native instruments, art work of various kinds, language newspapers, or references in English newspapers to concerts or exhibits of visiting artists.

TEACHER-PUPIL PLANNING

All students, even six-year-olds, should be given a share in planning the classroom program. There are many advantages, both linguistic and social, that will accrue to students from helping to plan classroom activities. A discussion (or in the beginning stages where discussion is impossible, responses to questions) of responsibilities, preferences, needs, and interests will certainly further the communication aims for our pupils. Sequential steps in outlining, work-study skills used in carrying out research activities, and other aspects of the language arts can be taught functionally through the planning phase of our teaching program.

Social values, which are of equal importance, will also result from careful teacher-pupil planning. Respect for the rights and opinions of others and acceptance of the majority will are but two of these social values.

It goes without saying that planning in which the teacher attempts to meet not only the linguistic needs but also the interests of his pupils, and in which pupils feel they have had a share, will provide the intrinsic motivation that will carry many lessons along. With older pupils especially, who may have only a limited amount of time to devote to language learning or who may have urgent social or vocational reasons for acquiring the language, planning together is not only a necessity but a professional courtesy.

A few cautions are necessary, however, particularly in dealing with older students. Because of their eagerness to learn quickly, they very often entertain the mistaken idea that the study of idiomatic expressions or lists of words—or an over-emphasis on reading—will result in increased language skills. Often, too, they feel that attention to pronunciation is a waste of time. Their eagerness to acquire the language may also make them impatient with the differing needs of their classmates or with the systematic methodology of the teacher. The skillful teacher should not summarily dismiss the opinions of these students. Rather, he will demonstrate, for example, that attention to pronunciation will increase reading ability and that structural items which are developed sequentially and systematically lead to more efficient and effective learning of communication skills.

After the teacher has ascertained interests or specific language needs of pupils, it is desirable that he decide on the daily *common core* of linguistic knowledge that he will present to the class as a whole or to a large group. For the sake of efficiency, individualized activities should be assigned *after* basic information has been presented and *after* a generalization or medial summary has been elicited from the students or, if necessary, given by the teacher.

Similar caution should be exercised in the presentation of the cultural aspects of the English program. Although the instructor will be aware of the specialized interests of individual members of his group, he will use as his point of departure the *present,* common environment and experiences of his students. Then, in ever-widening circles of interest—classroom, school, community, country, other countries—he will arrive at the points of shared cultural interests of the majority of the group. Areas of specific interest to individuals should be made the subject of special assignments.

With older students who are interested in creative writing and who have some proficiency in the language, additional individual planning is important. Special research, reading or writing assignments, and individual correction and discussion will be necessary. Errors found in written work by the teacher or by a trained assistant may serve both as the basis for further planning with the individual or, at the discretion of the teacher, for general class or group work.

Our attention has been turned primarily to older students because of the special problems that sometimes arise with them in planning. Let us look for a moment at some of the ways in which all pupils can have a share in planning in a language-learning class. Planning can run the gamut from participating in routine classroom management to writing and producing an original play based on a holiday program.

With language beginners in the early stages, planning may have to be brought about by pantomime and gestures and as a response to simply worded requests. Pupils can assume responsibilities for making the room attractive—cutting and mounting pictures, building boxes and shelves, preparing bulletin boards, arranging centers of activity—and for keeping it attractive and functional. By means of gestures and pictures pupils can help decide which trip into the community they prefer to take first. By means of pictures again or by thumbing through pages of a reader or a magazine, students may express their preference for listening to, or reading, one story or another.

With relation to committee work the older children can certainly help decide whether they prefer to do research, keep a log of activities, assist in the preparation of instructional materials, or perform the many other tasks that are part of our current dynamic teaching approach.

A class secretary, if he is capable of writing, can keep notes on important decisions and on follow-up activities needed to carry out the decisions.

The daily plan, or the plan for the English period alone, can be drawn up by the teacher and the more advanced pupils through such questions as "What should we do first?" (copy the assignment; correct the homework). "Then what should we do?" "Should we practice _____?" (naming vocabulary, pronunciation, pattern). The wording of the questions can be varied to give practice in expressions such as *should, need, have to, must,* etc. The plan may then be written on the board by a more able student after writing has been introduced.

None of the suggestions above is a contradiction to what has been stated—that the teacher is the firm guide and leader of the class. In the modern classroom the teacher does not abdicate his position as leader, but he does permit the maximum of flexibility and pupil planning, guiding such flexibility and planning so that it will lead to increased motivation, greater efficiency, and desirable language and social outcomes.

CENTERS OF ACTIVITY

Well-defined centers of work, play, study, or research, which enrich the regular program of the class, or where pupils can engage in worthwhile activities while the teacher is occupied with another group, form an important part of the modern classroom.

Nowhere, perhaps, are these areas or centers as important as in classes with pupils who are learning a language. They serve many purposes in addition to the primary ones of helping pupils develop language ability and cultural appreciation. Pupils gain status by contributing to the centers; they gain security in the manipulation of familiar, concrete materials; they learn to express themselves through a medium other than language; and they live in an environment that offers motivation for learning.

For those schools where pupils may be placed in special English classes for one or two hours daily, it may be advisable to provide a common core of materials in the centers of activity for all classes on the same grade. In this way pupils who are not ready to participate in the regular class program may continue an activity or an assignment agreed upon by the regular class teacher and the instructor of the special English class. The language learners may work independently or with an assistant to fix new concepts or vocabulary, which have been presented to them by the special English teacher.

Carefully chosen objects in various curriculum areas can be

used to stimulate curiosity and learning. Study and discussion of these objects will permit the pupils to move from the narrow vocabulary of a limited situation toward the fuller English suggested by the realia. If the objects, then, are those that exist specifically in the English-speaking environment, they will open up to teacher and students additional channels of cultural orientation.

The number and type of centers will depend, of course, upon the space in the room and the age of the pupils. Although the library corner is a must from the kindergarten through the secondary school, a block building or doll center will not be needed after the first or second grade. (Dolls and doll houses are useful in upper grades, however, to teach parts of the body and furniture arrangements in the home.)

The centers need not be elaborate or store-bought. Orange crates, shoe boxes, and hat boxes, gaily decorated by pupils and teachers with construction paper or paint, serve many useful purposes. In addition, parents, other community members, or shop teachers may be called upon to help construct shelves or partitions.

In classes with younger pupils, careful planning is necessary to make the room really functional. A library corner where quiet is needed should not be placed near a housekeeping corner where two or more children may be playing. Partitions (a small chest of drawers, an ironing board, a set of shelves) should be set up so that areas of play, research, and reading are clearly marked off.

It is essential that the material related to the current unit of work be prominently displayed in the classroom. Experience charts, based on the *current* unit of work, should be the *only ones* prominently displayed. Others based on preceding units may be on an easel or on a string in a corner of the room. Charts may be attached to a string by means of spring clips generally used for hanging clothing.

It will be found desirable to preserve *all* experience charts for ready reference. Charts may be used over and over again either in working with newcomers or in building new structural items on known experiences and patterns; for example, "I wash my teeth" may become "Does he wash his teeth?" or "Does he wash his teeth every morning?" or "I don't wash my teeth." The possibilities for language practice through the use of experience charts are endless. The preparation of charts is explained in the section on The Stages in Reading Growth (page 146).

Centers may include any or all of the following:

1. Library	Colorful picture books, magazines, picture dictionaries, a regular dictionary, interesting readers on various reading levels, an encyclopedia, books in the students' native languages on various reading levels, magazines, newspapers
2. Games	Word and picture games (either commercial or prepared by teachers or pupils)
3. Nature-Science	Aquarium, terrarium, plants, shells, magnet, microscope, thermometer, barometer, weather calendar
4. Social Studies	A neighborhood map, a map of the country, a map of English-speaking countries, a globe, a list of community resources (this may include a map), a bulletin board of current events, dioramas of historical scenes or scenes from stories
5. Dramatic Play and Communications	Puppet stage, puppets, telephones, a record player, records, miniature furniture and home furnishings, microphone, blocks, tape recorder with listening jacks for small group or individual instruction

| 6. Construction Corner | Materials for handicrafts, expendable magazines, scissors, glue, boxes, construction paper |
| 7. Current Unit | Pictures, flannel board, experience charts, dioramas, bulletin board, real objects (realia) |

The following suggestions should help make the centers more functional. It is desirable to:

1. Use concrete, tangible materials.

2. Have a *few* meaningful objects attractively displayed.

3. Be sure the materials are on the pupils' level of understanding.

4. Allow pupils to share responsibility for planning and caring for centers.

5. Keep objects within easy reach.

6. Label objects (at least some of them) in large print.

7. Change centers frequently. Relate them to emerging interests of pupils and to the unit of work being studied.

8. Make sure that all pupils have the opportunity to use the materials and to become familiar with their names and their varied uses.

9. Prepare language lessons based on the materials found in one of the centers. An example of a possible lesson with younger children will be found in the chapter on materials. Another plan, in which the library corner serves as the springboard for a series of teaching lessons, will also be found in Chapter 25.

CLASSROOM MANAGEMENT—ROUTINES AND RECORD KEEPING

The most inspired teaching can produce poor results unless careful attention is given to those details of management which make for smoothness and efficiency of teaching and learning. With young and older pupils alike, it is important that routines be established during the first few days. Time and procedure for leaving the classroom should be clearly understood as early as possible. For example, pupils should not be permitted to come in late without an excuse or an apology. Although the teacher will try to end the lesson on time, students should be guided to sit politely until they are dismissed by word or gesture. Many of these details may seem trivial—and they are—but they do set the emotional and work tone of the classroom.

A regular procedure should be agreed upon for taking and recording attendance. It may be desirable, in fact, to train a student assistant who will help the teacher in this chore.

Procedures for the copying and correcting of the assignment should be decided upon at the beginning of the semester. Systematic and efficient procedures for distributing and collecting materials such as textbooks, test papers, assignments, art, and construction work should be clearly demonstrated and practiced from the first day. Unless there arises a good reason for change, established routines should be maintained throughout the semester.

All teachers have individual preferences as to seating arrangements for pupils. In order to facilitate the learning of pupils' names, an alphabetical arrangement may be more desirable during the first part of the semester. The teacher may wish to retain the alphabetical arrangement for the entire semester in order to expedite the taking of attendance, the entering of ratings, or the collection of materials. Pupils can join members of their group or they may join their "buddies" or assistants later during the class period when the alphabetical seating is no longer necessary.

Service squads—to keep boards clean, to pass a wastepaper basket, to get materials from closets—should be organized as soon as feasible on the basis of student volunteers. Where audio-visual materials (projectors, record players, sound recorders) are used, a group of students from the teacher's own class if pupils are sufficiently mature or from another class in the school should be trained to keep the machines in working order and to operate them when necessary.

Of primary importance in classroom management is the attention devoted to record keeping. The preparation and scrupulous maintenance of pupil and teacher records will ensure continuity of instruction for learners.

With relation to the pupils the teacher should know such pertinent items as name, address, family members, country of origin, years of schooling, number of years of study of English, place of study, and (where the information is pertinent) traveling experience. It is also desirable to know their age, achievement level and literacy level (on the basis of observation or test). With older pupils vocational or professional interest information should also be ascertained. If possible, interest and hobby questionnaires should be prepared, and the relevant information recorded.

It will also be found helpful for special English teachers to learn what the pupils are studying in other classrooms or in other areas. This will give the teacher the opportunity to integrate the language work, wherever possible, with other known concepts or experiences of pupils. Information about English books already read and units of work studied will permit the English teacher to extend or to reinforce the knowledge of his pupils.

Other pertinent background information as to physical, emotional, or social condition will be of value as well as records of formal achievement tests, reading ability tests, or intelligence tests if they are used in the school.

In addition to background information it is essential to keep up-to-date records of students' progress in all phases of the work. These will include ratings on tests, the groups in which a pupil may be in the various aspects of the language arts, the extent and type of group participation (leader, secretary), the recitation marks as noted by the quality of oral work, by the answers to questions, or by the number of times and situations in which he volunteers. Records should be kept, too, of individual assignments or projects and of special language needs as they have been noted during the course of the semester.

Anecdotal records of students' progress in class and of their attitude toward their work, their classmates, and the teacher form an important part of our "battery" of records. Since it is virtually impossible to make notations for each student every day, the teacher may wish to prepare one or two anecdotal records of outstanding or atypical pupils for further evaluation and study.

Let us now consider the types of work or lesson records that the teacher will find helpful. He will want to keep a notebook with daily plans, a unit plan, and a term plan with broad outlines of the linguistic and cultural items to be covered. Some procedure, a daily log perhaps, should be maintained to indicate work that has not been covered, additional work done, and special needs—for example, further work required on a sound that nearly all pupils have mispronounced. Any unusual happening and reminders for the next day should also be recorded.

In the event of absence the teacher should make some provision for informing the substitute or the assistant where lesson plans and other necessary materials are kept. Plans should be prepared at least a week in advance so that a substitute teacher can continue the work without undue loss of time for the class.

The alert teacher will also keep such records as a list of community resources (both people and places) that he can utilize, a calendar of important school or community events (tests, assembly programs, festivals, clean-up drives, elections), and a list of instructional materials available in the school or in the district that he might borrow.

SUMMARY

We have touched upon the importance of creating and maintaining a pleasant but workmanlike attitude in the English classroom. Various practices for establishing rapport with class members have been recommended. One such way—permitting pupils to participate in planning—has been explained in more detail. We have suggested some linguistic and cultural contributions that may be derived from centers of activity. The importance of pupil records for placement purposes and for curriculum planning has been emphasized. It is only by paying scrupulous attention to details, which may appear unimportant at first glance, that teaching will become a science and an art.

UNIT IV

THE ROLE OF THE SUPERVISOR

CHAPTER 12

Training and Utilizing School Personnel

In cooperation with teachers, school supervisors and administrators play a key role in the English-teaching program. Their policies with regard to organization of classes, to gradation of classes for varying ability and social maturity levels, and to the number of pupils in each classroom will certainly affect the instructional program. The help administrators give the clerical staff and other personnel in receiving and testing new pupils for placement purposes will also influence intraclass grouping and subsequent teaching practices. The over-all school or center organization (clubs, social activities, special rooms, time schedules, parent reception, and parent organization practices) cannot help but bring about changes in the class program.

Every aspect of the instructional program will reflect the philosophy and attitude of the supervisory staff. Whether there is provision for continuous curriculum reorganization, whether a teacher is encouraged or permitted to experiment with new techniques or to take the class out on community visits, whether he has a sufficient allotment for maps, textbooks, and other audio-visual aids, whether necessary school supplies are on hand, whether a formal testing program is in operation in the classroom, whether the teacher is asked to keep many and varied reports—these and many other administrative and supervisory policies will modify actual teaching practices. Where younger learners are involved, the question of parent relations will also be pertinent. This important area of school life will be discussed in a separate chapter (see page 311).

Perhaps the most important activities of the school administrator are the selection, training, utilization, and supervision of personnel.

There are too few school systems that require a special license for teaching English as a second language. There prevails a general fallacy that anyone who knows English can teach English as a second language without too much preparation. Nothing could be further from the truth.

As we have observed, teachers of English as a second language need—in addition to innate qualities of empathy for nonnative learners of English—a willingness to study characteristics of their pupils' background and language, the time, devotion, skills to prepare instructional materials on numerous learning levels, a knowledge of English structure and pronunciation, and special training in the teaching of English as a second language.

If no licensed or trained teacher of English as a second language is available, the first duty of the supervisor, then, is to choose from among the teachers on his staff who volunteer to teach English those who have demonstrated unusual skill in teaching as well as innate personal qualities of sympathy and professional devotion. If there are no volunteers, teachers with these qualities will have to be selected from among the staff or recruited.

TEACHER TRAINING

The training of these staff members is a long-term process. The supervisor will first have to become familiar with methods of teaching English as a second language and with the culture-language patterns of the majority of the pupils. Then, slowly and sequentially, through various supervisory techniques, he will have to guide the volunteer or selected teachers to the point where they will become self-sustaining and capable of self-evaluation and where they can assume roles of leadership in various school and community committees.

The supervisory techniques should include:

1. A series of conferences—group, grade, faculty—in which resource people would be called upon to give information related to: (1) cultural backgrounds of various ethnic groups; (2) brief descriptive analyses of the major languages represented in the school; (3) the contributions of psychology, linguistics, sociology and anthropology.

2. Lectures or materials providing a descriptive analysis of the English language.

3. Conferences on methods of teaching English as a second language, stressing the fact that principles of foreign language teaching and of early childhood methodology (such as reading readiness) should be used *in conjunction with* accepted techniques and principles of teaching English and speech.

4. Model lessons given by the supervisor himself or by specialists in the field on various aspects of the language program; for example, the development of an active vocabulary, techniques for making structures a matter of habitual control, the development of skills that will help pupils to read with ease and enjoyment, and the presentation of cultural facts in a language context—in dialogues, for example.

5. Provision for visits to other schools or centers where English is being taught. It is essential, however, that these visits be preceded by a short conference in which the observers are advised to focus their attention on specific aspects of the teaching situation. The observation should be followed by a conference with the teacher who gave the lesson in order for him to clarify any question in the observers' mind. If possible, the observation should be followed by still another conference at the home school in which the methodology observed is discussed in order to determine how the techniques observed can be applied or adapted to fit the situation in the home school.

6. Provision for intervisitation in the school itself. The super-

visor may train one teacher in a particular technique—for example, grouping in reading or giving a dictation—and arrange for other teachers of English to observe. It is not essential that the teacher observed be a teacher of English as a second language. If a social studies teacher has developed excellent techniques for grouping or if a mathematics teacher has unusual methods of securing full pupil participation, the supervisor should arrange for visits to the rooms of these teachers.

7. Workshops in which teaching problems or a discussion of areas of special teachers' interest lead to action research projects or to experimentation.

8. Meetings with committees who will prepare picture files, worksheets, graded reading materials, and other necessary instructional materials.

9. Organization of a professional library devoted to literature in the field, to sample instructional materials from other schools or communities, to graded texts, and to resource units and materials that are particularly appropriate for the local school situation.

10. Assistance to teachers in the preparation of units and plans—day, week, semester, year.

11. Training of teachers in the preparation of tests and in the evaluation and application of test results.

12. Preparation of regular newsletters (short, concise, schematic) keeping teachers abreast of community resources, of new techniques, of recently published materials, and of experiments in the teaching of English as a second language.

13. Conferences with staff members *other* than the English teachers to familiarize them with the English program in order to enlist their cooperation, to stimulate integration of subject matter, and to effect smooth articulation when the language learners are ready to enter the regular stream of the school.

14. Frequent supervisory visits both when invited by the teacher to observe a special activity and, at other times, according to need and to school policy. (Samples of observation check lists will be found on p. 440.) It is urged that the visit be fol-

lowed by a conference in which the teacher is asked to evaluate his own performance. Only *one major* point in the lesson should be taken up at any one time as a follow-up of the visit even though the lesson may have had serious shortcomings in various aspects. Other points of criticism may be made the subject of staff workshops (the teacher remaining anonymous, of course) or of other postobservation conferences.

Teachers, beginning or experienced, will not resent supervision if it is creative and constructive. Just as teachers guide their pupils to acquire insight into language and culture, so should supervisors guide teachers cooperatively to gain insight into possible weaknesses in their teaching procedures. We have already stated that supervision is a long-term process. Another truism with relation to supervision is that it should be continuous. Beginning teachers, experienced teachers, and those teachers aspiring to supervisory posts will profit from a well-spaced flow of bulletins and from regular dynamic teaching demonstrations, which will vitalize their own teaching.

UTILIZING SCHOOL PERSONNEL

The supervisor who utilizes strengths within his own staff and resources within the community will find that he is in the position to offer a well-rounded training program enriched by the contributions of individuals of varied talents and experience. There are many persons in the community who can be called upon to give lectures, to assist in the preparation of materials, or to serve as consultants on phases of methodology in which they have specialized.

Within the school all members of the teaching and clerical staff can contribute to the enrichment and vitalization of the curriculum for speakers of English as a second language. Some members of the teaching staff, naturally, are in a better position than others to help because of similarities in methodology, in approach, or in content between their field of specialization and English. For example, where there are elementary school classes in the language center, the teachers of the early grades can demonstrate the "readiness" techniques in reading which are an integral part of their approach. These same "readiness" techniques are valuable to English teachers in presenting vocabulary and concepts. In schools where there are teachers of foreign languages such as French, Spanish, Italian, or German, the supervisor will find that he can utilize their training and experience in numerous ways.

Since so many principles of language methodology are identical in teaching Spanish as a foreign language, for example, and in teaching English as a second language, the special skills of the Spanish teacher can be valuable in training teachers, in developing a curriculum, and in preparing instructional materials. Moreover, teachers of foreign languages have always been aware of the importance of teaching the foreign language within the cultural frame of the country whose language is being learned. Activities designed to increase the competency of pupils learning the English language are those that have always been the stock in trade of foreign language teachers. The instructor of any foreign language, therefore, can render the English teaching program considerable assistance.

Especially valuable in an English-speaking community where there are large numbers of language learners is the foreign language teacher who knows the language of the non-English speakers in the school and community. The supervisor should call upon this person to assist in every step of the teaching-learning situation.

In addition to the ways mentioned above, this staff member can render valuable assistance to the pupils, to other teachers in the school, to the administration, to parents of non-English speaking pupils, and to community leaders.

With relation to the pupils, the teacher who knows their native tongue can help in the following ways: He can (1) prepare materials for their reception at the school (such as signs in registration rooms and corridors); (2) assist in the actual reception of the pupil and his parent; (3) prepare materials to determine the pupil's level of literacy in both English and the native tongue; (4) explain placement procedures to parents and pupils, particularly in cases where pupils are being placed in ungraded English-orientation classes without regard to previous grade or schooling; (5) interpret simple rules and regulations of the school, such as time for arriving and leaving and procedure for eating lunch in school; (6) organize and write materials in both languages explaining the school program and the necessity for parent cooperation; and (7) list school and community resources.

Perhaps of even more vital interest to the pupil is the fact that the teacher who knows his language and his customs and mores can be assigned to the guidance program. Guidance in the true sense of the word depends so much on the rapport between pupil and teacher that the use of an interpreter during an interview may vitiate the efforts of the guidance staff.

With older pupils in an English-speaking community, there is another aspect of the problem that causes some concern to educators and which requires the special skills of bilingual teachers. We refer to the need for some telescoped program of education for children who may come to school at the age of fourteen or fifteen with little or no school background. Only with a curriculum designed especially for them will they become functioning, working, and participating members of the English-speaking community. Can we afford the luxury of teaching these students by the "direct" method, with a necessarily limited vocabulary and with time-consuming methods, when they must acquire vocational skills and knowledge and when they have an urgent need to learn *full* English quickly in order to become self-sustaining members of the community? Would it not be more expedient to teach them English *through the medium of their own language* and to furnish them *in their native tongue* with the educational, social, and vocational facts which they need immediately? The bilingual teacher or aide may help supply the answer to this complex problem. (See page 434 for a possible program for these youngsters.)

With relation to other teachers in the school who teach English or other subject areas to students whose native language is not English, the teacher with the knowledge of the pupils' language and mores can make outstanding contributions in the construction of instructional materials, in teaching successful approaches in methodology, and in bringing about acceptance of these language-handicapped pupils by other pupils. He can help by suggesting the language items that should be given priority in the teaching of English. The suggestions will be based on the teacher's more intimate knowledge of the native language structure and his awareness of items that are similar to or radically different from English. He will be able to translate materials from English to the native tongue. He will be able to point out cognates (if such exist) so that his colleagues will not feel forced to use simple, one-syllable words in presenting their subject.

Every teacher in the English speaking school with students whose native language is not English should be first a teacher of English and then of a curriculum area. The language teacher can suggest ways of developing or clarifying vocabulary and structures by means of cognates (where possible), dramatizations, pictures, and other devices prior to the content development, so that the basic subject matter of the lesson can be presented more smoothly and efficiently and with greater comprehension on the part of the learner. He can also explain procedures for teaching intensive reading (see page 149).

The question "When does a person know English?" educationally speaking is one that also puzzles school administrators. The answer will depend in great measure upon the acceptance by school personnel of students who may be linguistically handicapped. Just when does a person "speak" English? When may he be considered ready to enter the regular current of the school?

The teacher whose native language is that of the pupil may be able to help in the solution of this knotty problem. Acceptance is among other things a question of communication, of feeling secure either as teacher or as pupil, of feeling success in one's assignment, and of having respect for the other person's way of life. The native-born teacher is in an ideal position to bring about understandings and appreciations that underlie mutual acceptance.

With reference to the total school program, the teacher who speaks the native language of the pupils can assist in various ways. To cite just a few: he can teach the basic elements of the language to staff members, help to devise tests to determine native ability or to effect interclass promotion, plan assembly programs utilizing special abilities of the pupils, translate forms to be sent to the home, and serve as liaison between the school and the Parents' Association.

He can help to develop leadership within the non-English-speaking community by planning orientation and other meetings and by opening channels of communication between new and established community members. He can give courses for parents in many areas of interest in addition to English.

Summary

The supervisor's role is of vital importance in formulating and carrying out an effective English program. Dynamic guidance and leadership are particularly crucial in the areas of teacher selection, training, and utilization.

Where no licensed teachers of English are available, the selection of teachers from among the staff should be based on an evaluation of the qualities that the supervisor knows will result in successful teaching.

The training of teachers for the program should be systematic, continuous, creative, constructive, and democratic. Bulletins, workshops, conferences, and visits to other schools should be among the supervisory techniques that are planned cooperatively by teachers and supervisors. Observations of teachers in the classroom should be followed by constructive suggestions for improvement (if such are necessary) and by group meetings in which common problems are analyzed and concrete solutions are recommended.

The strengths of all school personnel should be utilized in developing the English program. The approaches or special skills of teachers other than the teacher of English should be brought into play whenever such skills can make a contribution to the growth of children's knowledge or attitudes and to more effective community involvement.

CHAPTER 13

Placing Pupils

Another essential function of the supervisor is to provide for the proper placement of children in the English program, since placement and classification seriously affect the quality of the instructional program. Wide ability and age ranges in a classroom, which might be avoided through more effective placement policies, will lead the conscientious teacher to organize numerous groups, making the planning for adequate instructional materials extremely arduous and resulting, perhaps, in decreased efficiency.

There are three main stages in the pupil's life in the English program where the supervisor, working with his staff, will have to define policy very clearly. The first is the policy on the pupil's initial placement into the school's English program; the second is the policy on his progress within the English program; the third is the policy on the certification of the pupil as ready to enter (1) a higher school, or (2) the regular stream of the school, where all instruction is given in English.

In this chapter we will concern ourselves primarily with practices in the initial placement of pupils. The measurement of achievement and progress within the English program is discussed in a later chapter (see page 342).

PROBLEMS AND PREMISES IN INITIAL PLACEMENT

The supervisor will be confronted by many problems when formulating policies for the *initial placement* of children into

English classes. He may have to provide for pupils who have never had instruction in English and for those who are coming into the school with previous English instruction received in other schools, in other communities, or in other countries.

Pupils with No Previous Instruction in English

Let us consider first the pupils beyond primary school age who have had no previous instruction in English.

Since education is compulsory in most English-speaking countries, these pupils have to be given immediate intensive instruction in English and helped to enter the regular school program *irrespective* of native literacy or previous school achievement. Admission policies and practices differ from school to school and district to district.

Some school systems have organized "pre-first" classes to which pupils, regardless of age, are assigned for intensive oral English instruction. After these pupils have acquired a minimum oral and sight vocabulary, they are placed in the regular English classes of the school. Other school systems place children in classes with children of their own age and provide special instruction in English in one of the ways described in Chapter 1.

It is recommended that, especially with older pupils who have had previous schooling, a study of records be made to ensure the best possible placement within the school organization. Where there are large numbers of entrants into the school from the same non-English community or country it would be helpful for the supervisor to study the school program of that community (its curriculum, its standards, and its promotion policies) as a guide to more effective placement of the incoming pupils. Any administrative measure that will enable the teacher to start with the pupil "where he is" and help him to develop from that point is worth the expenditure of time and effort.

Pupils with Previous Instruction in English

Initial placement of pupils who have studied English outside the receiving school presents more complex problems because of the variations that exist in organizational and curricular policies of schools and communities.

In addition to making a study of the pupils' school records, the school or language center often prefers to administer a test or a battery of tests to determine specific levels of ability in the various aspects of the language arts. Some schools feel, also, that native intelligence should be measured. (Limitations of intelligence tests for placement purposes will be discussed later in this chapter.) Still other schools prepare tests in the pupil's native language as a further measure of the pupil's general ability. Some schools use a combination of all these procedures.

FORMULATING CRITERIA FOR INITIAL PLACEMENT

The problem of preparing and administering informal classification tests to incoming students who have had previous instruction in English is a difficult one, since many related factors must be taken into consideration. These include:

1. The natural timidity of some pupils taking a test in a new situation, which may mean that even some of the English they know will be temporarily forgotten.

2. The different standards that the pupil had to meet in the previous school (based on different curricula or other environmental factors).

3. The difference of opinion among authorities as to what constitutes "knowing a language."

4. The varying degrees of acceptance of language disabilities on the part of teachers in the school who may have to teach English as well as other subjects to the language learners.

5. The different classes on one grade level within the school organization.

6. The lack of administrative time and qualified personnel to ensure reliable testing and follow-up.

Because of these inherent difficulties, which often influence the content and the results of tests, initial placement of students should be extremely flexible. Criteria and rating standards for admission should be formulated by each school on the basis of a realistic study of its organization and its personnel.

Naturally, where only one class may exist in a school for newcomers of all age and ability levels, the discussion of placement and classification tests will remain solely of academic interest, although tests and other measures can be used to assess the pupil's knowledge as a basis for intraclass grouping and individualized instruction. Where the school can organize two or more classes for incoming students who have had little previous English study, one class may include pupils who have practically no knowledge of English and those with the ability to understand and use only limited words and structures. A second class may be made up of pupils who can read English at a second- or third-grade level. If the size of the language center or school warrants the formation of even more finely graded classes for new students, these may be organized on the basis of such criteria as whether English is a second or third language for the student, and whether the pupil has a good command of his native language.

An older pupil who has attended junior or senior high school and who has studied English in an accredited school may qualify for placement in an upper grade (or term) of English. Admission into the higher term of the subject should again be based upon (1) a study of school records, (2) a realistic knowledge of the offerings of the pupil's previous school, (3) a battery of tests, and (4) an oral interview at the time of registration.

In schools where a specific number of points is required for "certification" or "graduation," the question of credit for higher work becomes important. The amount of placement credit given to pupils is subject to varying practices. Some schools may give credit for the exact number of years or months of English study which the pupil has had in accredited schools. Others may give a maximum of one or two years' credit and insist that the pupil spend a definite period of time in the school's English program.

Criteria for admission that serve the purpose in one school or center may not be at all appropriate in another. We shall not attempt, therefore, to delineate specific standards for entrance.

With relation to the testing program used with incoming pupils, a few additional words of caution are advisable. No one test or battery of tests will fit every situation. If, for example, a truly bilingual person should administer the test (both for purposes of rapport and for evaluation), and no such person is available, the test results should not be considered too valid or reliable.

If, as is true in some areas, so many students come in at one time at the beginning of the semester that the administration of tests or the interview becomes a routine thirty-second affair, many errors in classification are inevitable.

It is important, also, that the supervisor take steps to measure the language ability of incoming pupils at times during the semester other than the initial registration period. Since it is often difficult to release teachers or counselors to conduct interviews and to administer tests, it may be necessary to defer the interview until a time when the staff member is free or to seek the assistance of community members or college students and staff. The written tests, however, can be administered, where practicable, if directions (in several languages) are on a tape recording so that a clerk or a pupil office monitor can give the newcomer the test material.

Experiments have been conducted involving the use of the tape recorder instead of an interviewer to determine the aural-oral abilities of incoming pupils. Children listen to utterances, paragraphs, or questions. Their responses are recorded for evaluation by a staff member at some later time. Unfortunately the mechanical difficulties often encountered and the timidity of the students have limited the application of this procedure for all but experimental purposes.

The practice in some schools of using intelligence tests alone to determine classification or to predict success has several serious limitations:

1. Research studies have shown that the correlation between general mental ability and capacity to learn a foreign language is less than .30. For prognostic purposes, the IQ test alone has very limited value.

2. Intelligence tests measure not only capacity to learn but also *acquired* knowledge, skills, and habits.

3. Most tests of intelligence measure the *experiential background* of the person taking the test in addition to his general mental ability.

4. Unless norms are based on a population and a cultural background *similar* to those of the pupils being examined, the tests are not reliable in a new situation.

5. Research studies indicate that a stay of approximately two years in a new language environment is needed before the score on the IQ test can be considered valid.

6. General mental ability, although bearing some slight positive relationship with ability to learn a foreign language, must be coupled with motivation, volition, and high interest on the part of the learner.

7. Even pupils with very low IQ's are capable of acquiring sufficient *oral proficiency* for communication purposes.

Regardless of results of intelligence tests, in bilingual areas or in English-speaking communities, students *must* be taught English for everyday living. It will be the teacher in these communities who will need to gear his procedures and instructional program to the pupils' capacity and ability. By providing rich language and other curriculum experiences, the levels on intelligence test scores will undoubtedly be raised since, as noted above, scores are affected by experiential background.

TESTING MATERIALS—PREPARATION AND SCORING

There are few standardized tests for young pupils in the field of English as a second language. Thus, it becomes the responsibility of the staff of the school or community to prepare adequate informal measures of ability in the English language arts. In any case, since the pupil is coming into a school that follows a definite program and sequence of English, it is important to find out where the child will fit within *that* program and not how he achieves on a standardized English test which may bear little or no relationship to the specific curriculum in that school.

Materials used in the testing program will differ from school to school. One school may prefer to prepare *one* written test with items ranging in difficulty from the very simple to the relatively more complex ones in the curriculum for the upper grades. With relation to the scoring of such a test, it is recommended that a definitive rating scale be devised only *after* a study has been made of the correlation between scores received on the test by a number of children and their achievement in classes into which they have been placed.

Let us assume—for students above the primary grades—that it has been tentatively decided by supervisor and staff members that all pupils who receive 40 per cent or less will be placed at the first level of English, that those receiving 40–60 per cent will be placed in the second level, and so on up the scale. It is only by careful observation of many pupils in the English classes over a period of time that the staff can determine whether this measure of evaluation is valid. Experience may show that the scores on rating scales for admission into a certain level have to be raised or lowered. Only through continuous evaluation of a testing measure in the teaching situation can we ascertain its value and usefulness.

The same analysis would have to be made by the school that prefers to use the following procedure for determining initial placement of pupils: Tests covering the work of each level of English are prepared. After the interviewer ascertains the length of time of previous study, the pupil is given a test at that grade level—or perhaps the level below or above, depending upon factors that have been mentioned, such as achievement record and school system from which the pupil is transferring. A minimum rating for entrance into a specific level will be required. A pupil not achieving the passing grade on the test may be given a test on the lower level or may be placed in the lower class at least temporarily—until he can be brought up to a level of achievement commensurate with the time he has spent in his study of English and with the admission standards of that level.

In general it is preferable not to use for placement purposes school achievement tests that have been prepared to measure progress of pupils in a specific level. Such tests, although built around the syllabus for the level, may contain specific emphases (linguistic or cultural) depending upon the personality, viewpoints, and interests of the teacher and upon the areas that have been highlighted during the semester.

Tests for initial placement should measure only basic skills and abilities in the language arts.

ABILITIES TO BE MEASURED

At any given time, the school will wish to find at which point the pupil is in his ability to:

1. Understand spoken English.
2. Make himself understood when speaking English.
3. Read English with comprehension.
4. Use the language in written communication.

There is, in addition, the important outcome of cultural understanding or of "area" appreciation, as it is often called, which some authorities consider as important as the development of language competency. Some schools may also wish to evaluate this aspect of the English program.

Each of these abilities to be tested will require the preparation of a specific scale, consisting of carefully graded items or standards.

For example, in measuring ability to *understand spoken* English—normal for the pupil's age—the broad points on the scale may be:

1. Can understand no English.

2. Can understand one-word utterances.

3. Can understand short, simple sentences about limited situations (the weather, the classroom) when spoken slowly.

4. Can understand simple sentences about general everyday topics.

5. Can understand and react to a connected passage related to a general situation when spoken slowly.

6. Can understand the unlimited flow of speech of a native speaker.

7. Can understand broadcasts and recordings.

In ability to *speak* English, the broad points on the scale may be:

1. Can speak no English.

2. Can utter one or two words haltingly.

3. Can utter short, simple sentences on limited situations but with no accuracy of structure; e.g., "Eat yesterday bread."

4. Can utter short, simple sentences on limited situations with a fair degree of accuracy.

5. Can utter short sentences with structural accuracy on general situations.

6. Can utter longer sentences correctly but with poor pronunciation and intonation.

7. Can sustain a conversation on nontechnical material with a native English speaker.

Similar scales will be prepared to judge reading and writing capacity. There are many intermediate points, of course, on the scales, which the trained interviewer will observe.

If the tests are to have value, the interviewer should record the errors in pronunciation, in structure, and in choice of words that the pupil makes. It will then be possible to inform the classroom teacher of these findings so that he can plan remedial work for the pupil in those aspects where he reveals weakness. Careful notation at the initial interview can serve many additional purposes. Later tests can demonstrate the effectiveness of the remedial techniques used in eradicating certain errors or they can prove that certain types of teaching presentations were more effective than others in developing fundamental language abilities.

The informal tests that the school will prepare should attempt to measure *productive* knowledge of English on the part of the pupils, that is, their ability to *speak* and to *write*; and receptive knowledge, that is, their ability to *understand* and to *read* with comprehension. In schools and communities where the basic structural items, vocabulary items, and pronunciation features to be learned within the total program have been divided and classified for inclusion in delimited levels or courses, the primary purpose of the test will be to measure the pupil's level of ability in those language items. In schools where the teaching may unfortunately be less systematic because of the widespread belief that pupils will acquire much English incidentally, testing is usually more general. In this situation, the school may seek only a broad picture of the child's knowledge of English. Less attention may often be paid to the specific features of language. It is strongly recommended that, even in this situation, the interviewer take specific notes on such items as correctness, poverty or richness of the pupil's vocabulary, his ability to understand, manipulate and generate utterances, and the control of pronunciation and intonation for purposes of future teaching and testing.

SOME TESTING TECHNIQUES

One or more of the following informal tests may be planned to measure students' language abilities. (Note that there will be an inevitable overlapping of abilities measured.)

In tests of *listening comprehension,* incoming pupils may be asked to:

1. Imitate minimal pairs; that is, words whose pronunciation differs in only one sound; for example, rag, rack; yellow, fellow; very, berry; hat, hot.

2. Imitate sentences of varying length.

3. Carry out a request (first one request alone can be used; then more than one); for example, (1) Go to the door, (2) Go to the door and open it, (3) Go to the door, open it, and look to the left.

4. Point to the picture about which a statement is being made. Examples: The ship is white; the sheep is white. He's slipping; he's sleeping. He's washing the car; he's watching the car.

5. Answer specific questions about themselves, the weather, the room.

6. Take an aural comprehension exercise (see page 178).

7. Listen to a recording and answer questions on it.

In tests of *oral production*, pupils may be asked to:

1. Identify (in complete sentences) ten common classroom objects in a picture series.

2. Answer questions about themselves.

3. Tell what they see in a picture.

4. Tell what happened yesterday or during a recent holiday period.

5. Answer questions on various topics; e.g., "What did you do this morning?" "What did you have for dinner last night?"

6. Answer questions based on a passage that has been read.

7. Discuss a passage or an article that has been read.

To test *reading comprehension*, the pupil may be asked to:

1. Select the unrelated word from among a group of words.

2. Select the synonym of a given word from among four words.

3. Select the antonym of a given word from among four words.

4. Complete a sentence with a word selected from a group of words; e.g., The dog *moos, barks, crows, flies.*

5. Read a passage and answer questions about it with the book open.

6. Read a passage and answer questions about it without referring to the passage.

In tests of *writing ability* the pupils may be asked to:

1. Write the names of ten or more objects, which the teacher dictates.

2. Write a short sentence about each of ten objects in the classroom.

3. Write answers to questions about themselves.

4. Write answers to questions on a picture, a passage, or an article.

5. Take a dictation.

6. Write a short connected passage on a topic with which they should have some familiarity; e.g., their former school, their new home, the trip to school.

In addition to these tests, the school may wish to devise tests that measure specific skills in even greater detail. The ability of the pupil to use structural items will be noted, of course, in most of the tests suggested above. Other devices which focus attention on this aspect of language ability may include:

1. Asking the pupils to choose the correct word in sentences such as:

> He (go, goes) to the store.
> The (boy, boys) is walking to the door.

2. Asking the pupils to convert sentences from the present to the past or from the declarative to the interrogative, etc.

3. Asking the pupils to choose from two sentences the one that describes accurately the action in a picture. For example, in a picture in which a man is washing a car, the sentences would be:

> The man is washing the car.
>   or
> The man washed the car.

4. Asking the pupils to change a verb form in accordance with the expression of time given in the sentence.

> (Yesterday) I _____ to the store. (to go)
> (Every day) I _____ lunch at 12 o'clock. (to eat)

As a further test of pronunciation, pupils may be given words for which they will have to find the rhyming word from a list of words or they may be asked to find a word having the same sound as the specified sound in the first word of a group (see p. 225).

ADDITIONAL SUGGESTIONS IN TESTING

Some cautions and administrative problems with relation to testing have already been given. With relation to the test content it is recommended that:

1. The subject matter of the test be kept within the known experiential background of the pupil. For example, a pupil's not knowing the word "faucet" if he has never seen or heard of one would not constitute lack of ability in English.

2. The tests be planned to measure knowledge of English and not memory. For example, in preparing passages for aural comprehension, the examiner should make them short enough, so that the questions can be answered on the basis of comprehension rather than on ability to remember details of a long statement.

3. The tests be planned to measure knowledge of English and not native intelligence.

4. The tests not call for a high degree of literary skill on the part of the pupil. Unless the pupil is being tested for placement in a course of creative writing, imagination and richness of ideas should not be required.

5. The test not include incidents with which all pupils are so familiar—the discovery of America by Columbus, for example —that true comprehension of English is not being measured.

6. The test items (at least most of them) allow for objectivity of scoring. This means that many short-answer, objective-type tests should be prepared. If an essay is required, a definite point allotment for errors should be allocated and agreed upon *before* the pupils take the test.

7. The testing conditions be such that English ability and not familiarity with test directions is measured. It may be necessary

to prepare directions for the pupils in their native languages, since the wording in the directions and procedures may be unfamiliar to them.

RECORDING THE RESULTS OF TESTS

The supervisor should make careful provision for the recording and preservation of test data. The records related to the pupil's placement and growth in English may be kept in the department office or by the teacher specifically assigned to the English-as-a-second-language program. Duplicate entries of placement data and progress in English should be kept in the central office of the school along with all other information about the child.

In addition to permanent records indicating the cumulative growth of the pupil in all areas of school life, many schools keep "pupil sustenance" or "pupil maintenance" cards. The permanent central office records will contain all pertinent information about the child (date of birth, family members, standardized tests, personality ratings, health items, etc.) as well as general end-term ratings in English as a second language, which will be used to determine classification into the next higher grade or level of work. Some schools may have one over-all rating, whereas others may subdivide English ratings into the various aspects of English ability—understanding, speaking, reading, comprehension, etc.

The "sustenance" record contains data relating exclusively to the pupil's classification and progress within the English-as-a-second-language program. The following pertinent items are usually included:

At the top of the form:
Date of birth
Date of entrance into the school
Date of entrance into the English program
Language spoken at home

Initial placement (names of tests given, if any; results of test, and comments by interviewer; name of interviewer)

Provision is then made for the entry of notations at the end of each level of work:

Date
Name of teacher
Class designation
Over-all rating
Rating in pronunciation, structure, oral facility, vocabulary, reading comprehension, writing
Remarks (usually found on the reverse side): weaknesses; strengths
Recommended for placement in _____

The remarks include data which will help the next English teacher or the next school place the pupil in the group for which he is best fitted. There will be notations for special strengths, specific weaknesses, books read, units of work not covered in the syllabus for the level and any other useful information.

Other entries may be made depending upon local policy and conditions. Where such data are pertinent, a record may be kept of the pupil's complete program and of comments of teachers other than the English teacher as to the pupil's ability to maintain himself in subject classes where English is the medium of instruction.

Of even greater value than the "sustenance" card would be a folder for each child. The *face* of the folder would contain all the data found on the sustenance card. *In* the folder could be kept evidences of the pupil's work and progress. The initial test material, subsequent long tests, compositions, any letters or forms (hobby or interest questionnaires, for example) would be kept together so that interested personnel or parents (where this is advisable) could evaluate the growth of the pupil through the study of the material.

Such records are of vital importance in providing not only for the continuous development of learners but also for smooth articulation and pleasant relationships between one class or one school and another.

SUMMARY

It is recommended that placement and classification be based on a broad profile study of the pupil rather than on any one test or item. There should be extreme flexibility in initial class placement.

Continuous study of testing procedures and frequent evaluation of pupils' ability based on closer observation in the learning situation are the responsibilities of the supervisor working in cooperation with the school staff.

Through his leadership and direction in helping teachers devise and interpret tests, the testing program in the school can become a positive force in helping pupils attain the desired knowledge, skills, attitudes, and habits.

The testing program is only the first step in classifying and placing pupils. In addition to asking himself, "Who are the pupils to be placed in classes?" the supervisor should make certain, through continuous testing and objective interpretation of test findings, that the personnel, curriculum, and school organization are in step with the developmental needs of the children. Two ways of doing this are by providing for the recording of all test data and by keeping evidences of the pupils' work so that correctness of placement can be evaluated objectively from time to time.

Continuous evaluation of procedures and policies in this vital area of school administration is necessary. Teachers and supervisors working together should evolve criteria for placement of children that will result in optimum language development for the children and in practical class arrangements for teachers.

CHAPTER 14

Bringing the School and Community Closer Together

Current educational literature emphasizes the importance of a cooperative and cordial relationship between the school and the community. Today's school embraces the community in which it is located—its people, their needs and aspirations, and its resources. The school's curriculum is constantly enriched and vitalized by the resources—both people and places—that the community has to offer. The community, in turn, shares the activities and program of the school. The modern concept of home-school-community relations is the subject of many excellent textbooks. We shall limit ourselves, therefore, to practical suggestions and recommendations particularly pertinent to the teaching of English to speakers of other languages.

Obviously the reciprocal sharing and socialization possibilities will differ to a large extent in an environment that is primarily English-speaking from one that is not. In either situation the school can profit from community cooperation in many ways. Schools anywhere can:

1. Help pupils grow in conceptual and language development through purposeful trips into the community.

2. Enlist the aid of people who have traveled to the native lands or communities of the students to furnish staff members with insights and knowledge leading to the orientation and acceptance of their cultural background.

3. Procure financial aid and other assistance for improving

the school building, for buying audio-visual materials, and for setting up special exhibits and rooms.

4. Foster social growth of pupils through jointly sponsored community and school activities such as festivals, dramas, exhibits, group discussions, forums, panels, community improvement and clean-up projects.

5. Get assistance from the local newspaper bureau or the publisher in the preparation and distribution of an English newspaper.

6. Enlist the aid of language informants or community "buddies" to give students practice in language skills.

7. Ask for the help of interested community members in rendering many services to the school, such as assisting in the library, evaluating films (by means of a checklist prepared by teacher-community committees), accompanying younger pupils on trips, and helping to decorate rooms.

8. Enlist the aid of bilingual persons in receiving and orienting non-English-speaking parents, in translating materials for them, and in helping the clerical staff to fill out necessary pupil records.

In an English-speaking community, the necessity for school-community cooperation assumes great importance. The school's problems are often multiplied because of the presence of pupils in the school and in the community whose native language is not English. Established residents of the community may fear that newcomers create housing and employment problems. The old and new members may fail to accept each other because of the barriers of language. English-speaking parents may feel that their children are deprived of full educational opportunities because of the time to be devoted to non-English-speaking children. Mutually unfamiliar cultural patterns and social mores create suspicion and subsequent misunderstanding.

The school cannot ignore these conflicts within the community. It has the moral responsibility and the knowledge to bring about a necessary, mutually accepting relationship among community members. The school is also aware of the fact that the attitudes of pupils toward one another in classes will reflect parents' suspicions, prejudices, and fears and that learning cannot flourish in an atmosphere of antipathy and tension.

There can be little doubt that a carefully prepared program of school-community activities, in which old and new community members come together to share the satisfaction of seeing their children participate in a school project or meet to work out problems of general concern, will help to alleviate community tension. Some of the procedures the school can adopt may include:

1. Preparing welcome booklets for newcomers to the community in which the school program is outlined and in which community resources are listed. (Samples of welcome booklets will be found on page 321.)

2. Encouraging wide membership in the Parents' Association through invitations to parents in the language they understand, through facilitating attendance (hours of meetings, provisions for younger children), and through integrating social activities with discussions of value to parents (consumer education, housing, their children's progress, work opportunities, adult education, English).

3. Setting up workshops in such areas as housing, nutrition, consumer education, and child psychology.

4. Arranging festivals, bazaars, cake sales, and visits to classes.

5. Allowing recognized and reputable community organizations to use school facilities for educational and recreational purposes.

6. Sponsoring lectures, demonstrations, and exhibits by health, social, and other community agencies.

7. Participating, through representation and through active help, in worthwhile community projects.

8. Arranging for courses on an adult level in the learning of English.

9. Formulating interesting pupil programs in the auditorium in which many pupils take part and to which parents are invited.

10. Arranging for parents to participate in assembly programs in which pupils are awarded prizes for some meritorious school or community deed.

11. Enlisting the aid of parents (English-speaking and non-English-speaking) in a school activity such as accompanying classes on trips, helping to staff the cafeteria or yards, evaluating pictures and films, and assisting in the preparation or distribution of materials.

12. Encouraging the publication of a parents' bulletin or letter with articles in the pertinent foreign languages and in English.

13. Arranging for a social evening where talents of various community members will be utilized. For example, one group of parents can prepare their national dishes; another group can furnish the music and the dances.

14. Making provision for representatives of all community groups to serve with the principal or the director as a community consultation group to explore problems and programs of mutual interest.

15. Setting up various social and educational situations in which parents or community members of all ethnic backgrounds have the opportunity to sit together and plan together for the common good.

These are only a few of the ways in which the school can work with parents so that it will receive their wholehearted cooperation in guiding pupils to grow into responsible, prejudice-free community members.

The school cannot do the job alone. Community leaders, including those who may have no children of their own in school, must be enlisted to help. Community leaders need not be heads of government or social agencies. Leaders are found in places of worship, in stores, in banks—any place where there are people of good will. If leadership appears to be nonexistent, it should be developed. This can be done through many individual meetings with community members who seem interested in community and school needs, through a series of workshops—in short, through such supervisory techniques as visitation, intervisitation, conferences, and readings, which are helpful in developing latent qualities in all individuals.

Some words of caution may be needed here. It is wrong to equate the non-English-speaking parents' poor attendance at PTA meetings or lack of response to letters sent by the school with lack of interest in their children's education. It is the rare parent who is not interested in his child's schooling. Sometimes poor attendance at Open School Week or PTA functions by non-English-speaking parents is caused by the fact that (1) they do not understand or speak English, (2) they feel that their clothing is not appropriate, (3) they are working, or (4) they have younger children they cannot leave with anyone.

Even more important is the fact they have the highest respect for the teacher and other school personnel. They feel that once they have entrusted their children to the school, they should not interfere in any way. It is *not* lack of interest but, in most cases, this deference to school authority that keeps parents away from school.

Parents should not be forced to come to the school nor should children be punished or humiliated in any way because their parents do not come. If they can be encouraged to visit the school through some of the activities cited previously, it will no doubt be beneficial to the school, the children, and themselves.

On the other hand, whether parents come to school or not, teachers still have the responsibility of helping the children grow in desirable habits, attitudes, knowledge, and skills.

It may be useful at this point to note two other characteristics of many native speakers of other languages that are sometimes misunderstood by school personnel: the concept of the extended family and the respect due to older relatives. When grandparents or godparents or relatives (whom we might consider "distant") come to visit, children usually have to remain with them. It would be considered rude for them to excuse themselves even to do their homework.

Moreover, young adolescents would be expected to care for younger children in their family or for relatives in case of illness. Insight into these and other cultural facets of the students' lives is necessary in order to make them and their parents feel that we "accept" them and in order to avoid a feeling of frustration and insecurity on our part.

SUMMARY

One of the important functions of schools has always been to keep alive and transmit the cultural heritage of the people in its community. When the community includes peoples of varied ethnic backgrounds, the school must also assume the task of helping to bring about a mutually accepting relationship among all the members of the community.

The supervisor, working with his staff, can guide the organization of many projects both in and out of the school, which will not only encourage people to preserve their heritage but will also lead them to a deeper understanding and appreciation of the contributions which other peoples of different language or cultural background can make to the community.

Two topics of concern to parents, which can be depended upon to stimulate interest and cooperation, are the welfare of their children and the improvement of their own living or working conditions in the community. These topics should be used by the supervisor as the springboard for many cooperative undertakings which will bring the school and the community closer together with profit to both.

Supervisors and other school personnel should make every effort to develop insight into those facets of the culture of their students that will have an impact on the educational program and on school-community relations.

Materials That the School Can Prepare

COMMUNITY RESOURCES

In order to help newcomers in the English-speaking community toward more effective personal-social adjustment, it is important that the school prepare a list of community resources for early distribution. Although this section was prepared primarily for use in those communities where English is the predominant native language, a similar project will be found useful in rural communities anywhere. The school should help people living outside the large cities to become familiar with the resources available to them in the larger adjacent town or city.

The list may be prepared by an upper-grade class in social studies, by a service group in the school or community, or by the Parents' Association. If a more schematic, less detailed arrangement is preferred, a chart, in which the following minimum information is outlined, may be prepared.

Type	Name	Address	Director	Days & Hours	Fees	Special Services; e.g., Interpreters

The school or agency may wish to draw up a list of community resources that are available to *all* residents or of those that are especially geared to meet special needs of one or more groups. The information may be in English or in the native language or languages of the community members. An accompanying map with a numbered code for important buildings or areas would be extremely helpful.

The list may form part of a welcome booklet given to children; it may be distributed in mimeographed form in a guidance class, during a "reception" assembly, or at a parents' meeting. Any method of disseminating information that will bring about profitable utilization of community resources should be used if the school is to fulfill its role as an important agency of society.

RESOURCES IN OUR COMMUNITY

I. *What are our resources?*

  A. Recreational
    1. Playgrounds (Indicate name and address and any special information as to fees and hours.)
    2. Libraries
    3. Clubs or centers for leisure-time activities; settlement houses
    4. Movie houses, theaters, museums
  B. Welfare facilities
  C. Health clinics
  D. Places of worship and religious organizations
  E. Government agencies and other agencies
    1. Post office
    2. Police Department
    3. Fire Department
    4. Savings banks
    5. Stores
      a) Foods
      b) Home appliances and furnishings
      c) Clothing
  F. Schools
    1. Elementary

2. Secondary
3. Adult education centers
G. Ethnic organizations

II. *Which resources offer special services or facilities; for example, a Spanish-speaking staff or French materials?*
A. Recreational
   1. Parks
      a) _____ Park has a pool and baseball field.
      b) _____ Park has a pool and swimming instructor.
   2. Libraries
      a) _____ Library has a Spanish-speaking librarian. Books in Chinese are available for both children and adults. They also have a collection of books to help you to learn the English language.
      b) _____ Library [same as above]
   3. Clubs
      a) Boys' club (open to all boys)
         1) Dental clinic (fee 50¢)
         2) Library (books in Spanish)
         3) Swimming pool
         4) Varied activities such as sports and dramatics
         5) Group leaders who are Spanish-speaking
      b) Girls' _____ House
         1) Library (books in Italian)
         2) Game room
         3) Gymnasium
         4) Records and television
         5) Summer camp
         6) Citizenship committee
         7) Two other girls who are Italian-speaking and are the leaders
      c) _____ Center
         1) Two Spanish-speaking directors, one male and one female
         2) All types of play activities
         3) Dental and medical clinic
         4) Financial aid to families
         5) Summer camp

B. Department of Welfare
1. Financial aid
2. Dental and medical care
3. Spanish-speaking advisers and directors
4. Buys equipment needed in school such as sneakers

C. Health clinics
1. _____ —a general medical clinic, open to all, no fee
(There is a Spanish-speaking receptionist.)
2. Eye and ear clinic (open to all, no fee)
(There is a Spanish-speaking receptionist.)
3. Family shelter for women and children
a) Provides shelter for anyone in need
b) Medical care (free)
c) Spanish-speaking receptionist and director
4. Family shelter for men [same as for the women]

D. Religious organizations
Listed below are the places of worship which hold services for
Spanish-speaking people. There are many other places of worship in the neighborhood.
1. St. _____ (Girl Scout meetings are also held here)
2. Church of _____
3. St. _____
4. St. _____
5. Nativity Center (this church holds only its Masses in Spanish)
6. Temple of _____

E. General and governmental services
1. Post office (interpreter present all day)
2. Police Department (has interpreter when needed)
3. Bank (interpreter present all day)
4. Movies
a) _____, sometimes Spanish, sometimes American films
b) _____, only Spanish films
c) _____, sometimes Spanish, sometimes American films
5. Stores
a) About 90% of the food stores are either owned by or
have a Spanish-speaking person working there
b) All home furnishing stores have an interpreter
c) Clothing (nearly all have interpreters)

F. Ethnic organizations

F. Schools

    1. Every school in the neighborhood has an afternoon center

    2. _____ School.

        a) Afternoon center—teachers, Spanish-speaking

        b) Medical care (free)

            1) Nurse (Mon., Wed., and Fri.)

            2) Doctor (Fri.)

        c) Dental care (free, referred to clinics not in school district)

        d) Special personnel

            1) Two Spanish teachers

            2) One Spanish coordinator

            3) Two guidance counselors (Spanish-speaking)

            4) Special classes for children who are learning English

WELCOME BOOKLETS

Since the first contact between school and parents is important in establishing firm and friendly relationships, it is desirable that the school prepare an attractive booklet in which pupils and parents are made welcome and in which essential information for them is clearly outlined.

The booklets may be written in the foreign language, although some schools in bilingual areas prefer to prepare them in English with clear diagrams and illustrations. Other schools often have the foreign language on one side of the page and the English on the other. Certainly, the native language of the readers should be used if the aim of the booklet is to furnish information that will help pupils and parents make a smooth adjustment to the school and community.

It goes without saying that the booklet must be written carefully both from the standpoint of language and of psychological approach. It is strongly recommended, therefore, that a literate, native speaker of the foreign language be asked to cooperate in the preparation of the Welcome Booklet or for that matter in the preparation of any communication to be sent to the home.

To be really helpful, samples of items such as report cards and form letters sent out by the school should be included in the Welcome Booklet. Also essential is a list of community resources, which may or may not be part of the school program. Hospitals, clinics, libraries, employment agencies, and other resources should be indicated as illustrated above.

Sample I below is recommended for parents of younger children. The other sample given here outlines a booklet for parents of older pupils.

SAMPLE I

A BOOKLET FOR PARENTS

Dear Parents: *This Is for You.*

This little booklet will introduce you to our school. Your child will be with us for a good part of the day during these years when he is growing up. We want these years to be happy. We think they will be. They can be even happier, however, if you, too, know and understand what your child is doing here. We hope you will understand your child's school after you read these pages. We also hope that you will understand how important a role you can play in making your child's school a better place in which to live.

Your Child's Day

Your child will come to school five days a week, Monday to Friday, from 8:40 o'clock in the morning to 3:00 o'clock in the afternoon. He must come to school every day. He may be absent only when he is ill. It is important that he come to school for his own sake. It is very difficult to make up work he has missed. Naturally, if he has been ill, we shall do everything to help him.

Let us tell you what will happen to your child in school. First, we wish to assure you that he will be under the care and supervision of a teacher who is well-trained in handling children. She is there to help him learn. She is understanding and patient. She is ready to speak to you at any time about your child and about his progress in school. She welcomes your opinions and your cooperation.

What will your child do in school? Let us try to explain as clearly as we can what his school program will be:

1. He will learn to understand, speak, read, and write English. He

will use books that are interesting and colorful. Soon he will learn to enjoy reading and writing.

2. He will learn the mathematics and science that he needs in his everyday life.
3. He will learn about the places in his community and about its people. He will study the history of this country. He will learn about its people who have come from many lands, about its great men, and about its culture. He will also learn his rights and duties as a citizen of this country.
4. Besides these important studies, your child will learn how to take care of his body, what to do in case of sickness, and where and how he can get medical advice. He will learn about healthful foods, which will give him a strong body.
5. Your child will also learn how to get along with other boys and girls of his own age. He will have a chance to act in plays or to make drawings for his classroom. He will take part in many activities, which will teach him to work and live with others.

These are some of the many things that your child will do and learn at school. We are sure that you can understand how important school is for your child. Perhaps, at first, your child will have a little trouble in getting used to his new school surroundings. If this does happen, please do not be alarmed or upset. We know that with your help and encouragement and with the teacher's guidance, he will soon be well-adjusted and happy.

The School Staff

You may ask, "Where can I go if I want to speak to someone about my child? To whom can I speak if I want to know about his work? May I come in at any time? Will I be welcomed?" Of course you are welcome. For your convenience, we have prepared a list of the people in the school who are interested in you and in your child. Next to their names you will see where and at what time they can be found.

1. Principal—Mr. _____ Room _____ _____ Floor
   Hours: 9–3
   (If the principal is out when you arrive, you may ask for the assistant principal)
2. Assistant Principal—Mrs. _____ Room _____ _____ Floor
   Hours: 9–3

3. School Nurse—Miss _____ Room _____ _____ Floor

        Hours: Monday, Tuesday, Wednesday, 9–11

        Thursday and Friday, 12–3

4. School Clerk—Mrs. _____ General office _____ Floor

        Hours: 9–3

5. Attendance Officer—Mr. _____ Room _____ Floor _____

        Hours: Monday to Friday 9–11

6. School Guidance Counselor—Mrs. _____ Room _____

Floor _____

	Hours: Monday	9–12
	Tuesday	9–12
	Wednesday	9–12
	Thursday	1–3
	Friday	1–3

CLASSROOMS AND TEACHERS

1. Kindergarten	Miss _____	Room 204—2nd Floor
2. First Grade	Miss _____	Room 206—2nd Floor
3. Second Grade	Mrs. _____	Room 205—2nd Floor
4. Third Grade	Mrs. _____	Room 207—2nd Floor
5. Fourth Grade	Mrs. _____	Room 300—3rd Floor
6. Fifth Grade	Mr. _____	Room 301—3rd Floor
7. Sixth Grade	Miss _____	Room 302—3rd Floor
8. Boys' Gymnasium	Mr. _____	Room 100—1st Floor
9. Girls' Gymnasium	Mrs. _____	Room 110—1st Floor
10. Art Room	Mrs. _____	Room 200—2nd Floor
11. Music Room	Mrs. _____	Room 305—3rd Floor

The Parent-Teacher (or Parents') Association

Earlier, we mentioned that you could become a very active part of your child's school. We believe that a true spirit of cooperation and understanding can be developed between the school and the parents through our active Parent-Teacher (or Parents') Association. Everyone may join the Association. Parents and teachers meet regularly to discuss topics of interest to you and to your child.

You may hesitate to join the Parents' Association because you have never belonged to such a club and you know nothing about it. You may think, too, that your English will not be understood and that you will not understand what is being said. Please do not let that prevent you from joining the Parents' Association. Many other parents and some of the teachers speak and understand your language. Interpreters, who know your language, are always available at meetings.

The parents of this organization are people exactly like you. They live in your neighborhood. They have children who go to this school. The woman in charge of this group is Mrs. _____ She has two boys in this school. One is in the 4th grade and the other is in the 6th. Her husband is employed by the _____ Company where many men in this neighborhood are also employed. Mrs. _____ is a housewife like many of you. She works with the Association because she is interested in her children's education.

Parents help the school in many ways. Last year the parents came to help in the classrooms, in the lunchrooms, and in the yards. This year they plan to open a center on _____ Street, where the children can play after school. All of us, parents and teachers, working together can make the school and the community a safe, cheerful place for all the children.

From time to time, your children will receive a notice to bring home to you. It will remind you of the date when the Association is having its next meeting and what the program for the meeting will include.

Our first meeting this year will be on _____. Please try to come that evening. You will see the various rooms where your child works and plays during the day. You will meet the teachers and supervisors of the school and your neighbors and friends. Your visit will help you to understand your child and his school.

We hope that this little book has helped you to understand your child's school a little better. We realize, of course, that it has not answered all your questions. We wish to emphasize again that you may come to talk to one of the teachers or supervisors when you are free. In addition, your questions will be answered at the meetings.

This is your school. It is your right to be a part of it. Together, we can help to make your child a fine, happy, healthy member of the school, of his home, and of the community.

> Cordially yours,
> The Staff of _____ School
> _____, Principal

OUTLINE OF CONTENTS OF A HANDBOOK FOR
PARENTS AND OLDER PUPILS

I. *Introduction*

A. Welcome
B. Need for study, effort, and cooperation
C. Importance of learning English
D. Welcome to parents and invitation to the Parent-Teacher (Parents') Association

II. *General Information*

A. Attendance law
B. Regulations related to such matters as punctuality, attendance, and absence notes
C. Drills such as fire, shelter area, safety
D. Passes—out of room, out of building, transportation
E. Personal appearance
F. Care of property—building and books

III. *The School Program*

A. Class program
B. Assembly
C. Clubs

IV. *Shop Safety Rules*

V. *Records*

A. Report cards (samples) and translations
B. Record cards
C. Health cards

VI. *School Activities and Services*

A. General organization
B. Lunch program
C. Clothing fund
D. Milk
E. Library
F. Trips
G. Banking
H. Health (medical, dental)

VII. *Guidance Program*

    A. Group guidance
    B. Individual guidance

VIII. *Looking Ahead*

    A. Graduation
    B. Higher schools
    C. Employment opportunities

IX. *Parents' Association or Parent-Teacher Association*

    A. Meetings
    B. The year's program

X. *Community Resources* (including addresses)

    A. Hospitals, clinics
    B. Community centers
    C. Public library
    D. Parks
    E. Museums
    F. Other

XI. *Summary of Important Facts*

UNIT V

EVALUATING THE PROGRAM

CHAPTER 15

The Staff Studies the Pupil

The progress of pupils toward the linguistic and cultural attainments that are the desired goals of the English-language program should be measured continuously. Evaluation is essential in determining whether pupils are to be recommended for promotion from one level to another and whether they are to be "certified" as ready for "graduation" or admission to a higher school of learning, or both.

Just as essential, however, is the fact that measurement of the pupils' growth will help us determine whether there are serious gaps in our instructional program and whether our classroom procedures and methodology are bringing about effective development in the language arts. For these and other significant reasons an achievement testing program should be made an integral part of the instructional program of all schools.

WHY DO WE TEST?

Tests which measure achievement serve many purposes. They can be used to:

1. Determine whether initial placement policies need to be re-examined in the light of the pupils' capacity to maintain themselves in classes or to progress much more rapidly or slowly than other class members.

2. Permit teachers and supervisors to recommend pupils for intraschool promotion or for progress into a higher school on the basis of objective evidence.

3. Help set standards of achievement for pupils and for the school.

4. Diagnose areas of language study in which individual pupils or groups of pupils are weak.

5. Judge the effectiveness of experimentation in such matters as classification, teaching procedures, or use of instructional materials.

6. Compare achievements of one group with those of another group in the same school or in a school in another community.

7. Help us gauge our ability as teachers with full awareness, however, of any factor within the pupil or the school which may limit our effectiveness.

8. Focus attention on weaknesses in the total instructional program.

9. Point up the need for organizing more finely graded classes or, perhaps, more remedial classes.

10. Provide continuity of instruction for learners as they move either within the school or to other schools.

It is only to the extent, however, that the staff translates test findings into more effective teaching procedures that pupils will derive the full benefit from the evaluation program. If, for example, it is found that pupils cannot grasp the meaning of an unfamiliar paragraph, it is obvious that the reader will have to help children with word-recognition techniques or, perhaps, provide a wider range of experiences. If tests reveal that the entire class was unable to distinguish the difference between one structural item and another (the use of s in the third person singular, for example), the teacher will have to reteach the entire lesson, possibly using another type of presentation or even reteaching the items on which the incorrectly answered structural item is based.

From the supervisor's point of view tests may indicate the

need for the organization of remedial classes in reading or in writing, the need for sharpening of classification procedures to ensure the placement of pupils in classes that will better fit their language needs, or the need for more extensive teacher training in group dynamics or materials preparation.

Research workers in the school or in the community will also use the results of school achievement tests. On the basis of test results they may come to conclusions of benefit to school personnel with relation to such problems as the comparative efficiency of one method or another for the development of language skill. In the area of English as a second language there are many other moot questions that need to be resolved. Experiments are undertaken continually to determine whether oral proficiency is a prerequisite for reading ability or whether the use of the pupil's native tongue for teaching purposes will retard or aid him in learning the new language. Answers to these and other questions can best be found through carefully controlled objective testing procedures.

Who Does the Testing?

Although we are concerned primarily with the informal teacher-made tests, which the teacher gives at various times during the semester to measure general progress or the acquisition of one skill or another, the testing program may also include: (1) tests which the *supervisor* may wish to give as an *additional* technique in the supervision of teachers and as indices of needed administrative, curricular, or supervisory changes; (2) tests which *research workers* may give before, during, or at the termination of experimentation; (3) tests which *guidance workers* or *psychologists* may give in order to measure achievements of pupils in English in terms of mental ability or in terms of other personality factors.

A testing program, therefore, often goes beyond the confines of the classroom and becomes part of a schoolwide or countrywide project of evaluation.

When Does Testing Take Place?

The testing program of the school or of the school system should be carefully scheduled. Tests, such as uniform examinations in which all pupils on one level are given the same test despite the fact that they may have been taught by different teachers and with different instructional materials, should be planned ahead and should be conducted at specific times during the semester.

Teachers will thus be able to acquaint pupils with the type of format and directions they will find on the test so that the test will measure English ability rather than familiarity with directions. Teachers will also be aware of the amount of content they will be expected to cover before the test. Moreover, if the test is being conducted for experimental purposes—to measure, for example, the comparative value of intensive aural-oral practice and silent reading in developing language ability—teachers will have to prepare special instructional materials and techniques and carefully control their classroom procedure in order that the test results have validity.

The testing program in the *classroom*, on the other hand, should be continuous. Teachers often ask about the frequency with which tests should be given in classrooms.

If properly used, tests are as good a teaching device as any with older pupils. Five-minute tests consisting of several items of the short-answer type, based on vocabulary, structure, or cultural items taught the session before, may be given nearly every day and may serve as an excellent review or as the springboard for the new lesson. Nothing will give pupils such a sense of mastery as a perfect score or an almost perfect score on a test of material taught the previous day and studied that evening. The ratings will also give the teacher a clue as to whether the lesson taught the day before has been learned or whether there is need to reteach it. Longer full-period tests, including a variety of question types, should be given at the completion of each broad unit of work.

The pupils themselves or groups of the better pupils may help to rate the daily short-answer tests. Pupils enjoy rating papers. They gain status by doing so and reinforce correct language forms when working with an answer key. Pupil cooperation permits the teacher to have a large number of ratings on which to base his evaluation while relieving him of the chore of rating papers daily. It is recommended, however, that the teacher spot-check ratings.

What Will Be Tested?

The skills and abilities to be tested will depend, of course, upon the objectives and the curriculum of the English program.

Only those items, skills, or abilities that are in the curriculum for that level and which have been developed and practiced with the pupils should appear on a teacher-made test. However, the *degree* of mastery or skill within each ability demanded may differ from class to class in the school or from group to group within the same class. For example, whereas less able pupils may be expected to *choose* the one correct answer from among two or more structural items, the more gifted pupils may be asked to *complete* a sentence where no choice is given. Whereas the slower pupils may be permitted to consult their readers in answering questions on a story, the more able pupils will be expected to answer from memory after one reading of the page or passage.

Other factors should also be considered in preparing achievement tests for a class or in rating achievement tests which are given to all pupils on a grade.

A realistic appraisal of the pupils' general ability, of special limitations of materials or other resources in the school or the community, and of all the other elements that enter into a teaching-learning situation should be taken into account.

For example, children living in a predominantly English-speaking community might be expected to attain greater proficiency in a shorter period of time. Pupils who have done little or no reading will not be expected to demonstrate ability in reading. Classes that for any reason have lost instructional time could not be expected to achieve on the same level as those that have had full instruction. Pupils who have come into the class after the beginning of the semester cannot be expected to achieve the levels of learning of their classmates.

Although the teacher cannot afford to overlook these factors, there are still certain specific abilities that he will wish to test to measure the progress of his pupils or to diagnose weaknesses. In achievement tests, just as in placement tests, the teacher will measure the abilities of pupils to understand speech and to produce it. Tests, therefore, will include those which help the teacher judge the pupils' abilities to *understand*, to *speak*, to *read*, and to *write* English.

The teacher will also make provision for judging the pupils' attitudes and knowledge with relation to the cultural appreciations and understandings that are part of the English program.

Tests similar to those recommended in the chapter on classification can be used to gauge achievement. Conversion exercises and multiple-choice exercises are especially good for testing specific vocabulary and structural items. Moreover, since tests will duplicate the practice exercises done in the classroom (without, however, the benefit of the teacher's constant modeling, prompting, and help), any of the materials found under Language Learning Activities on pages 164–171 or under Individualizing instruction on pages 222–236 can also be used for informal testing purposes.

More general, longer tests of *aural-oral ability* may be prepared which will evaluate the pupils' ability to:

1. Say one sentence about an object or a picture, using correct structure and acceptable pronunciation.

2. Take an aural comprehension exercise on which the responses are given orally or in writing.

3. Answer questions on material that has been heard on a recording.

4. Summarize a paragraph that has been read or heard.

5. Discuss a paragraph that has been read or heard.
6. Sustain a conversation with a native speaker.

It will be noted that the items above are broad. The point in the English program at which pupils can be expected to attain all the skills and knowledge involved under each item will vary from pupil to pupil, from class to class, and from school to school. Through participation in the English program alone (that is, without additional benefits of living in a predominantly English-speaking community or of laboratory practice), some pupils may never attain the ability to sustain a conversation with a native speaker; others may need five years of one hour of English instruction each day; more mature pupils may be able to approximate that ability in an intensive program of about two years. Standards for intraschool progress or for promotion can be established only after a realistic appraisal of all the factors involved in the particular school or community.

In tests of *reading comprehension,* attention should be given to speed in reading, to proper phrasing—that is, to reading in thought groups—and to intonation and rhythm, as well as to comprehension. Tests may include those that evaluate the broad ability of the pupil to read a paragraph orally and to answer questions on it, to read a passage silently and to answer questions on it, to read an editorial or an article and to summarize it, and to read an article and to express an opinion on it.

Writing capacity can be judged by the pupil's ability to take simple words in dictation, to take longer dictation exercises, to use simple words in sentences, to write answers to questions or a summary, or to write a "freer" composition on some topic.

How Will These Abilities Be Tested?

No one test can permit the teacher to judge accurately and comprehensively the habits, attitudes, knowledge, and skills that should result from our English-teaching program. A series of varied tests, which measure receptive and productive abilities of children, will be required to obtain a total picture of a pupil's progress or disabilities. For diagnostic purposes, particularly, more than one test will need to be devised.

Many specific skills and capacities can be singled out and measured by means of techniques or devices that permit the teacher to measure the attainment of that particular skill. For example, if a teacher wishes to find out whether pupils can change one type of sentence to the interrogative, he will prepare a test in which attention is focused on changing sentences such as "He sees the boy" and "She sees the boy" to the interrogative.

If the teacher wishes to judge the pupils' progress in hearing contrasting sounds, he will devise oral or oral-written examinations that measure only the pupils' ability to discriminate between the two sounds.

Often, however, the relationships within the language arts make it difficult to test one aspect of language to the complete exclusion of any other. For example, an aural comprehension test will constitute not only a test of the pupil's understanding of spoken English but of his ability to *write* or to give *orally* the answers to the questions based on a passage—including items of pronunciation, structure, and vocabulary.

Achievement tests, again, will be either oral or written and will be of the short-answer (objective) type and, with older more advanced pupils, of the essay or discussion type. Both kinds of tests have a place in our program. Although it is true that essay and discussion type of examinations cannot be scored with any great degree of objectivity, they permit the teacher to evaluate the functional uses to which the pupil is able to put the vocabulary and structural items he has learned. Essay questions have the added advantages of being easily prepared and of testing one or more aspects of knowledge intensively. With older pupils and pupils who have acquired some proficiency in the language, they also permit the teacher to judge sustained writing ability, including organization of ideas and power of critical thinking. Through written essays, the teacher can also judge the level of language ability by noting richness of vocabulary, the variety of sentence structures, and the use of idiomatic English.

The newer type of objective tests are rated more easily and permit a wider sampling of knowledge. They do, however, require longer preparation. Among the widely used short-answer type of questions are the completion, the multiple choice, the matching, and the substitution or conversion questions (nouns for pronouns; singulars for plurals, etc.).

In some school districts the teacher may also wish to use translation as a further check of the pupil's language ability. Vocabulary items or cultural items can be tested through the medium of the foreign language. Except with a superior group of pupils, translation of long passages should be avoided since, as we know, it requires a high degree of literacy in both the native language and in English.

NEWER TECHNIQUES OF EVALUATION

Current testing philosophy emphasizes the value of class logs, of anecdotal records, of sociometric techniques, of pupil-prepared tests and of various types of culminating activities to supplement the written test. The teacher's judgment, based on his observation of the pupil's classroom performance, should also form part of a testing profile. In addition to studying folders of the pupil's work (reports, homework, notebooks), the teacher might ask himself the following questions:

1. Does the pupil volunteer in class?
2. How often and in what situations does he volunteer?
3. Are his answers sustained where required or merely "yes" and "no" answers?
4. Does he make use of the supplementary reading material in the library corner?
5. Does he use English with progressive frequency in the classroom?
6. Does there seem to be a carryover of English outside of

the classroom—in the corridors, in the lunchroom, in the play yards?

7. Does he show greater understanding of peoples of other cultural backgrounds?

It is impossible to offer a blueprint to cover all testing situations. One generalization that can be made, however, is that the formulation of the curriculum should precede the organization of the testing program in the class or in the school. A corollary to the generalization would be that there should be continuous curriculum revision on the basis of test scores.

Tests should be based on the curriculum of the school. Since the curriculum includes all the experiences pupils have, both in and out of school, informal tests that are reliable or valid for one school may have little or no value in another. Tests and promotional policies will depend upon the objectives and length of the program, the materials available, the standards or policies of admission of the higher level or higher school, and the teacher's judgment, based on objective evidence and personal observation, that the pupil will be able to sustain himself in the next level.

SUMMARY

There is no one best way of studying our pupils. All measures will be effective if they are flexible, if they are continuous, if they give pupils a sense of achievement and mastery, and if they help school personnel in the difficult task of placing pupils in groups or classes where they can be encouraged and stimulated to achieve language skills and social attitudes commensurate with their ability. Tests should be devised to measure basic language abilities of pupils, that is, their capacity to understand language and to produce it. Within these broad abilities the teacher should also measure specific pronunciation, grammatical, or word skills, for diagnostic and teaching purposes.

Many people in the school or in the community may use the

results of the class and school testing program. Test and research findings should lead to improved teaching-learning procedures so that pupils can be helped to develop facility in the language arts and understanding of the important "area" studies. Only in this way can we justify the time and effort that are consumed to prepare tests, to score them, to record their results, to interpret them, and to translate them into better English programs for pupils in the schools.

CHAPTER 16

The Teacher Analyzes His Procedures

There is general agreement that the teacher is the most important single element in any teaching-learning situation. It is his personality, his attitude toward his work and his pupils, and his desire for increased knowledge in his field that will determine the kind of instructional program children will receive. Although the supervisor, the parents, and the resource personnel may make it necessary for the teacher to modify certain techniques or procedures, it is the total impact of his personality, his attitude, and his scholarship in the classroom that will foster the growth of children toward socially and educationally desirable goals.

In bilingual areas or in predominantly English-speaking areas in which the language learners have an immediate urgency to acquire orientation knowledge as well as English, the teacher's role is of paramount importance. Many of the pupils have had school, home, and social backgrounds vastly different from those of established community residents. It is the teacher who, in the final analysis, determines how well and how quickly the newcomers to the schools will develop the ability to communicate in English. It is he who will help them gain the emotional and social adaptability necessary for living in an unfamiliar school and social environment.

Teachers very often take stock of themselves. Some of the questions they ask are:

1. Have I familiarized myself with the background of my pupils?

2. What do I know about their educational background, their living habits, their socioeconomic conditions, their hobbies, and their interests?

3. Am I learning something about my pupils' language and customs—first, to establish even greater rapport with them; second, so that I can make use of possible cognates in teaching English; third, so that I can anticipate their difficulties?

4. Am I taking additional courses or reading literature on special methods of teaching English as a second language?

5. Do I know how other areas in the country and world have met the problem of teaching English as a second language?

6. Do I use a variety of media to strengthen language learnings?

7. Do I differentiate assignments and class activities in order to provide for differences in educational background (pupils who never went to school; children of migrant workers; those who can read but are afraid to speak)?

8. Do my teaching plans include activities and experiences that the pupils feel they can use immediately in all classes and in the community?

9. Do I start with pupils' basic needs in vocabulary and pronunciation in order to enable them to communicate their wants, needs, and desires as quickly as possible?

10. Do I follow the progress of these pupils in other classes and in their life outside the school to make certain that what I teach is functional in real-life situations?

11. Do I make sure that fundamental grammatical items are reasonably habitual before I proceed to new learnings?

12. Do I modify my procedures, after consultation with other interested personnel, to achieve important language, social, and emotional objectives?

Affirmative answers to these and similar questions will reassure teachers that they are meeting their professional responsibilities.

In addition to seeking answers to these questions, teachers

may wish to study the following checklist, which permits them to analyze some of their classroom procedures and techniques in more detail.

If some technique or device has been inadvertently omitted by the teacher or by the writer, it is hoped that the items in the list will serve as a reminder and as a stimulus for continued effort in the direction of making teaching the art and the science of which we have already spoken.

A Checklist for Teachers

I. *Does your room have*

    A. A display of appropriate maps?
        1. the community
        2. the country
        3. other English-speaking countries
        4. the world
    B. Neatly labeled objects? (used at beginning level only)
    C. Specific evidence of current units of work?
        1. appropriate experience charts (at beginning reading level)
        2. tastefully arranged visual materials
        3. a display of pupils' work
    D. A library corner?
        1. picture books and picture dictionaries
        2. a wide variety of magazines and newspapers
        3. readers on various levels and in various subject areas
        4. a dictionary
        5. other research tools
        6. books and magazines in the students' native tongue
    E. Many centers of activity?
    F. A well-organized picture file with accompanying language cards?
    G. Charts indicating group and individual responsibilities?
    H. Devices such as the selection chart to vitalize learning?

II. *Do your pupils*

A. Welcome new arrivals?

B. Keep well-organized notebooks with a table of contents?

C. Participate in class recitation through choral and individual repetition?

D. Show real interest by volunteering answers, by asking questions, by doing research and supplementary reading, by using English increasingly in the school and community?

III. *Do your lessons*

A. Start with the "here and now" and branch out to the broader community?

B. Have a clear and definite aim of which the pupils are aware?

C. Grow out of socializing experiences such as visits into the community or known interests of pupils?

D. Provide both for the development of language competency and for the fostering of sociocultural appreciations?

E. Follow the *Hear, Say, See, Do** technique in which pupils *hear* the teacher *say* a new word in a sentence; in which they *say* it in chorus and individually; in which the teacher *writes* the new word on the board, *says* it again, and asks *pupils* to *repeat* again; and in which pupils *engage in many activities* involving the use of the new word or concept?

F. Include the use of a variety of materials?

G. Provide for stimulating, sequential language learning and practice based on sound psychological and linguistic principles?

H. Make provision for "nonverbal" activities, such as art work and construction, which will lead to communication?

* The "Do" is deferred until after writing has been introduced.

I. Provide for definite medial and final summaries in the pupils' own words?

J. Lead to the preparation of cooperatively prepared charts and the dramatization of dialogues, which may be used for review purposes or for building other language patterns?

K. Provide a well-balanced, integrated program of listening, speaking, reading, and writing activities?

L. Lead to future lessons?

M. Look back on work that has been done and ahead to other language possibilities?

N. Utilize the abilities and the talents of the class members?

O. Include integrative as well as differentiated activities?

IV. *Do you*

A. Give your pupils a sense of achievement and security?

B. Plan worthwhile activities with your pupils?

C. Keep a folder of materials?
  1. conference notes
  2. lesson plans
  3. lists of community resources
  4. lists of available materials
  5. anecdotal records of atypical pupils

D. Try to use English—judiciously, however—as the medium of instruction?

E. Act as a model for the pupils' speech?

F. Speak naturally and normally to accustom pupils to habitual use of full English?

G. Plan to evaluate pupils' progress systematically?
  1. to determine changes in class grouping?
  2. to recommend pupils to higher classes or to other schools?

H. Individualize your instruction?

I. Know which agencies are available for pupil or parent assistance?

J. Enlist the cooperation of parents?
K. Keep professionally alert by attending meetings, reading literature, experimenting with new techniques and materials, visiting other teachers, and welcoming visits and constructive supervision?
L. Make the students feel proud of their cultural heritage?

CHAPTER 17

The Supervisor Assesses the Program

There are many facets of supervisory activity too numerous to mention in a small volume not specifically devoted to supervision. The following checklist of some of the essential activities has been collated with the conviction that it will reassure supervisors that they have been following the very practices indicated and that it will stimulate continued self-evaluation and changes if needed.

A Checklist for Supervisors

I. Reception of Newcomers

    A. There are signs in the appropriate foreign languages indicating the rooms in which registration will take place.

    B. Interpreters are assigned to the registration rooms. (A teacher, a parent, a student, or any member of the staff is used for initial registration and collection of data.)

    C. A welcome booklet explaining school procedures is given to the parent and to the child.

    D. Previous school records are carefully checked to ensure proper placement.

    E. The pupil is accepted and placed in a classroom, pending receipt of birth or other certificates.

    F. The registration form, which includes the data on the

cumulative record card, has been translated into a number of foreign languages.

G. The principle underlying English-orientation classes is explained to parents if the child is to be placed in such a class without regard to age or previous records.

H. Provision is made for an interpreter (child, parent, or teacher) to be available for later registrants.

I. Simple school routines such as time of arrival, lunch, and dismissal are explained orally to parents (or guardians) and to pupils.

J. Provision is made for immediate luncheon privileges if the child is entitled to them and if the school provides such services.

K. The pupil is directed to another school if he does not belong in the school to which he first reports.

II. Placement of Pupils and Programing

A. All speakers of other languages are programed for special help in English. Placement for children under approximately eight years of age may differ from community to community. For example, in "disadvantaged" communities where many six-year-olds usually need to learn everyday concepts related to age, shape, form, and direction, non-English speakers may be placed in regular classes. They are given special instruction as needed, however, for about an hour a day (divided into three or four periods) by the classroom teacher or a teacher aide. (Some schools provide early-morning or after-school instruction.) In predominantly English-speaking neighborhoods in which English-speaking children of six have a good grasp of oral expression and have had many reading experiences, it might be desirable to place non-English speakers in special language learning classes for a flexible period of two or three months before placing them in regular classes.

It is imperative, however, that children in the special classes spend several hours a day with children in the regular classes to prepare for their placement in regular classes.

B. Pupils above the age of eight are placed in special classes with other pupils who need to learn the language, if the number of pupils warrants formation of these classes. Where only three or four children are involved, individual children may be placed in regular classes but given a bilingual "buddy" where possible and offered special instruction as often as feasible during the school day.

C. Pupils are placed in special English-orientation classes on the basis of age where possible.

D. Where there is only one English-orientation class in the school, newcomers (even with a two- or three-year age span) are placed together for a short, flexible period of intensive instruction in the English language arts and school and community customs. Subgroups are organized within the classrooms on the basis of age.

E. If numbers warrant the formation of more than one homogeneous class, pupils are grouped on the basis of one or more of the following: (1) previous schooling, (2) literacy in English, (3) literacy in their native tongue, (4) previous schooling in an English-speaking school.

F. Attempts are made by application to school authorities to form special classes or to get special services such as a language teacher or a special teacher assistant.

G. Language learning classes are organized at the discretion of the principal where the education board makes no provision for special language classes.

H. *All pupils* below or above the age of nine, whether they are placed in an English-orientation or in a regular class, are assigned a "buddy," or a student assistant, to help them.

I. Pupils are programed immediately to assemblies, art,

music, recreation, physical education, shops, and other areas where language competency is either not necessary or less necessary.

J. Attempts are made to program non-English-speaking pupils in shops, gyms, etc., with English-speaking pupils.

K. Pupils are encouraged to participate immediately in school service squads, clubs, and organizations.

L. Pupils who have been placed in regular classes are programmed for special English instruction during those subject periods where they cannot profit fully from the regular program because of language difficulties.

M. Pupils are *not* taken out for special English instruction during periods like shop, health education, or visual instruction.

N. Provision is made for teachers of English-orientation classes or of regular classes and for special teachers of English as a second language to meet. Conferences are devoted to the planning of joint units of work, to a discussion of progress or problems of individual pupils and of pupils who need additional follow-up, and to evaluation procedures.

O. Provision is made for group guidance periods, *preferably in the students' native tongue,* to supplement orientation and language learning periods.

P. Provision is made for individual guidance with staff members or guidance workers who *know* the pupils' native tongue.

Q. There is continuous evaluation and screening of pupils.

R. Pupils are placed in the next higher English-orientation class (if more than one exist) or are placed in regular classes as soon as they can profit from instruction in regular classes. (In general, they may not be up to grade in reading and writing but they may have fair aural-oral competence.) *All* teachers in the school are encouraged to provide continuing help where needed.

S. Pupils are given additional instruction in all phases of

the language arts *for as long as is needed,* even after they have completed the initial English-orientation program. Special classes in pronunciation or in reading are organized as needed.

T. Advantages and disadvantages of "pull-out" programs and "self-contained" classrooms are carefully studied. Organizational changes are made where warranted to provide maximum help to pupils.

U. The advantages of setting up bilingual programs in which pupils study a given curriculum area both in their native tongue and in English are explored. Age of pupils and availability of qualified personnel are considered.

V. Wherever feasible, pupils are programed to classes where they can increase their literacy in their native tongue.

III. The Curriculum

A. All pupils, whether in English-orientation or in regular classes, are given knowledge and skills within the language and sociocultural topics listed in Chapter 2.

B. Early emphasis is placed on developing the language arts within areas of health, nutrition, and safety.

C. Attempts are made to utilize previous school experiences of pupils in curriculum planning.

D. Provision is made for the utilization of cultural contributions of pupils.

E. Trips and other real or vicarious experiences form an important basis of learning.

F. Every teacher is a teacher of language. New vocabulary and difficult structures or patterns are clarified in all subject areas before the new subject material is taught.

G. Methodology emphasizes an aural-oral approach. The students' native tongue is used judiciously; reading and writing are introduced with materials that pupils have understood and said with reasonable facility.

H. Instructional materials are prepared by a committee of teachers where possible. There are samples of the following kinds of instructional materials in a central file:

1. Orientation material to be used in English-orientation classes, in special English classes, and in regular classes. This material should include language drills and practice activities, reading selections and vocabulary worksheets, which can be checked easily by pupils themselves or by a student assistant and which can be used to meet needs of pupils coming in at any time during the semester.

2. Material for developing good habits of pronunciation.

3. Material for teaching and for reinforcing fundamental structures and basic sentence patterns in English.

4. Material to be used by the regular class teacher or by an assistant in mathematics, social studies, science, language arts, etc. (The activities for pupils should be based on the units of work found in the regular curriculum of the school but should also give concurrent practice in developing or reinforcing items of structure and vocabulary.)

5. Where such gradation is important, the material should be on at least two levels of literacy and reading ability.

6. Audio-visual aids—particularly flat pictures.

I. The English-orientation class teacher or the special English teacher has a complete file of flat pictures, which includes illustrations of the vocabulary and concepts within the topics found in Chapter 2.

J. *After* the initial orientation topics are studied, simplified units of work in all other regular subject areas (social studies, mathematics) are developed.

K. The curriculum is modified or adapted continuously to ensure a basic fund of knowledge, particularly for those pupils for whom the school is the terminal point of education.

L. Learnings (concepts, vocabulary, language structures, and sentence pattern variations) from all subject areas are included in the language arts program.

M. Only the simplest audio-visual aids are used. Teachers recognize that flat pictures are often more effective than a sound film, particularly in the early stages of instruction.

N. Students are encouraged to contribute as soon as possible to all those creative activities in which they excel and which will help to give them status.

O. Provision is made for the continuous integration of language patterns and cultural items.

P. The four aspects of the language arts program *are developed separately* for teaching purposes but they are *practiced* together in listening, speaking, reading, and writing activities, in which they are used functionally and meaningfully.

Q. Articulation and thus continuity of instruction for pupils is provided at every step of the program.

R. Special provisions are made for "pull-out," or self-contained classrooms; for bilingual programs; for classes designed to increase the native literacy of pupils.

IV. Teacher Selection

A. Teachers are selected on the basis of their ability, knowledge, and flexibility. They have demonstrated skill in such important teaching procedures as the grouping of children, the preparation of materials, and the evaluation of pupil progress.

B. They are willing to learn and to master effective techniques in teaching English as a second language.

C. They are willing to help prepare instructional materials.

D. They show a deep appreciation of pupil problems, they have a mental-health approach to teaching, and they believe in continuous curriculum adaptation and revision.

E. Teachers, who will be assigned to the guidance program, are chosen because they are bilingual, because they have a knowledge of the customs and mores of the students, and because they have empathy.

F. In general, new teachers are not assigned to teach classes in English as a second language unless they have a license or special training in the field.

G. If new teachers must be assigned, they are assigned a teacher assistant, or buddy, to whom they can turn for help.

H. New teachers are furnished with all available materials.

V. Teacher Training

A. The entire staff, not just the teachers assigned to the English-teaching program, are alerted to policies and needs with regard to non-English-speaking pupils, by means of such administrative practices as general faculty or grade conferences and schoolwide circulars.

B. Resource people are consulted about effective practices in other schools, about current research findings, and about available materials.

C. Available materials are placed in a central file. These include pamphlets, brochures, and other materials in the following categories:

1. The customs and mores of various ethnic groups.

2. The educational programs in schools from which students may have come.

3. General methods of teaching English as a second language.

4. Specific techniques that have been developed in other areas for teaching English as a second language or for giving cultural orientation.

5. Free and inexpensive materials that will vitalize teaching.

      6. Materials from community agencies that can be used with parents, such as nutrition materials and health and safety pamphlets.

      7. Samples of instructional materials prepared in other schools or districts.

      8. Examples of successful units of work or projects prepared by teachers in the school.

      9. Language teaching materials for use by the teacher or by a buddy, or teacher assistant.

  D. Teachers are encouraged to visit other teachers in the school who have shown excellence in one or more phases of the program.

  E. Teachers attend carefully planned demonstration lessons in other schools or district centers.

  F. Individual teachers are released to attend conferences (district, state, national, agencies). Provision is made for them to report to the entire faculty or to groups of teachers.

  G. Teachers are encouraged to enroll in pertinent courses.

  H. A committee is formed to prepare materials listed in (C) above.

  I. Teachers of English-orientation and special English classes and the regular teachers of the grade or school meet periodically to plan materials, to discuss problems, and to recommend changes in administrative or teaching procedures.

VI. Relations with Parents and Other Community Members

  A. Letters, messages, notices, and report cards are prepared in the appropriate languages.

  B. The content of this material is carefully checked by a native speaker for accuracy of the native tongue and for proper psychological approach.

  C. Special meetings of non-English-speaking parents are conducted.

  D. Persons who speak the language of the parents are invited to interpret or to speak at these meetings.

E. The topics presented at the parents' meetings are those which have immediate value and interest for adults. Topics may include discussions of:
   1. Routines and regulations in the school
   2. Forms such as report cards, prepared bilingually
   3. Nutrition
   4. Community resources
   5. Consumer education
   6. Housing and employment opportunities
F. Parents are encouraged to come to school. However, children are not scolded because their parents do not come. There is understanding of the fact that non-attendance is often considered a great compliment to school personnel.
G. Letters of praise about their children far outnumber letters about infractions, if any.
H. Children are often permitted to take home work that has been graded A or 100% or with some other symbol of excellence.
I. Leadership is developed among non-English-speaking parents.
J. English-speaking parents and non-English-speaking parents meet together at parents' meetings during part of the evening for socialization.
K. Provision is made for a community activity jointly sponsored by English-speaking parents and non-English-speaking parents, which will result in bringing various ethnic groups in the community closer together.
L. Every effort is made to give parents and community leaders a meaningful voice in the school program and to use their talents and strengths wherever possible.
M. Special classes in English are organized for the parents at hours convenient for them. The English teaching program may be offered by the school alone or by the school in cooperation with a community or religious agency. Teachers, materials, and equipment such as record players or tape recorders are made available.

N. Parents are encouraged to take other courses offered by the school to meet their needs as they perceive them; e.g., Homemaking, Nutrition, Child Care, Sewing.

O. Other kinds of help (housing, legal, consumer education) are provided in cooperation with other community agencies.

UNIT VI

MATERIALS AND TEXTS

CHAPTER **18**

About These Materials

In the preceding chapters we have indicated various principles that will guide teachers and supervisors in the organization of effective programs for pupils who are learning English as a second language. We feel, however, that principles and general suggestions are not enough in a program that may present many new and unfamiliar challenges even to veteran teachers and supervisors. As we stated above in discussing the characteristics of our learners and in discussing methods of teaching, there is no one method, technique, or "system" that will fit all situations. Approaches and techniques that have been successful in various curriculum areas should be drawn upon by teachers if they are to organize effective teaching-learning programs. For example, the teacher of English as a second language would do well to give careful attention to the techniques of developing "readiness" for reading, which the elementary school teacher has at his command. He should also familiarize himself with the procedures for presenting pronunciation, sentence patterns and vocabulary which foreign-language teachers have found successful.

This is not a herculean task but one within the scope of all teachers. The materials we have included throughout the book will undoubtedly elicit remarks such as "I've done that" or "That's what we do in language arts or foreign languages." That is exactly the kind of response we hope these materials will produce. We would like experienced teachers to feel secure in the procedures they have undoubtedly tried, and new teachers to find some concrete examples that will give direction to their initial planning and upon which they can build.

We hope that *all* teachers will find an idea, a new variation, or a device which will make teaching English to speakers of other languages both a challenging and a gratifying experience.

The materials throughout the book have been centered about the objectives of developing language competency and cultural orientation in a classroom atmosphere that is conducive to learning. We have attempted to translate theory into practice in some detail. Specific illustrations have been provided of many of the principles and suggestions that have been advocated. In this section we have prepared additional concrete suggestions for analyzing the students' language, for teaching pronunciation, for setting up a picture file, for utilizing a center of activity, and for preparing lesson plans.

It is recommended that none of the lesson plans or reading materials be adhered to rigidly, but that they be adapted or rewritten depending upon the classroom organization, the pupils' age and ability, and upon your own teaching personality and strengths. We repeat: No two classes are alike, no two teachers, no two schools.

Just as we believe that an eclectic approach is best suited to the teaching of English as a second language, so do we ask that you use an eclectic approach in the selection and use of these materials. Use what is best for you, in your classroom, in your school, in your community, with your pupils.

CHAPTER 19

A Checklist for Contrasting English with the Student's Native Language

This is a brief, general listing of questions that will point up the possible conflicts your pupils may experience in learning English. In this text, we can only hope to direct the school staff's attention to the difficulties learners may face. For analyses in greater depth, you should examine books listed under Resources and Texts or consult bilingual members of your community.

The value of a brief contrastive study as a means of preparing more efficient and more effective instructional material cannot be underestimated. Awareness of similarities and differences between English and the native language of the pupils and knowing in advance what the problem features of English may be for them will alert us to prepare more intensive drills to overcome them. It will help us too to feel less frustrated when an item obviously dissimilar to English—the target language—requires numerous carefully prepared, sequential lessons before pupils can use it with reasonable control.

PRONUNCIATION

1. Vowels and Consonant Sounds
   a. Does English have vowel sounds which do not exist in the native language of the students?
   b. Which English consonant sounds do not exist?

c. Are any sounds *phonemic* in English which are not phonemic in the native language? For example, /b/ and /v/
are two separate phonemes in English but not in Spanish.

d. Does the native language have diphthongs such as in
"boy," "brown," "pie"?

e. Are consonant clusters distributed differently in the native
language? For example, /sk/ is not found in *initial* position in Spanish; /nd/ is not found in *final* position, nor
is our commonly used past signal /kt/, as in "walked."

f. Is there more than one sound for the plural? In English,
we say *books* /s/, *boys* /z/, and *boxes* /iz/.

g. Is there a phenomenon similar to our "ed" ending for the
past? Note: *walked* /t/, *combed* /d/, and *wanted* /id/.

h. Does the native spoken language reduce any vowels to the
schwa (mute "e") sound /ə/, as does English?

2. Intonation

a. In the native language, does the voice fall at the end of a
statement or a *"Wh"* (who, when, etc.) question as it
does in English?

b. Does the polite request in the native language use a falling intonation (as is the case in English)?

c. Does the voice rise with inverted questions? (In English it
usually does.)

3. Rhythm, Stress, and Pause

a. Is word stress phonemic in the native language? For example, convért and cónvert are not the same in English
and would fill different sentence slots.

b. Are there words that are generally unstressed in spoken
speech, as are our articles (*a, an, the*) and many of our
function words such as *of*?

c. Does the native language stress all syllables equally or
does it stress only accented syllables, as does English?

d. Is pause phonemic in the native language, as it is in English? For example, /ai – skrim/ (I scream) and /ais –
krim/ (ice cream) have different meanings in English
although the sounds are the same in both utterances.

e. Does the native language contract words; e.g., He's, I'd, Don't.

STRUCTURE

1. What are the major sentence patterns in the native language? Basic patterns in English include the following:

> Birds fly.
> The boy is here.
> The man is a doctor.
> I have a book.
> I gave him a book.
> There's a book on the table.
> He speaks well.
> Let's eat now.
> She expected me to speak.

2. What does the native language do about *word order?* For example,
   a. Does the noun subject precede the verb?
   b. Does the noun object follow the verb?
   c. Does the pronoun object follow the verb? (E.g., I see him.)
   d. Does the adjective precede the noun?
   e. Do determiners (*a, the, each, some,* etc.) precede the noun?
   f. Does word order change meaning? (As in English an *arm-chair* is not the same as a *chair arm.*)
   g. Are the subject and "be" verb ever inverted to form a question?
   h. Can other verbs and subjects be inverted? (Can he go? Must I study? *But,* Does he have to study?)
   i. Where is the word indicating negation placed?
   j. Do "adjectival nouns" exist? (In English, we can say "a ham sandwich" or "a Navy yard.")
   k. How is the reflexive-reciprocal relationship expressed?

(In English, "we wash *ourselves*" and "we speak to *each other*.")

3. What does the native language do about inflection? For example,

   a. Is anything added to a noun to indicate plurality?

   b. Are adjectives inflected to agree with the nouns they modify?

   c. How are the comparative and superlative of adjectives formed?

   d. Are the verb forms for *he, she,* and *who* inflected?

   e. How is possession with a noun expressed? (For example, in English we say "the man's hat" but "the leg of the table.")

   f. Are pronouns inflected? (English: I, my, mine, me.)

   g. Do subjects and verbs agree? (In English, we say "The boy is here" but "The boys are here.")

4. Does the native language have function words? Are these used as they are in English? For example,

   a. Is future time expressed by means of a function word? (In English, we may say "I'll go" or "Will he go?")

   b. How is "mood" expressed? Note English modals: You *should* go; You *have to* go; You *ought to* go; You *may* go; You *must* go.

   c. Are prepositions—e.g., on, in, to, for, by—used as they are in English?

   d. What verbal expressions are needed after certain conjunctions or subordinators such as *if, while, after, although?*

   e. Is a word similar to English "do" added to express questions or negation?

5. Other questions may include:

   a. Is the pronoun subject always expressed?

   b. Does the native language have *two* verbal constructions to express the present? In English, we say, "I walk" (every day, always, usually) and "I'm walking" (now).

   c. Is the definite article ever omitted or used in ways different from English? For example, we say, "Coffee is grown in Colombia" but "The coffee here is good." We omit the definite article with days of the week; we don't use the article before names of people.

d. How are tag questions expressed? For example, English says: He's going, isn't he? They're rich, aren't they? He likes you, doesn't he? I can go, can't I? Other languages use a *set* formula for tags. Spanish: *verdad?* French: *n'est-ce pas?* Italian: *vero?* German: *nicht war?*

VOCABULARY AND CULTURE

1. How many forms of "you" are there?
2. Do verb forms change depending upon the person addressed, the person speaking, or the person about whom one is speaking?
3. Are words formed as derivatives of other words? (E.g., bright, brighten, brightness, brightly.)
4. How are prefixes and suffixes attached to words? Does the sound and *spelling* of a word change because of the addition of a prefix? (For example, the prefix *in,* meaning "not," changes in *il*legal and *im*moral.)
5. Do word meanings change according to the context? For example, in English, the word "time" means different things in the utterances "What a good time we had!" "Get here on time." "What time is it?"
6. Does the native language use a form of "be" in expressions such as "I'm ten"; "I'm hungry" (tired, sleepy, bored, etc.)?

THE RELATIONSHIP OF SPEAKING TO READING AND WRITING

1. Is there a one-to-one correspondence between sound and visual symbol? (Note "dough," "through," "enough," "cough," "hiccough.")
2. What does the native language do about punctuation marks?
3. Is a page read from left to right and from top to bottom?
4. How are numbers, dates, addresses, and telephone numbers spoken and written?

CHAPTER 20

Pronunciation Aids

THE PHONETIC ALPHABET

The following is a slight adaptation of the International Phonetic Alphabet, the IPA. Some linguists use other symbols for some of the vowels and consonants. A few common examples are č for tʃ, ž for ʒ, š for ʃ, ʌ for ə.

The vowels are in the order found in the vowel triangle on page 369. The reasons for the order will be obvious as the triangle is examined.

The phonetic symbols are always enclosed in brackets.

VOWELS

Symbol	Word
[i]	eat
[ɪ]	it
[e]	ate
[ɛ]	let
[æ]	hat
[ɑ]	hot
[ɔ]	law
[o]	go
[ʊ]	pull
[u]	food
[ə]	but

THE VOWEL TRIANGLE

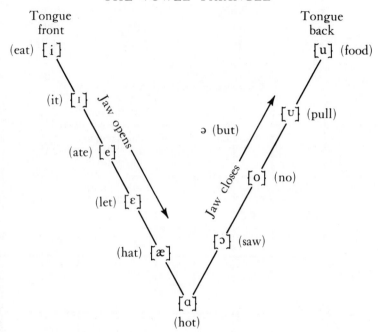

DIPHTHONGS

Symbol	Word
[ai]	buy
[aʊ]	brown
[ɔi]	toy

CONSONANTS

Symbol	Word	Symbol	Word
[b]	bird	[ʃ]	shop
[d]	day	[t]	tie
[f]	fat	[θ]	thick
[g]	go	[ð]	this
[h]	hat	[v]	village
[k]	cat	[w]	was
[l]	let	[y]	you
[m]	May	[z]	rose

[n]	no	[ʒ]	azure
[ŋ]	ring	[tʃ]	chew
[p]	pull	[dʒ]	John
[r]	rip	[ʍ]	while*
[s]	sing		

CONSONANT CHART*

Passage of air	Vibration of vocal cords[†]	Two lips	Lower lip and upper teeth	Tip of tongue and upper teeth	Tip of tongue and back of upper teeth	Front of tongue and front of palate	Back of tongue and soft palate	The vocal cords
Completely stopped	no	p			t		k	
	yes	b			d		g	
Two sounds	no					tʃ		
	yes					dʒ		
Through a narrow opening	no		f	θ	s	ʃ		
	yes		v	ð	z	ʒ		
Through side of tongue	no				l			
	yes							
Through nose	no							
	yes	m			n	ŋ		
No stoppage	no							
	yes	w			r[‡]	y		h

*Adapted from a chart by the author published in *English as a Second Language: From Theory to Practice* (Regents Publishing Co.).

[†]When cords vibrate, the sounds are "voiced," and when the cords do not vibrate, the sounds are "voiceless."

[‡]Tongue curls back.

* Many speakers of English do not differentiate between [w] and [ʍ]. They use [w] exclusively.

SELECTED LIST OF SPECIAL PRONUNCIATION PROBLEMS
ACCORDING TO STUDENTS' NATIVE LANGUAGE*†

All Students: Vowels, r; θ/δ; stress and intonation

Most Students: 3; final stops; s/z; t/d; w/v; y/j; ʃ/ts; l/r; initial and final clusters (bl, sk, rth, etc.), words of more than one syllable

Asian students: initial, medial, and final l/r; l/r clusters (fl, fr, gl, gr, bl, etc.) ; final clusters, especially ks, kz, kt

Chinese students: all the vowels; b; d; g; v; θ; δ; all the final consonants except n and ŋ; h/ʃ; ʃ/ts; y/z

French students: ɔi; ɪ/i; ʊ/u; h; θ/δ; tʃ/ʃ; y; s/t/θ

German students: θ, δ; all voiced finals; p/b; d/θ; d/δ; s/z; w/v; dʒ/y; tʃ/ʃ; n/3; s clusters

Italian students: i/ɪ; ʊ/u; h; θ; δ; s/ʃ; initial fl, pl, bl; final clusters; unstressed syllables; word stress

Japanese students: all vowels; unstressed i, u; θ/δ; f/h; s/ʃ; z/3; t/ts; ʃ/tʃ; w/v; l/r; all clusters

Polish students: ə; long vowels; diphthongs; θ/δ; w; l; z/3; final w/l; unstressed syllables; g/k

Spanish students: ε/e; ɪ/i; ʊ/ə; final voiced consonants; b/v; y/dz; s/z; s/θ; s/ʃ/ts; d; final m/n/3; s clusters; final clusters

---

* Adapted from E. C. Trager and S. C. Henderson, *Pronunciation Drills,* English Language Services, Washington, D.C., 1965.

† Please refer to the International Phonetic Alphabet, p. 368, for symbols.

CHAPTER 21

Materials Related to Speaking, Reading, and Writing

STRESSED VOWEL SOUNDS: SOME COMMON SPELLINGS: *

Note: Unstressed vowels are usually pronounced [ə].

Symbol	*Common Spellings*
[i]	me, need, read, belief, receive
[ɪ]	hit, mitt, been, build
[e]	hate, wait, ray, neigh, break
[ɛ]	red, head
[æ]	hat, laugh
[ɑ]	hot, father, star, heart
[ɔ]	all, walk, paw, for, aught, frost
[o]	go, oh, toe, bold, boast, though, tow
[ʊ]	good, wolf, full
[u]	food, move, threw, through, rule, blue, shoe
[ai]	aisle, night, child, ice, buy, sky, height
[aʊ]	house, now, loud, brown
[ɔi]	boy, boil
[ər]	girl, pearl, nerve
[ɛr]	hair, hear, bare

* See the chart on p. 368 for phonetic symbols.

ENGLISH CONSONANT CLUSTERS*

The Thirty-nine Consonant Clusters in *Initial* Position

[pr]	pray, press	[gl]	glow, glue
[tr]	tray, tree	[dw]	dwell, dwarf
[fr]	fray, free	[kw]	quick, quack
[gr]	gray, grass	[tw]	twine, twig
[dr]	drew, drip	[sw]	swine, swear
[kr]	crew, crow	[hw]	whine, where
[θr]	through, throw	[θw]	thwart, thwack
[br]	brew, broad	[fy]	feud, few
[šr]	shred, shrink	[ky]	cute, cube
[st]	stay, stem	[my]	mute, music
[sp]	span, spend	[by]	beauty, bugle
[sm]	small, smoke	[py]	pure, putrid
[sk]	skin, scare	[vy]	view
[sn]	snow, snare	[hy]	hue, huge
[sf]	sphere, sphinx	[str]	stray, string
[sl]	slay, slow	[skr]	screw, scroll
[pl]	play, plow	[spr]	spray, spread
[kl]	clay, claw	[spl]	splash, spleen
[bl]	blow, blue	[skw]	square, squint
[fl]	flow, flay		

The 151 Final Consonant Clusters of English†

I. Single Morpheme Words

[nd]	lend, bend	[dθ]	width
[nt]	tent, hint	[dz]	adze
[st]	fist, must	[ln]	kiln
[ns] [nts]	fence, tense	[rb]	curb
[ld]	old, cold	[rd]	card
[ks]	box, wax	[rf]	turf

* From Charles Fries, *Teaching and Learning English as a Foreign Language* (Ann Arbor, Michigan: University of Michigan Press, 1948).
† *Ibid.*

[lf]	wolf, golf	[rg]	iceberg
[ŋk]	sink, rank	[řj]	surge
[kt]	act, sect	[rč]	search
[nǰ]	change, hinge*	[rk]	fork, bark
[lv]	valve, solve	[rl]	curl, girl
[lt]	belt, bolt	[rm]	worm, warm
[sk]	desk, task	[rn]	turn, barn
[lp]	help, gulp	[rp]	chirp, carp
[ls]	false, pulse	[rs]	curse, hoarse
[lk]	silk, milk	[rt]	court, hurt
[lθ] [ltθ]	health	[rv]	curve, nerve
[mp]	limp, pump	[rz]	furze
[nč]	bench	[rš]	harsh
[ft]	soft, left	[rθ]	worth, hearth
[sp]	lisp, wasp	[rps]	corpse
[lm]	film	[rst]	first
[lj]	bulge, bilge	[rts]	quartz
[lb]	bulb	[mpt]	tempt
[lš] [lč]	mulch, welch	[mps]	glimpsed
[lč]	belch, gulch	[kst]	text
[mf] [mpf]	nymph	[ksθ]	sixth
[ps]	copse	[ndθ]	thousandth
[pt]	crypt, apt	[lfθ]	twelfth
[nθ] [ntθ]	tenth	[nks]	lynx, sphinx
[nz] [ndz]	lens	[nkθ]	length
[fθ]	fifth	[rmθ]	warmth
[tθ]	eighth		

II. With *bound inflectional* morphemes added

    A. [z] added. *Plural* and *3rd singular, present*

[bz]	bibs	[lnz] [lz]	kilns
[gz]	figs	[lvz]	shelves
[lz]	balls	[rbz]	curbs
[mz]	rooms	[rdz]	cards
[vz]	lives	[rgz]	icebergs

* Notice that Fries uses [ǰ] for [dz] of the IPA; [č] for [tʃ]; [š] for [ʃ].

[ŋz]	rings	[rlz]	girls
[θz]	breathes	[rmz]	worms
[lbz]	bulbs	[rnz]	turns
[ldz]	colds	[rvz]	curves
[lmz]	films		

B. [s] added. *Plural* and *3rd singular, present.*

[fs]	coughs	[pts]	crypts
[ts]	rats	[sks]	desks
[θs]	breaths	[sps]	lisps
[dθs]	widths	[sts]	fists
[fts]	tufts	[tθs]	eighths
[kts]	acts	[ksts]	texts
[lfs]	gulfs	[ksθs]	sixths
[lks]	milks	[lfθs]	twelfths
[lps]	helps	[mpts]	tempts
[lts]	belts	[ndθs]	thousandths
[lθs]	healths	[nkθs]	lengths
[mfs] [mpfs]	nymphs	[rfs]	surfs
[nθs] [ntθs]	ninths	[rks]	works
[ŋks]	sinks	[rps]	chirps
[fθs]	fifths	[rsts]	bursts

C. [d] added. *Past tense* and *past participle.*

[bd]	rubbed	[lmd]	filmed
[gd]	hugged	[lvd]	solved
[jd]	raged	[nǰd]	changed
[md]	roamed	[rbd]	barbed
[ŋd]	wronged	[rǰd]	surged
[ðd]	breathed	[rld]	curled
[žd]	rouged	[rmd]	stormed
[vd]	lived	[rnd]	warned
[zd]	raised	[rvd]	curved
[lǰd]	bulged		

D. [t] added. *Past tense* and *past participle.*

| [št] | pushed | [nčt] | lunched |
| [čt] | touched | [nst] [ntst] | danced |

[lft]	engulfed	[ŋkt]	linked
[lšt] [lčt]	welched	[pst]	lapsed
[lkt]	milked	[skt]	asked
[lpt]	helped	[spt]	lisped
[lst] [ltst]	waltzed	[rčt]	perched
[mft] [mpft]	triumphed	[rkt]	worked
		[rpt]	warped

CHAPTER 22

Teacher-Prepared Materials

Where no books are available or if the teacher feels that those available are inappropriate for his students, he can prepare, alone or working with a committee of teachers, short selections or dialogues to be used for intensive or extensive reading practice. The same material can be used for other language work such as dictation or dramatization. The reading materials can be extensions or variations of the experience charts or they can be designed to develop and give practice in specific concepts or language items.

It is desirable, of course, to prepare some of the reading material on at least two levels of ability. It is recommended, however, that the entire class or group engage in the same preliminary or motivating activity (trip, film, speaker, etc.) and that then the differentiated material be distributed.

Following are some dialogues that illustrate the use of language in normal, everyday situations.*

SOME SAMPLE DIALOGUES

I

"What's your name?"
"John. What's yours?"
"Harry."

* For an explanation of dialogue presentation, see p. 174.

II

"How old are you, John?"
"I'm eleven. How old are you?"
"I'm eleven, too."

III

"What's the weather like today?"
"It's beautiful."
"Is it warm enough to go swimming?"
"Of course."

IV

"What are you doing after school?"
"Nothing. Why?"
"Let's play ball together."
"O.K. I'll meet you in the yard."

V

"I always help my mother with the shopping."
"So do I."

VII

"Mom, may I go to the movies this Saturday?"
"What's playing?"
"A Western. Joe asked me to go with him."
"All right. But don't go before two o'clock."
"Why not?"
"I'd like you to go to the store first."

EXAMPLES OF SUGGESTIONS FOR NARRATIVE READING
BASED ON THE PRECEDING DIALOGUES*

I

My name is John. I have a new friend. His name is Harry.

II

I'm eleven. My friend is eleven too.

III

The weather today is beautiful. My friend is sure it's warm enough to go swimming.

* It is obvious that the same dialogues could produce many other reading selections.

VII

I asked my mother's permission to go to the movies on Saturday. She asked me what was playing. I told her that it was a Western and that I was going to the movies with Joe. She said I couldn't go before two o'clock because she wanted me to go to the store first.

READING PASSAGES

Shopping for Food (Simple Version)

My mother wants me to shop for food. This supermarket sells everything. I can buy the sugar, soup, and salt in the grocery department. I can buy eggs, butter, and milk in the dairy department. I have to get meat. I can buy bacon and roast beef in the meat department. My mother gave me ten dollars. I hope (that) ten dollars is enough.

Question: What does your mother want you to buy?
  Answer: She wants me to buy food.
Question: What can you buy in the grocery department?
  Answer: I can buy sugar, soup, and salt.
Question: What can you buy in the dairy department?
  Answer: I can buy eggs, butter, and milk.
Question: What can you buy in the meat department?
  Answer: I can buy meat.
Question: How much money do you have?
  Answer: I have ten dollars.

(In addition to questions and answers, any appropriate completion, matching, or other short-answer type of exercise can be prepared orally or in writing. You may also wish to allow pupils to study and *copy* both the question and the answer. Moreover, the answer can be a word or utterance *and not* a complete sentence.)

Shopping for Food (More Difficult Version)

Mrs. Smith needs groceries, meat, and dairy products. Her

food closet is empty. She must prepare a list so that she can remember everything.

She always goes to the same market. The service is excellent. The food is also of fine quality and the prices are right.

In the grocery department, she's going to buy a pound of sugar, two cans of soup, and a box of salt. In the dairy department, she's going to buy a dozen eggs, a pound of butter, and a container of milk. She's going to buy a package of bacon and a two-pound roast in the meat department.

She thinks she will need more than ten dollars for all this food. The bill will be fifteen dollars at least.

What is empty?
What does Mrs. Smith need?
Why must she prepare a list?
Why does she always go to the same market?
What is she going to buy in the grocery department?
What is she going to buy in the dairy department?
What is she going to buy in the meat department?
How much will the bill be?

The reading selections and questions can be made more complex still. The language can be extended to include adjectives or more adverbs; for example, "She's going to buy a dozen white, medium-sized eggs," or "She's going to buy a half-pound of sweet butter." The structures can be varied so that pupils are given practice in distinguishing between two or more similar or contrasting patterns or so that they can review many types of patterns or pattern combinations.

Again it is suggested that one selection be made the jumping-off point for varied language work. Pupils may be asked: "Use *he* instead of *she*." "Change the affirmative to the interrogative or to the negative." "Tell us, do you go shopping?"

AN EXAMPLE OF RECOMBINED READING

Let us assume that the function words (prepositions), *on, under,* etc., have been introduced and practiced. The teac.

prepare a passage similar to the following, which will allow the students to *hear, say, read,* and perhaps *write* the prepositions in a normal, everyday situation.

John got a watch for his birthday. One day John lost the watch in his house. He looked for it everywhere. He looked under his pillow. Then he looked under the bed. He looked in his dresser drawers. He looked on the floor of the closet. He even looked behind the sofa and under the carpet. But he could not find the watch.

One day his mother found the watch. Where do you think it was?

The pupils should try to guess where the watch might have been found, affording practice in talking about location, rooms in the house, objects, and furniture, and, of course, in practicing prepositions.

TEACHER-PREPARED DICTATION OR AURAL-COMPREHENSION PASSAGES

I

Tom and Peter are good friends. Their houses are close together. Tom lives in a large house. He belongs to a large family. Besides Tom, there are his parents, his two brothers, a sister, and Tom's grandparents.

Peter lives in an apartment. He belongs to a small family. He lives in the apartment with his parents and one sister.

Possible questions for use in aural-comprehension exercises

1. Are Tom and Peter good friends?
2. Where does Tom live?
3. With whom does Tom live?
4. Where does Peter live?
5. With whom does Peter live?

II

It's Sunday afternoon. The Fenton family is planning activities for the afternoon. John would like to go to a ball game. Clara would like to visit a friend. Mr. and Mrs. Fenton would like to stay at home. There's going to be an excellent TV program at six o'clock.

They decide to meet at seven o'clock. They plan to have dinner together and then go to the movies.

Possible Questions

1. What day is it?
2. What's the Fenton family planning?
3. Where would John like to go?
4. At what time is the TV program?
5. What do they plan to do after seven o'clock?

CHAPTER 23

Materials for Vitalizing Learning

A Suggested Minimum List of Pictures for a File
on City Living

I. Pictures related to the school

  A. Personnel—principal, nurse, custodian, guidance coun-
  selors, librarian, faculty members
  B. Rooms—gymnasium, auditorium, cafeteria, shops,
  nurse's office, principal's office, general office, classrooms
  C. Instructional materials—bulletin boards, books, charts
  D. Rules and regulations—fire drills, safety on stairs, etc.

II. Pictures related to the home

  A. Rooms—bedrooms, bathroom, kitchen, (dinette), living
  room, (dining room), hall
  B. Furniture—dresser, closet, tables, chairs, lamps, rugs,
  Venetian blinds, stoves, refrigerators, iceboxes, book-
  cases, beds (mattresses, sheets, blankets), pillows
  C. Utensils and tools—knives, forks, spoons, plates, sau-
  cers, cups, broiler, pots, pans, hammer, scissors
  D. Home activities—cooking, eating, sweeping, washing,
  sewing, dressing, reading, studying, health habits
  (brushing teeth, combing hair, etc.)
  E. Meals—setting the table, serving, types of food for
  breakfast, lunch, dinner, snacks, parties
  F. Recreation—radio, television, cards, word games,

checkers, parties, books, phonograph, crossword puzzles, knitting, sewing, cooking, dancing, singing, playing musical instruments

G. Exterior—sidewalk, entrance, stoop, letter box

III. Pictures related to the community

   A. Neighborhood
      1. Post office—various departments, stamps, air mail, envelopes, parcel post, inquiry window, money orders, forms (overseas money, parcel post), mailboxes
      2. Police—receiving desk, radio room, radio cars, uniforms, equipment, different types of police jobs, traffic
      3. Fire—fire house, equipment, uniforms, people performing various duties
      4. Business establishments—stores, grocery, meat store, candy store, vegetable market, beauty parlor, pet shops, chain stores, drugstores, supermarkets
      5. Sanitation—street cleaners, exterminators, garbage cans
      6. Health—doctors, nurses, ambulances, clinics, hospitals
      7. Occupations—factory, mechanics, sales clerks, manual labor jobs, armed services, professional
      8. Places of worship

   B. Transportation
      1. Signs such as—stop, go, right, left, uptown, downtown, one way, detour, this way out, exit, entrance
      2. Types of transportation in neighborhood—bus, train, car, bicycle, scooter, wagon, carriage, truck
      3. Terms (in transportation) outside of the neighborhood—boat, airplane, escalators, elevators, bus, train, terminals, stations, bus stops, shipping dock, coin box, turnstile, taxi, railroad, subway, trolley, transfer

C. Recreation
1. In the neighborhood—playgrounds, schoolroom, gym, street, parks, afternoon centers, community centers, settlement houses, sports equipment (such as gloves, bat, ball)
2. Out of the neighborhood—skating rinks, movies, libraries, museums, beaches, pools, ball parks, bowling alleys, zoo, organizational activities such as Boy Scouts

IV. Pictures related to an understanding of cultural values

Historic landmarks—buildings, statues
Holidays—religious, political, special days of national groups
Heroes
Documents

V. Miscellaneous

A. Pets—dogs, cats, turtles, fish, pigeons, rabbits, canaries, monkeys
Care of pets—bathing, feeding, training, responsibilities
B. Leisure-time activities—stamps, coins, doll house, scrapbooks, photography, sewing, knitting, painting, baking, science, reading, musical instruments, concert- or playgoing, fishing

Suggested Pictures for a File on Country Living

I. The General Scene

A. Farmhouses (various types)
Barn
Silo
Chicken houses
Well (pump, buckets)
B. Fields
Crops

Orchards

Pastures

C. Brooks

D. Woods

E. Farm implements—tractors, trucks, threshing machines, automobiles, hoe, spade, fork

F. Animals—cows, horses, pigs, sheep, chickens, ducks, geese, dogs, cats

Wild animals—deer, rabbits, squirrels, bears

Fish and wild birds

II. Pictures Related to Community Life

A. Recreational—country dances, hay ride, skating, sleighing, swimming, horseback riding, country fairs, carnivals, picnics

B. Places of worship

C. Schools, library

III. Pictures Related to the Home

A. Interior views

Farm kitchen	Bunks
Wood or coal stove	Utensils
Electric washer	Living room—fireplace
Outhouses	Potbelly stove
Bathrooms	Lamp (kerosene)
Washstands	Electric lights

IV. Pictures Related to Transportation and Communication

A. School bus, automobiles, station wagon, trains, bus

B. Telephone, mailman, mailboxes, letters, mail-order catalogues, magazines, newspapers

V. Miscellaneous

Drugstores

General store

Volunteer fire company

Roads—dirt, concrete, macadam, highways
Bridges—country bridges, large bridges
Depot

CHORAL READING

Here is a fun poem for older students for choral reading. It it excellent for rhythm and intonation, as well as for enjoyment.

POOR OLD WOMAN*

Solo	There was an old woman who swallowed a fly. Pause
All quite shocked slowly	Oh, my! Swallowed a fly! Poor old woman, I think she'll die.
Solo	There was an old woman who swallowed a spider; Pause
slowly	Right down inside her she swallowed a spider; She swallowed the spider to kill the fly Oh, my! Swallowed a fly! Poor old woman, I think she'll die.
Solo	There was an old woman who swallowed a bird. Pause
said in an aside	How absurd to swallow a bird!
more quickly	She swallowed the bird to kill the spider,
All	She swallowed the spider to kill the fly,
Slowly, sadly	Oh, my! Swallowed a fly! Poor old woman, I think she'll die.
Solo	There was an old woman who swallowed a cat, Pause

* From *Grade Teacher*, Spring, 1966, issue.

incredibly	Fancy that! She swallowed a cat!
	She swallowed the cat to kill the bird,
All	She swallowed the bird to kill the spider,
	She swallowed the spider to kill the fly.
	Oh, my! Swallowed a fly!
	Poor old woman, I think she'll die.
Solo	There was an old woman who swallowed a dog. Pause
slowly—	She went the whole hog! She swallowed a dog!
what next?	She swallowed the dog to kill the cat,
All	She swallowed the cat to kill the bird,
	She swallowed the bird to kill the spider,
	She swallowed the spider to kill the fly.
Slowly, sadly	Oh, my! Swallowed a fly!
	Poor old woman, I think she'll die.
Solo	There was an old woman who swallowed a cow. Pause
deliberately	I don't know how, but she swallowed a cow.
	She swallowed the cow to kill the dog,
All	She swallowed the dog to kill the cat,
with increasing	Group 1
momentum	She swallowed the cat to kill the bird,
	Groups 1 and 2
	She swallowed the bird to kill the spider,
	Groups 1, 2, and 3
	She swallowed the spider to kill the fly.
	Groups 1, 2, 3, and 4
Slowly, sadly	Oh, my! Swallowed a fly! All
	Poor old woman, I think she'll die.
Solo	There was an old woman who swallowed a horse! Pause
casually	She died, of course.

—Unknown

SOME LANGUAGE GAMES

As has been mentioned earlier in this text, games should be played with three basic criteria in view: (1) They should lend interest and variety to lessons; (2) They should increase the students' understanding of English; (3) They should induce them to produce the new language.

Although people at all age levels enjoy games, you may wish to adapt some of the games for use with younger or older students. For example, with the Simon Says game, younger students can stand while they perform some of the actions and older students can remain seated throughout the game.

Games should be played quickly. Explicit directions should be given. The key sentence should be modeled several times. If the game is to be played competitively—that is, to score points —two or three "run-throughs" should be engaged in before scoring is begun. Naturally the number of "run-throughs" and the competitions, if any, will depend on such factors as age, interest, needs, and goals. As quickly as possible, the teacher should let students lead the games.

An excellent source of language games will be found in the books by Gertrude Dorry and by W. R. Lee (see Resources and Texts).

General Games

I'M THINKING OF _____

A student will choose one item from a list. He will jot it down on a piece of paper or whisper it to the teacher or leader. He will then say to the class, "I'm thinking of a _____" (number, name, date, month, time, a sport, an activity, etc., depending on the lesson emphasis). Students are to guess what the leader is thinking of.

> Individual student: "Is it _____?"
> Teacher or Leader: "No, it's not _____."
> Teacher or Leader: "Yes, it is. It's _____."

Notes:

1. In later stages, individual students may ask, "Are you thinking of _____?" eliciting the appropriate response.
2. The student leader may eliminate some possibilities; e.g., "I'm thinking of a number. It's not four. It's not seven."

ADD-ON

This is played with pictures, real objects, or verbal cues alone.

> Student 1: "I see a living room."
> Student 2: "I see a living room and a kitchen."
> Student 3: "I see a living room, a kitchen, and a bathroom."
> Etc.

or

> Student 1: "I like milk."
> Student 2: "I like milk and pie."
> Student 3: "I like milk, pie, and cake."

Notes:

1. You may wish to play the game within categories (food, rooms, games, etc.) or with random items placed on your desk or in a box.
2. This is a good game for practicing unstressed words or syllables (e.g., "milk 'n' pie").

OH, NO; NOT I

The teacher or a student makes a statement beginning with such words as "I hear that," "I understand that," "I see that," "I've heard that." What the teacher "heard" should be a statement which the student to whom it is made will want to deny. He will say that someone else is responsible. That student will say someone else is responsible, etc.

Teacher: "I understand you came to school late this morning."
Student 1: "Oh, no; I didn't come late. He did."

Notes:

1. Responses can be varied and expanded in many ways depending upon the knowledge of the students; e.g., "I always come to school early (on time)," or "I'm *never* late to school."

POOR JIM

Draw a sketch on the board or use a flannel-board cut-out. Pupils touch or remove the item "it" doesn't have.

This is perfect for practicing forms of *have; there is; there's not;* and the negative. Many versions can be played.

a. Student 1: "Poor Jim, he has a headache."

   Student 2: "No, he doesn't have a headache; he has a stomachache."

   Student 3: "No, he doesn't have a stomachache; he has a _____."

b. Student 1: "Poor Jim. He doesn't like spinach."

   Student 2: "You're wrong. He likes spinach. He doesn't like carrots."

   Student 3: "You're wrong. He likes carrots but he doesn't like _____."

c. Student 1: "What an unusual [silly, rare] house. It doesn't have a kitchen."

   Student 2: "Oh, no. It has a kitchen. It doesn't have a bathroom."

d. Student 1: "What a silly story!" (The Pied Piper)

   It doesn't have rats, etc.

SIMON SAYS

This is good for practicing parts of the body, the use of prepositions of place, and clothing.

Directives are given by the teacher or a student leader; e.g., Hands on head, pencils in desk, hands on tie, hands behind your back, etc. When the directions are preceded by *Simon says,* the students are to carry them out. When *Simon says* does not precede the directions, the students remain motionless.

Games for Number Practice

BUZZ

The teacher, or leader, indicates a number, which number and all its multiples the student will omit in counting. They will say "Buzz" in its place. E.g., if 3 is chosen, "One, two, buzz, four, five, buzz," etc.

WHICH NUMBER IS MISSING?

The teacher or a student will give a list of numbers quickly, omitting one. He will ask, "Which number is missing?"

IT'S MORE

To a list of prices or hours, students will be expected to *add* an amount set by the teacher or a group leader.

IT'S LESS

Same as the preceding except that students will deduct an amount.

WHO HAS NUMBER _____?

Make out number cards with numbers from 1 to 25, from 25 to 100, from 100 to a thousand, and above a thousand, depending on what has been taught. When calling on students to recite, to play games, etc., use the numbers instead of names.

HOW MANY ARE THERE?

Use number cards and pictures of any object, person or animal. Hold a number card in one hand and a picture in the other. Ask "How many _____ are there?"

HOW MUCH?

In addition to the buying activities suggested in the text, you may want to write lists of clothing [food, sports] items on the board, with prices. Ask, "How much did you pay for the _____?" Engage in chain practice or call on people through the "Who has number _____?" technique.

Games for Vocabulary and Structure Practice

OPPOSITES

Two teams are formed. The first person in Team 1 says a word and the first person in Team 2 has to say the opposite word. If he cannot his team loses a point.

THE SAME

As in above, except that a synonym is called for.

Guessing Games

Played with two teams for points or by the class as a whole.

WHAT IS IT?

A description is given; e.g., "It has four legs. It's made of wood. You sit on it." Students on the other teams have to say, "It's a chair."

WHO AM I?

A job description is given: "I cut meat." A student or a member of a team says, "You're a butcher." Another version of this is to give a description of a well-known person. Students have to guess who the person is.

TWENTY QUESTIONS

One student is sent out of the room while the others decide on an object, person, or animal. When the student returns, he asks questions such as "Is it in the room?" "Is it big?" "Is it red?" etc.

PANTOMIMES OR CHARADES

A proverb, a familiar concept, or a sentence which has been taught can be acted out by a member of one team. Members of the other team have to guess what the action is. They then make a statement identifying the situation being acted out. For example, The book is difficult; The boy is tall and handsome; A stitch in time saves nine.

WHAT DOESN'T BELONG?

Members of one team give four words orally, one of which doesn't belong in the list: milk, bread, hat, pear. The other side has to tell which word does not belong before the count of three.

IT'S NOT (OR HE'S NOT)

Another version of the "I'm thinking of" or "Twenty Questions" game consists of having the person (teacher or leader), who knows the answer, tell the class three things the object or person is *not;* e.g., He's *not* a butcher. He's *not* a tailor. He's *not* a mechanic. (Notice how stress may be practiced.) The class then proceeds to make other guesses.

Games for older students at more advanced levels of language learning

SCRABBLE (A MODIFIED VERSION)

Make numerous small cards with the letters of the alphabet, at least 10 cards for each except X and Z, of which fewer will be needed. The students sit around a desk. Each turns up one card in the pack at a time with which he tries to make a word. The minimum number of letters for the word should be previously agreed upon. He places the word in front of him. The next player may use his neighbor's word as well as the card he has turned up to make other words.

WORD DIVISION

Take a long word—e.g., imagination—and have students make as many words as possible from it. Have the small words written on the board by a student. Use them for further pronunciation practice, for making statements, and for learning new meanings, as well as for fun.

Note: Dictionaries should be available for verifying or checking.

CHAPTER 24

Examples of Lesson Formats and Units of Work

POSSIBLE LESSON PLAN FORMATS
With Emphasis on the Teaching of Structure

I. General Aims
   A. Linguistic
   B. Sociocultural

II. Specific Aims

   A. Language items to be introduced:
      1. Basic patterns or structures
      2. Vocabulary
   B. Sociocultural concepts to be stressed; e.g.,
      1. Usual time for meals
      2. Courtesy formulas at mealtime

III. Learning Experiences

   A. Warm-up (entire group)
   B. Pronunciation drill (entire group)
   C. Presentation of new material (entire group)
      1. Motivation
      2. Statement of aim
      3. Related review
      4. Oral presentation of model sentences by the teacher
      5. Repetition by the group, subgroups, and individuals

6. Generalization (a statement of the recurring feature of form, function, or meaning)
7. Oral Practice (all groups)
8. Group and Individual Work (as needed)

D. Dialogue presentation or dramatization (entire group)
E. Related activities (group and individual work); e.g., taking dictation, looking at projected materials, listening to tapes, role playing, participating in committee work, individualized work
F. Oral and (where possible) written summary of the lesson
G. Looking ahead to the next lesson

With Emphasis on Reading

I. General Aims

A. To develop the pupils' ability to read with comprehension, ease, and enjoyment
B. To guide the pupils in gaining knowledge of cultural facts through reading

II. Specific Aims

A. To give pupils a knowledge of language or cultural items found in the reading
B. To give practice (e.g., in finding details)

III. Learning Experiences

A. Warm-up (entire group)
B. Pronunciation practice (entire group)
C. Presentation of the new lesson
1. Motivation (relating the reading to students' experiences or to the longer story of which this lesson is a part)
2. Statement of aim
3. Clarification of new words, structures, or concepts
4. Oral reading by the teacher, followed by questions to

ensure comprehension and to find details (see p. 149 for technique)

5. Summary of the passage

D. Related activities, according to the pupils' ability and level; e.g., reading parts of the story in chorus after the teacher, formulating questions for classmates, taking a brief dictation, discussing the reading, preparing a dramatization, engaging in word-building activities—e.g., finding synonyms, antonyms, "family" words

E. Oral summary

F. Looking ahead to the next lesson

EXAMPLES OF UNITS OF WORK

These lesson plans are teacher-prepared. They are not found in any of the commercial materials currently available. For commercially prepared materials, consult the brochures of publishing companies, magazines, and bibliographies.

A Possible First Day*

(Beginners—Ages nine and above†)

Aims

Cultural: To teach patterns of identification and some greetings.

Linguistic: To teach form, function, and meaning of "My name's _____;" "Good morning;" "Good afternoon" followed by first or full names.

Materials needed

A list of pupils' names; a cardboard clock with movable hands; pictures of a man, a woman, a boy, a girl; chalk; name cards, to be pinned on children or placed on their desks.

Procedure

1. Greet the class: "Good morning."

2. Introduce yourself: "My name's Mr. (Mrs., Miss) _____." Point to yourself as you repeat several times, "My name's _____." Write your name *only* on the board.

3. Call a child's name. It is desirable to learn to say the children's names in their native language. Help him say his name preceded by "My name's _____" as he stands and presents himself. Give him his name card.

4. Follow this procedure with about ten children.

5. Put the first names of the children on the board in two columns. If you have a mixed class, label one column "boys" (with a simple stick figure) and the other "girls" (the stick figure of the girl can have a bow and a skirt).

---

* The time actually used in presenting the above lesson is thirty minutes.

† With younger children, all writing would be omitted and only steps 1 through 11 might be attempted.

6. If experience in your school and community has proved that children can be given their English names soon after they enter school, place the English equivalents (where these exist) next to the other name.

7. Give much repetitive practice in the names as preparation for the game "I'm Thinking of a Name" (see page 389 for the procedure.)

8. Play the game several times. It might be desirable to ask a native informant to give you the equivalent for the name of the game, but a hand to the head and a squint of the eyes usually gives the children the idea. Allow the pupils to give the first name. Indicate "yes" with a downward movement of the head and "no" with a shake of the head.

9. Show a morning scene. On the clock, point to the hour at which you greeted the children. Say, "Good morning." Greet several children whose names have been studied.

10. Dramatize the following dialogue with several pupils:

"Good morning. My name's Mr. (Mrs.) _____."
"Good morning. My name's John."

11. Have several pairs of students come to the front of the room and dramatize the dialogue.

12. Show an afternoon scene, perhaps some children leaving school as you point to the time of dismissal in your school on the clock. Introduce and give repetitive practice in "Good afternoon."

13. On the board, write two columns of hours: (1) 8, 9, 10, 11, 12; (2) 1, 2, 3, 4, 5.

14. Point to each of the numbers in the first column as you say, "Good morning." Have group, subgroups and individuals repeat.

15. Follow the same procedure for the afternoon hours.

16. Point to the numbers at random, give the appropriate greeting, and ask students to repeat after you.

17. Ask a student to come to the board, to point to a number, and to call on a student to give the greeting.

18. Dramatize the dialogue using "Good afternoon," first you with students, and then pairs of students.

19. Place four pictures of people on the ledge. Above each put a name: Mr. Jones, Mrs. Jones, John, Mary.

20. Engage in a substitution drill using "Good morning" with each of the names.

21. Engage in a substitution drill with "Good afternoon" and the names.

22. Play the game *"I'm Thinking of a Name"* again, including "Mr.," "Mrs.," and the first names.

An Intensive Lesson in Teaching Intonation*

BEGINNING LEVEL: ELEMENTARY AGE GROUP

Aims

1. To use falling inflection at the end of statements and question-word questions.

2. To use rising inflection at the end of inverted questions requiring a yes-or-no answer.

Motivation

Reference to previously learned poem: Yesterday we learned a poem about the people on the bus who went up and down. Let's say it together.

Statement of Aim

Today, let's learn when to make our voices go up and when to make them go down, especially at the ends of sentences.

Review

Previous learning is assumed.

1. What number is this: That's number one.
2. What color is this? That's red.

New Material

Language items and structure assumed to have been taught, although with no specific emphasis on intonation.

---

* Because of the time limitation and the nature of the lesson, little time was spent on actual practice. It was the teacher's goal to suggest possible formats for teaching intonation through a multiplicity of techniques. It was her opinion that intonation should be taught incidentally and integrated in Level I.

FALLING INTONATION

Numbers and notes refer to Miscellaneous Techniques, page 403.

1. What's this? It's a red balloon. (4)

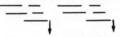

2. Where's the red balloon? There's the red balloon. (5)

3. Who has a red one? You have a red one.

OPTIONAL DRILL

4. Who has a red one? I/she/he (have/has) a red one.

5. How many are here? Six are here. How many are left? Five are left.

6. Which hand has the red balloon? The right hand has it.

INVERTED QUESTIONS: RISING INTONATION

1. May I have a balloon? Yes. (cat)
2. May he have a balloon? Yes. (7 ♪ ♪)
3. May she have a balloon? Yes. (8 ↗ ↘)
4. Is this a red balloon? Yes. (9 • • • • ♪)
5. This is red. Is it red? (thumb-finger)
6. I have a balloon. Do you have a balloon? Does she? Does he? (10—stair steps)
7. Who am I? Am I a red balloon? (10 ＼ ／)
8. Who is he? Is he a red balloon? (elbow-arm)
9. Who is she? Is she a red balloon? (head nod)
10. Who are you? Are you a red balloon? (body)

Miscellaneous Techniques
for Teaching Intonation

1. Vocal imitation, one of the best methods

2. Use of tape recorder—enables student to evaluate imitation

3. Use of the piano

4. Use of the harmonica, pitch pipe

5. Use of Klinghardt's System, alone or underneath phrase

   • • ， ♪

6. Use of Klinghardt's System, charted according to pitch levels.

   •
   •
   Dogs often bark.   •   ，

7. Showing position of words going down or up

   Dogs

   often

   bark.

8. Use of dashes

   —

   ‑‑

   —

* I am grateful to Miss Audrey Hayes, Language Arts Coordinator, New York City Board of Education, for permission to reproduce these techniques and this lesson. (The lesson was presented originally in my course entitled "Teaching English as a Second Language" at Hunter College.)

9. Stressed syllables capitalized and charted

DOG

The   often

BARKED.

10. Use of stairsteps diagram

11. Markings such as ⌒ rising; ⌍ falling; ⌒⌣ both

12. Numbers for levels with lines 1-4 2

13. Use of musical staff (for rhythm, too)

14. Arm, hand, or thumb movement up or down

15. Arrows rising ↑ ; falling ↓ ; variation ↗ ↘ ↩

16. Use of symbols such as ✍ rising, ✎ falling; ᷆ ᷇ circumflex; ⟞⟝ level

17. Rabbit puppet with ears rising or falling

18. Cat model with tail rising or falling

19. Use of mountain or hill with train or car going uphill or downhill

20. Plane taking off or landing (cutting motor)

A Lesson For Younger Children*

Level: Beginning (Kindergarten)
Curriculum Area: Language Arts
Lesson Topic: Introducing a Flannel-Board Story (*The Little Red Hen*)

Aims

TEACHER'S

1. To tell a flannel-board story.
2. To develop language through oral communication.
3. To provide an experience in listening for the purpose of sequential recall.
4. To use the structures "I won't" and "I will."

CHILDREN'S

1. To listen carefully so as to be able to retell parts of the story in sequence and to answer questions based on the story.
2. To enjoy themselves.

Materials Used

1. Flannel board
2. Cut-out, flannel-backed figures
3. Stick puppets

* Slightly adapted version of a demonstration lesson presented by Miss Lorraine Schulman, a teacher in the New York City schools, in the author's course.

Procedure

1. Based on previous experiences of planting and on current unit—The Wind.

2. "We have learned that the wind does many things. One of the things it does is blow the seeds from one place to another. What would you do if you found a seed blown by the wind?" (Plant it.)

"I know a story about the Little Red Hen who found some wheat seeds. Let's listen to find out what she does with the seeds and all the things that happen afterward."

1. Tell the story with the use of the flannel figures. The children join in on the repetitive responses (e.g., I won't).

1. Initiate *group* response to the following questions:
   a. What did the animals say every time the Little Red Hen asked them to help her with the work? (I won't.)
   b. What did they say when she asked, "Who will help me eat the bread?" (I will.)

2. Initiate individual language pattern responses and sequential recall by asking questions pertaining to sequence. For example:

   What did the Little Red Hen do with the seeds? What happened next? Children holding animal hand puppets (replicas of animals in the story) answer using language pattern responses.

3. Were the Little Red Hen's friends nice or not very nice? Why?

Evaluation

TEACHER'S

1. Note ability to respond sequentially.

CHILDREN'S

1. Did we answer the question of what the Little Red Hen did with the seeds?

2. Do we remember what happened afterwards?

Homework

Think about the story. We'll act it out tomorrow.

Follow-up

1. Reread the story. Elicit oral group and individual responses.

2. Dramatize the story and eventually adapt the story to other situations.

Teaching the Concepts of Big and Small to Kindergarten Children*

Motivation

"Yesterday we learned a poem that we liked very much. You listen while I say it first." (Teacher recites and gestures.)

> I'm big, I'm very big
> I'm small, I'm very small
> Sometimes I'm big
> Sometimes I'm small
> Guess what I am now?

"Let's all do it together. Everyone stand." (Repeat song play with gestures.)

Statement of Aim

"Today, children, we're going to learn more about what is big and what is small, and then we're going to have fun playing a game."

Review Basic Vocabulary

"I have some things I think you'd like to look at. Let's see if we remember their names. What do I have? I have a _____." (Hold up objects: ball, flower, car. Individual children respond.)

* Slight adaptation of demonstration lesson given by Mrs. Carole Cannechia, a teacher in the New York City schools, in the author's graduate course.

Oral Presentation

"Everyone watch me." Teacher holds up a big ball and a small ball. "Look. I have a big ball. I have a small ball." "Let's pretend we have a big ball and a small ball. Let's all do that together. Now the girls will say it. Now the boys will say it. You say it, Caroline. Now you say it, Tom." Use similar procedure for:

I have a big flower.
I have a small flower.
I have a big car.
I have a small car.

Teacher then holds up objects and asks individuals to frame the question. "What do you have?" The teacher will answer, "I have a big flower."

Practice: Picture Identification and a Game

"Now children, we're going to look at some picture cards." Cards are on blackboard ledge. "Who will show us the big car? What do you have, Tom?" Proceed with all pictures in similar fashion.

"Now we are ready to play our game. It's called the fishing game. This is a fish. Let's say 'fish.' " Choral repetition. "This is our pond, and we're going to put all our pictures in the pond. This is our fishing pole. Let's say 'fishing pole.' " Choral repetition. "We must fish for a picture and tell what we have. I'll be the first fisherman. Oh, look. I have a _____. If you say the right name you may keep the picture. If you don't, you have to put the picture back into the pond. Who would like to be our next fisherman?" Proceed with game.

A Lesson for Younger Children Arising out of a Center of Activity

Bathing a Baby in the Housekeeping Corner

Materials Needed

Doll, tub, water, towel, soap, washcloth, baby powder, clothes, clothesline

Demonstration by the Teacher

"I'm going to bathe our baby. Let's see. What do I need? I need water, soap, a tub, a washcloth, and a towel." (As the teacher touches each, she has the children repeat the words several times.)

The teacher tells the class what she is doing as she performs each action. "I'm putting water in the tub. Now, I'm taking the clothes off the baby."

When she has gone through the process once or twice, she may say, "Do you want to bathe the baby now?"

The teacher will capitalize on the pupils' enthusiasm by saying, "We should learn all our new words carefully before we start."

In the recommended manner, the teacher develops the words "water," "soap," "towel," "tub," etc. (Substitution and question-answer drills follow.)

The teacher calls on individuals and requests them to "Put water in the tub." "Get the soap." As the pupils dramatize the action, she teaches each to say, "I'm putting water in the tub." "I'm getting the soap."

A number of the pupils are given the opportunity to dramatize the situation. Each pupil gives one sentence to describe the action he is performing.

As a summary, an experience chart can be written by the teacher with sentences suggested by the pupils. Pictures of soap, towel, etc., can be used to illustrate the appropriate sentences on the chart.

As a follow-up, children can be asked to describe what their classmates are doing as these perform the actions; e.g., "She's getting a towel."

A Lesson on Structure

(Time: thirty minutes)

(Intermediate Level—Ages twelve and above)

Aim

To teach the form, function, and meaning of "if" sentences with "Be" and "Have."

Materials Needed

A picture of various kinds of fruit, a picture series with "count" nouns, an empty purse, a picture series with "mass" nouns.

Motivation

Tell the students that you passed a fruit store on _____ Street (naming a street near school) and that they had beautiful fruit. Ask the children if they like fruit; what their favorite fruit is. Show them some apples. Say that you love apples and you want to buy them when you leave school but you have no money. Show the empty purse.

Presentation of New Structure: I

1. "I have no money. If I had money, I'd buy the apples." Repeat the "if" sentence several times.

2. Repetition of the model sentence (whole class, subgroups, individuals).

3. Study of the model sentence, which you will place on the board; e.g., "Do I have the money? Notice the word 'if.'" Box *if*. Underline *had*. Ask from which word it comes; what form it is. Underline *I'd*. "What is the full form of 'I'd'?"

4. (Optional) Indicate that the sentence could start with "I'd." Give practice in the sentence.

Practice of the New Structure:

1. "Let's practice sentences like these with other words." Review the vocabulary items. "I'll give you another word, and you'll put it in place of 'apples.'" Conduct a substitution drill with known words; e.g., cake, meat, grapes, books.

2. "Sometimes we have the money but we don't have time. Let's use the word 'time' instead of 'money' in the sentences we'll make with these pictures." Substitution drill: pen, pencil, ruler, book, notebook, box.

3. Replacement Drill: "Now let's talk about other people. We'll use other words instead of 'I.' If he had time, he'd buy the pen." Use He, Mr. Smith, the boys, the children, the girls, our friends, etc.

4. Transformation Drill: (with picture series of *pen,* etc.). E.g., I'd buy a pen, if I had money. What about him? He'd buy a pen, too.

Oral Presentation: II

"Very good. We've used a form of 'have' in all these sentences." Point to "had." "Now let's practice sentences with a form of 'be.' Look. Listen." Show picture. "If I were thirsty, I'd drink water."

5. Practice of sentences with "were."

    a. REPLACEMENT DRILL: The same sentence with *he, she, they, the boys, the girls,* etc.

    b. SUBSTITUTION DRILL: "If I were hungry, I'd eat cake." (Meat, bread, fruit.) Show picture series.

"Freer" Practice

1. Question-Answer: "What would you buy if you had time?" Teacher asks questions pointing to things on either of the picture charts. Individual students answer, "I'd buy a _____."

2. "Choose one or the other. If you had money, would you buy a pen or a pencil? If you were hungry, would you eat bread or fruit?"

3. Add-on Game: "What would you buy if you had a thousand dollars?" The first student gives an answer. The second says that he would buy that and something else. The third student adds to the sentence of the second student, etc.

A Suggested Plan for a Unit
on the Library

(Age Group—ten and above: Intermediate Level)

Note: This brief unit will again illustrate some of the possibilities of integration inherent in any of the topics found in Chapter 2. Three lessons are outlined here, but the teacher may wish to telescope or expand the material suggested, depending upon the time at his disposal and other factors.

The unit is divided into three sections. In each of the three the focus of attention will be on one of the major aspects of language study. The first will emphasize the oral development of new concepts and of new structural patterns. The second will be devoted to studying a reading selection that places the new vocabulary and some of the patterns in a functional language activity. The third will select a grammatical item for further development and more intensive study.

There will be overlapping, of course. Some teachers may prefer to place the lesson for structural emphasis during the second third of the unit, leaving the reading as the culminating activity of the entire unit. Others, as is done in this plan, will treat the items in the reading as "recognitional" items and then teach them intensively, since the functional reading exercise has "readied" pupils for the more active grammatical emphasis. Skill and experience will tell the teacher what is best in his situation after he has tried both approaches a number of times.

415

The reading selection found in the second lesson is offered solely as a suggestion. Where books are available, the teacher may not find it necessary to prepare his own reading selections but will present a related story from a reader in the manner suggested under Reading on pages 149 and 150.

Please evaluate and adapt this material. It is suggestive, not prescriptive.

FIRST SESSION (EMPHASIS ON ORAL DEVELOPMENT)

Teacher Preparation

1. Arrange to take the class to the school library or the public library.

2. Notify the librarian of your visit so that she may prepare material or a guided tour.

3. Get copies of library cards and index cards.

4. Prepare oaktag labels—Sports, Adventure, Science, etc., for your library corner.

5. Prepare flashcards with such words as *dictionary* and with verb forms such as *I went, he found, she said,* etc. (found in the lesson).

Steps in Development

APPROACH

Oral class discussion—The teacher elicits responses to the following comments and questions (language errors, except glaring ones, should be ignored during this step):

There are many books on the table and shelves at the side of our room. What do we call the section where we keep our books?

Who can read the labels over each set of books?

Can you tell our class where the public library is in our community?

Are any of you members of the public library?

What books do you find in the public library?

How has the library helped you? (research, enjoyment, information)

ORAL PRESENTATION BY TEACHER

(Remember to speak at normal tempo but in simple sentences. The pupils may understand much more than they can say themselves.)

Importance of the library

Its location in the community

Borrowing facilities

Types of materials found in it for: leisure-time reading; research and information

STATEMENT OF AIM

"Today we're going to look at some books in which we can find information." You may want to place this aim on the board —"Books for Information."

ORAL DEVELOPMENT OF VOCABULARY

"This is a dictionary. Let's all say 'dictionary.' " (Method of presentation of *each* item follows as always, *hear, say, see, do*; see page 111.)

This is the encyclopedia.

This is the *Book of Knowledge.*

This is the *World Almanac.*

This is *Who's Who.*

ORAL PRACTICE

"Show us the dictionary." Teacher asks pupil; then pupil asks teacher; then pupil asks other pupil.

"Point to the *World Almanac,*" etc.

After sufficient practice has been given on the new words, the teacher will give or attempt to elicit some basic information about each of the books above; for example, "Let's look at the dictionary. What do we find in it?"

ORAL DEVELOPMENT OF NEW CONCEPTS AND STRUCTURES

"We find the *meanings* of words in a dictionary. Let's all say 'meanings.' "

"We find the *pronunciation* of words in a dictionary. Let's all say 'pronunciation.' "

(Under the word *dictionary* on the board, the teacher will write: "Meanings," "Pronunciation.")

ORAL AND WRITTEN PRACTICE

1. Questions such as:

    What do we find in the dictionary?
    In which book do we find meanings?

    (These two question patterns may be selected for practice in this situation.)

2. Let us complete these sentences:

    a. The book corner in our room is called the _____ corner.
    b. We can _____ books from the library.
    c. We look up words in a _____.
    d. We look at _____ _____ to find out about the life of an important person.
    e. We look at _____ to get information about a recent event.

3. Please copy the sentences.

SUMMARY

1. "What did we learn today?" (This is still an excellent way of summarizing if pupils have reached a fair level of competency.)

    and/or

2. Questions such as:

    Where is the library in our community?
    Who may belong to the library?
    For how long may books be borrowed?
    Can you name two types of books we may find in the library?
    Can you tell us the names of two books in which we find information?
    In which book do we find the pronunciation of a word?

Second Session (Emphasis on Reading)

Approach

Teacher recalls yesterday's lesson or the visit to the library. "Yesterday we learned about books of information that we may find in the library. Can you tell us what they are?" (Pupil response.)

Statement of Aim

"Today we're going to read a story about a boy and his parents who joined the library. They wanted to take part in community activities."

Clearing of Difficulties

"But before we start reading, let's look at (study) some of the words we're going to find in the story. There are many words you know already. Let's review them together." (These words may be placed on the board *before* the lesson.)

1. to know
2. the opportunity
3. to join
4. to prepare
5. to make sure of
6. to take out
7. to have to
8. fortunately
9. of course

"There are other words and expressions in the story that we need to learn." Teach these five at a time.

1. to take advantage of
2. wonderful
3. the research
4. the costume
5. the detail
6. so
7. the librarian
8. the bill
9. large
10. foreign

(These words are first modeled, then repeated in chorus and explained through pictures, realia, etc.)

Oral Reading and Questions by the Teacher

The word study, reading, and questions may be divided into two or three sections depending on pupils' interest and ability.

"Now let's read the story. I'll read one or two sentences and ask you a question. Please listen carefully. Our friend Juan is telling the story."

1. Last week, Mother, Father, and I joined the community center. (Teacher's question: "Who joined the community center?" Possible response: "Juan, his mother, and his father.")

2. Mother joined the sewing class, Father joined the musical group, and I joined the arts and crafts group.

3. The community center is preparing a Spanish fiesta. Mother's class is preparing the costumes for it.

4. Mother wants to make real Spanish costumes for my sister Maria and for me. Maria is going to be a gypsy dancer and I am going to be a toreador.

5. Mother wanted to see some costumes. So we went to the public library near the school.

6. At the desk, we asked, "Do you have books on Spanish costumes?"

7. The librarian said, "Of course, we have a good collection of books on Spain."

8. She showed us the section of Spanish books. Mother looked through a few books. The librarian asked, "Did you find what you wanted?"

9. Mother said, "Yes, thank you very much. I found an excellent book on Spanish costumes. May I take the book out of the library?"

10. The librarian told Mother that she had to join the library. She wanted to see some paper of identification, a letter or a bill.

11. Fortunately, Mother had a gas bill. She filled out a card. I filled out another card.

12. Before going home, we looked at the different sections of the library.

13. There were sections on sports, on travel, and on science. There were biographies. There were adventure stories.

14. There was a large section of books in Spanish, in Italian, and in other languages.

Summary

Individual pupils give a summary in sequence or the teacher asks questions to elicit a *sequential summary.*

Practice: Oral and Written

1. Complete the expression in Column A with the correct expression in Column B.

A	B
1) Mother joined	a) the arts and crafts group.
2) We have a good collection	b) a gypsy dancer.
3) The community center is preparing	c) a library card.
4) The librarian wanted to see	d) the sewing class.
5) Juan is in	e) some paper of identification.
6) I filled out	f) of books on Spain.
7) Maria is going to be	g) a Spanish fiesta.

2. Complete each sentence. Copy it. (Do this exercise orally first.)

a. Last week we _____ the community center.

b. The community center _____ a Spanish fiesta.

c. Mother wanted to _____ a real Spanish costume for Maria.

d. We _____ to join the library.

e. We _____, "Do you have books on Spanish costumes?"

Supplementary Exercises (for the less able group)

1. Copy the following groups of words and cross out the word in each group that does not belong.

a. library, book, bill

b. dictionary, sports, *Book of Knowledge, Who's Who*

c. music, fiesta, clay, dancing

    d. songs, ceramics, musical instrument

    e. painting, easel, librarian, artist

2. Tell the things you must do to become a member of the library.

Supplementary Exercise (*for the more able group*)

Answer the following questions in complete sentences:

    a. What is the community center preparing?

    b. What is Juan's mother preparing?

    c. What does his mother wish to make?

    d. Why did Juan and his mother go to the library?

    e. What did they ask at the desk?

Restatement or Summary

1. Why is a library important?

2. Name four books in which you may find useful information.

3. How can you join the library?

4. How did Juan's family use the library?

Assignment

Groups A and B

    Go to the library. Ask the librarian for the names of other books of general information.

Group B (more able group)

    In the encyclopedia look up the life of _____. Write ten lines about him.

THIRD SESSION (LANGUAGE EMPHASIS)

Approach

If in a previous lesson the teacher has taught the past tense ending in *ed* (all three sounds), he may ask questions such as:

"Why did you join the community center?"

The answers elicited are placed on the blackboard by an able student or by the teacher.

Connection with Previous Knowledge

Individual pupils may be asked to give the other pronouns, *you, we, they, he, she,* with each sentence on the board. *One* verb—with all the pronouns—is placed at the board by an able student. The teacher underlines the *ed* endings and asks questions such as: "When do we add the *d* sound?" "What two letters did we add to *each* action word?" "Are we talking about something that is happening *now?*" The teacher elicits the fact that the *d* sound is added to an action word or verb when we are talking about something that happened in the past (*yesterday* or *last week* or *this morning*).

Transition to New Development

"Now let's look at these sentences (or now listen to this sentence) in our story. Juan says, 'I went to the library *yesterday.*' Later he says, 'I found the books.' "

Statement of Aim

"Today we're going to learn to use words like I *went* or Juan *went* and I *found* or Juan *found.*"

Development

"Listen carefully—'Juan went to the library yesterday.' "
Choral and individual repetition: "Juan went to the library yesterday."
The teacher writes the sentence on the board. It is repeated again in unison and by several individuals. The teacher asks, "Where did Juan go yesterday?" while she points to the correct response. Pupils answer, "Juan went to the library yesterday." (Notice that we elicit the complete response here to give practice in the verb.)
The teacher now asks, "When did Juan go to the library?"

and points to the answer, which pupils repeat in chorus and individually.

The teacher then asks that pupils change *Juan* to *he* (if the substitution had not been made automatically by the students). This form with "he" is written on the board in the center (so that *I* and *you* as developed can be written above it).

When *I*, *you*, and *he* have been developed the teacher elicits that *went* is used as the past of *go*. He may say, "Notice that I said, 'When *did* Juan go to the library?' In our answer we said, 'Juan *went* or he *went*.'"

"Let's talk about *you*." Engage in a substitution drill:

I went to the park (cafeteria, gym, movies, etc.)

After this medial drill, the other pronouns are developed. These are written by the teacher or by an able student *above* and *beneath* "he went" so that pupils observe that the action word remains the same. (*I, you, we, they,* above; *she,* below)

Generalization

The teacher elicits that this is not a *regular* action word (which adds [d], [t], or [id]); that it is the past of "go"; that it is used with yesterday, etc.; and that the word "went" does not change with any of the pronouns.

Practice

1. Substitution drill changing "yesterday" to "last week," "last Monday," etc., and *retaining* "library."

2. Replacement drill with "went" using *all* subject pronouns, *using one noun only*: "I went to the library yesterday. You went to the library yesterday."

3. Questions by the teacher: "When did the boys go to the library?" "When did he go to the library?" "When did Harry go to the park?" "Where did they go yesterday?" "Where did you go yesterday?"

Summary

Questions by the teacher to elicit the facts within the generalization but not the generalization itself.

Connection with Future Lessons

Other "irregular" past forms such as *said* and *found* can be developed easily in functional situations either later during that same session or during another session, by reminding the pupils of *went,* and indicating that there are other verbs which do not form the past by adding a [d], [t], or [id] ending.

Adapted Version* of
The Pied Piper of Hamelin

(*A Brief Unit of Work for Grades Seven or Eight—*
Intermediate Level)

Far away in Germany, there was a little village. The name of
the little village was Hamelin. The little village of Hamelin
was next to a large river. Everyone in the village loved the river.

Many years ago, the little village was filled with rats. There
were all kinds of rats. Some of the rats were very big; some
were small; some were fat and some were thin. Big and little
rats filled the village. The people of the village tried to kill the
rats but there were too many of them. So they went to the mayor.
The mayor wouldn't listen to them. The mayor told the villagers
to go out and kill the rats.

A little man heard of the rats. He told the mayor he would
take all the rats out of the village for $500. The people said,
"Pay him so that we won't have any more rats." The mayor
promised to pay him.

The little man went out into the street. He blew a little horn.
All the rats came out to listen. Each time he blew the horn more
rats came out to listen. Soon the village streets were filled with
rats. The people hid in the houses. When the little man walked
down the street blowing the horn, the rats followed him. The

* Prepared by three students in the author's course: Sister Casella, Grace
Gonzales, Vicki Jaffee.

man walked into the river. The rats went after him and they were all drowned. The little man stopped blowing his horn.

He went to get his $500 but the mayor would not pay him. He laughed at him instead. So the little man took out the horn and began to blow. This time no rats came but all the children came. There were big children, little children, fat and thin children. All were happy when they heard the little horn. They followed the man while he blew the horn. He went over the hill. The children went over the hill after him. The man and the children walked far away from the village. The people could not see them any more. All the mothers and fathers cried out but they never saw their children again. The man with the horn never came back to Hamelin.

Long-Range Aims

1. To help children develop the ability to read and enjoy this story.
2. To help them develop a sense of social significance and of moral obligation.
3. To increase reading comprehension in English.
4. To stimulate an appreciation for English literature.

Short-Range Aims

1. To teach unfamiliar vocabulary and concepts found in the story.
2. To practice the language patterns involved.
3. To help children develop greater confidence in their reading ability.
4. To help children perceive the relationships between the aural, oral and reading skills.

FIRST SESSION

Motivation

1. Write the word "promise" on the board.
2. Ask, "Who can tell us what this word means?"

3. Call on several children in order to elicit from them the meaning best suited to the word.

4. Discuss "a broken promise." "Has anyone broken a promise to you? How would you feel if someone promised you a gift and then forgot or didn't bother to keep the promise?" Ask several individuals.

Statement of Aim

1. After some discussion on the above point, say, "We're going to read a story about a broken promise. The name of the story is 'The Pied Piper of Hamelin.' "

2. Write the title on the board.

3. Repeat the name "The Pied Piper of Hamelin."

4. Show a picture of the "pied piper." Tell them that Hamelin is a village in Germany.

5. Show Germany on the map.

Related Review

1. "Here on the board, children, are two lists of words. The list to the left is a list of words we learned in our last lesson. Let's go over them because we're going to find them in our new story."

little	small	fat	big
street	away	rat	thin
mother	father	great	happy

2. Call on children to make sentences to ascertain whether they can use the words effectively.

3. Give brief practice on synonyms, antonyms, etc., from the review. Also use such questions as: "Do you live in a street or on an avenue?" "In a city or in a town?" "Is there a river near your house?" etc., etc.

Oral Presentation of New Material

1. After the brief review, point to the list of new words and say, "Here are some of the important words we must know for our new story."

2. "Say them after me." Teach the words in groups of five. Point to each word, pronounce it, and have students repeat them chorally.

village	everyone	mayor
river	loved	short-tailed
Hamelin	people	long-tailed
wouldn't	kill	$500
rats	Germany	villagers

3. After each word has been carefully repeated, give a sentence, and show an appropriate picture where feasible, in order to clarify its meaning. These are a few sample sentences.

    a. A *city* has many *big* houses, but a *village* is *small* with just a few small houses.

    b. *Hamelin* is a *village* in *Germany.*

    c. *Hamelin* is near a *river.* This is a river. A river is a stream of *water* where boats sail or boys go to swim or fish.

    d. *Villagers* are the *people* who live in a *village.*

    e. *Everyone* means *each* person.

    f. *Everyone* in *Hamelin loved* the *river.*

    g. This is a rat. A *rat* has a *long tail.*

    h. Some *rats* are *long-tailed.* Look. This is a long-tailed rat.

    i. Some *rats* are *short-tailed.* Look.

4. After all the sentences have been presented and drilled orally, have several children give a word and use it in a sentence orally.

5. All the children should copy the new words into their notebooks under the title of the story.

Homework

Each child is to write each word learned in an original sentence, underlining the word listed in the new vocabulary.

Summary

1. Quickly repeat each word and the title of the story. If necessary repeat one or two definitions.

2. In order to summarize the discussion, return to the idea presented in the motivation. "I promise that we'll start to read the story in tomorrow's lesson. But you must know the new words so you can understand the story. Please study hard so you can help me keep my promise."

SECOND SESSION

Motivation

1. After they have given them orally, have several children write one or two of their homework sentences on the board. Designate the word to be used by each.

2. Correct the sentences with the entire class.

3. Then have the pupils read the sentences first chorally then individually *after* you.

4. Review the discussion of the preceding lesson.

5. Discuss the fact that the story took place a long time ago.

Procedure (This will be an "extensive" reading lesson.)

1. Distribute copies of the story.

2. Read the first three paragraphs aloud.

3. Ask questions such as: "Where does the story take place?" "Where is Hamelin?" "Where is Germany?" "Who can point it out on the map?" "What is it near?"

4. Present a picture of a river with a bordering village. Have them discuss the picture. Have them point out several things they recognize. Show a picture of rats. Ask the children to find sentences in the story in which the word "rat" appears. Ask questions such as, "Why do people hate rats?" "Why did the villagers of Hamelin want to get rid of them?" "What is a mayor?" "Why did the villagers go to him?" "What was their problem?" "Find as many words as you can that describe or tell about the rats."

5. "Now let us read on and see what happened to the rats." Read aloud to the class the next three paragraphs.

6. Reread the paragraphs and have pupils read chorally after

you. Then they may be asked to reread them silently in order to find answers to these questions (written on the board).

Who came to Hamelin?
Why did he come?
What pay does he expect?
Do you think it is a fair price? Why?
Who promised to pay?
What did the Pied Piper do then?
Why did the rats follow the piper?
What happened to all the rats?
Did the Piper keep his promise?
Did the mayor?

Summary

1. "Who can tell me what has happened so far in the story?" Have several children give one or more sentences each.

2. Ask children to make a list of important words used so far in the story.

3. Have children tell what part of the story these words tell about.

Homework

Write ten sentences about the story in correct order. Leave a blank space into which may be written an important word used in this story.

THIRD SESSION

Motivation

1. Have a pupil go to the front of the room, read the sentence he had prepared, clapping his hands in place of the missing word. Another child will be called on to give the word.

2. When all sentence and vocabulary review is completed, show a picture of the rats running from the building and another of the children following the Piper.

Procedure (This portion is also treated "extensively.")

1. "How many know why the children are running?" Let's read to find out.

2. Read several paragraphs orally.

3. Have all the children read the last three paragraphs in chorus, after you.

4. Ask the following questions:
   a. Who can tell us what happened when the Piper went for his pay?
   b. Had the Piper kept his promise?
   c. Did the mayor keep his promise?
   d. Which one do you think was right?
   e. Why was the Piper angry?
   f. What did he do to punish the mayor?
   g. Why is it wrong to break a promise?

Summary

1. "What lesson have we learned from 'The Pied Piper of Hamelin'?"

2. "Why should boys and girls keep a promise they make?"

3. "Tell why you think this is a good story to know and to tell."

4. "Write a short story in your own words in your notebook about the Piper of Hamelin."

Homework

"Draw a pencil sketch of one of the scenes that impressed you most in the story. Be original. Make the picture simple and direct. Give it a name."

Evaluation

The writing of sentences from dictation could help determine:
1. Increased knowledge of word forms and structures.
2. Reading comprehension.
3. Content retention.

4. Vocabulary growth.

The aural-oral responses to questions regarding the broken promise could help determine:

1. The value of teaching stories containing a moral.

2. The increased awareness on the part of the children of social or moral obligation.

3. The sense of justice and fair play inculcated by the story.

4. Growth in language ability.

CHAPTER 25

Materials for Supervisors and Teachers

A Course of Study for Older Illiterates

The course of study presented below is intended for the completely illiterate or the functionally illiterate, older student. It is assumed that he is functionally illiterate in both his native tongue and English.

It is unreasonable to expect that the majority of such students who have not had the benefit of schooling beyond the fourth grade—if that—can enter an eighth- or ninth-grade class and achieve any measure of success without a special program.

Many of these students will remain in school only while a compulsory education law forces them to do so. Many will go directly from the classroom to employment and later to marriage and parenthood. Schools have a responsibility to help these students meet situations they will face. They have a responsibility also to the community in which these students will make their homes.

The school program, which may, unfortunately, become a terminal program for many of the students, should concentrate on preparing them for their responsibilities as parents, consumers, and participating citizens. Therefore, much of the knowledge the student will need will have to be given in their *native language* by a sympathetic, bilingual teacher.

It is proposed that these students be given an intensive course in English for about two hours a day and an intensive course in their native tongue for two hours a day. The rest of the school day should be spent in joint activities with English-speaking students. The content in both the English and the native language should be designed to give the students the *fundamental* skills of listening, speaking, reading, and writing within vocabulary areas they will need (1) to find employment; (2) to become intelligent consumers; (3) to fulfill their role as parents; (4) to assume some civic responsibility. The English and native language courses should complement and reinforce each other. The important aspect of "self-realization" should not be neglected. While students will undoubtedly develop a sense of pride as they learn to read and write their native tongue, this feeling can be enhanced through programing them in music, art, shops, film, and physical education periods with other students in the school.

Although the course may be terminal for some, it is hoped that others will continue their education at a later date as they become aware of the advantages of further schooling. This will only be possible if a special program and a sympathetic teaching and administrative staff lay a good foundation in English and the native tongue and foster in each student the desire to take advantage of the greater opportunities which schooling can offer.

It is recommended that emphasis in the program be on understanding and speaking. However, as much reading and writing should be done as students are capable of doing. In English, reading of important signs, numbers, abbreviations, and simple employment, housing, or welfare forms should also be emphasized. Writing should begin with material needed for self-identification (name, address, social security number, names of family members, etc.).

Instead of switching constantly from English to the native language, it may be desirable to give material in English for two hours and then similar material in the native language. Some knowledge, e.g., consumer education (the preparation of budgets, cautions re installment buying, etc.) may best be given in the native language. There should be no set formula. More than ever, the factors in the student and community mentioned in Chapter 1 and which play a part in learning and teaching should be considered in developing topics, in allocating time, or in determining the language to be used for any activity.

POSSIBLE TOPICS TO BE TAUGHT (ENGLISH AND THE NATIVE LANGUAGE)

1. Self-Identification and Orientation (see page 31)
2. Community Living (see page 32)
   Emphasis should be on:

> Shopping for Food and Clothing
> Transportation
> Health Services
> Getting Things Done
> Communication

3. Employment Opportunities and Qualifications Needed
   Wages, social security, union membership, hours, responsibilities, taxes, safety rules.

SAMPLE PATTERNS FOR IMMEDIATE USE (ORAL MATERIAL IN ENGLISH, WITH NATIVE-LANGUAGE EQUIVALENTS)
   (*Possible responses* to questions must also be practiced.)

Emergency Needs

1. My name is _____.
2. I live at _____.
3. I need a doctor.
4. I need a policeman.
5. I need an ambulance.
6. I need a (priest, rabbi, minister, etc.).
7. Where is the clinic?
8. Where is the hospital?

9. Where is the police station?
10. Where is the post office?

Shopping

1. How much is _____?
2. Do you sell _____?
3. Where can I buy _____?
4. Please give me _____.
5. (A pound, a can, a jar, a bunch, etc.)

Transportation

1. How do I get to _____?
2. Where is _____?
3. Does this (bus) go to _____?
4. Do I have to change?

Consumer Services

1. Where can I get my hair cut?
2. Where can I get my laundry washed?
3. Where can I get my shoes fixed?

READING

1. Signs such as *Uptown, Downtown, Danger, Ladies, Gentlemen, Keep Out, Do not enter, Walk, Don't Walk.*
2. Simple housing, employment forms; post office and banking forms.
3. Signs in supermarkets.
4. Advertisements and other pertinent information in newspapers (employment, housing, TV and radio programs, recreational opportunities).
5. Safety rules (in school shops and various jobs).

WRITING

1. Self-identification.
2. Address.
3. Names of family members.

SYSTEMATIC TEACHING OF

Reading

1. Recognition of letters and words (see page 140).
2. Gradual growth of vocabulary needed for vocational and civic responsibilities.
3. Learning to recognize prefixes, suffixes, compounds.
4. Developing comprehension, e.g., instructions for drivers and road signs.

Writing

1. Printing.
2. Cursive writing (e.g., signature).
3. Pattern sentences.
4. Simple letters (needed to request services, to buy something, to explain absence, to ask for certificates).

Mathematics

1. Basic processes of addition, subtraction, multiplication, and division.
2. Knowledge of measures and weights (English equivalent of kilometers, kilograms, etc., where pertinent).
3. Reading timetables, simple graphs, charts, roadmaps.
4. Simple fractions.
5. Reading recipes, descriptions of processes.
6. Preparing a family budget (per cent for rent, clothing, food, recreation).
7. Interest rates, installment buying, saving.

Social Studies (Citizenship)

1. The contribution of various ethnic groups to the life of the community and country.
2. The rights of citizens.
3. The responsibility of citizens.
4. Geography of the community.

5. Industry and trades in the immediate and wider community.

Science and Health Concepts

1. Weather, clothing.
2. Electricity.
3. Repairing things at home (including cautions).
4. Health and Hygiene
   a. Illness, e.g., how to prevent it, what to do about it, calling a doctor, medicines to be kept at home.
   b. Care of teeth.
   c. Nutrition.
   d. Fire prevention.
5. Facts versus superstition.

Art, Music, Physical Education

Both for personal, creative expression and for audience participation.

Shorter Observation Checklist

	Poor	Fair	Good	Superior
The Lesson				
Aims	____	____	____	____
Achievement of aims	____	____	____	____
Motivation	____	____	____	____
Utilization of pupils' experiences	____	____	____	____
Clarity of presentation	____	____	____	____
Sequential development of lesson	____	____	____	____
Teacher modeling of new material	____	____	____	____
Use of gestures to elicit varied pupil participation	____	____	____	____
Variety of practice activities	____	____	____	____
Skill in questioning	____	____	____	____
Skill in dealing with answers	____	____	____	____

	Poor	Fair	Good	Superior
Use of teaching aids	___	___	___	___
Ability to maintain interest	___	___	___	___
Summary of lesson	___	___	___	___
The Pupils				
Extent of participation	___	___	___	___
Quality of participation	___	___	___	___
Social interaction	___	___	___	___
The Teacher				
Personal fitness: personality, vitality, speech, knowledge	___	___	___	___
Ability to establish rapport	___	___	___	___
Pronunciation and use of English	___	___	___	___
Classroom management (grouping)	___	___	___	___
Attention to routines	___	___	___	___
Comments				

Longer Observation Checklist

Teacher

Date

Major teaching activity (presentation of structure, dialogue,
  reading)

Teaching level (beginning, intermediate, advanced)

Materials used and purpose (blackboard, real objects, pictures,
  pocket chart, flannel board, etc.)

THE TEACHER

  A. Personality

  B. Manner

  C. Sensitivity to students (overcriticism, reasonable praise,
etc.)

  D. Voice (clear, audible, well-modulated, etc.)

  E. Appearance (appropriately dressed, well-groomed)

  F. Scholarship (ability to answer questions or to introduce
and explain linguistic, literary, or cultural allusions)

  G. Questioning Ability

   1. Asks questions of all students, then calls one by name

   2. Calls on volunteers

   3. Calls on nonvolunteers

   4. Varies types of question (yes-no, multiple choice, full
      answer, short answer, cued response)

   5. Avoids choral response to questions

6. Asks appropriate, logical questions (e.g., does not ask a child, "Do you like your job?")
7. Does not repeat answers except when necessary to give a correct model
8. Provides opportunities for students to question him and to question each other

H. Skill in using gestures and instructional materials

THE LESSON

A. Is the aim clear to students? How is it made clear (stated by teacher, written on blackboard)? Is it logical, important? Is it adhered to during the entire lesson? Is it achieved?

B. Is the lesson development smooth, sequential, logical?

C. Is the content too much, too little, geared to the age level, geared to the language level?

D. Is the method appropriate? Is it suitable to the age level? Is it in accordance with accepted principles (i.e., listening and speaking before reading and writing)?

E. Is there a variety of drills (repetitive, pattern practice, question-answer)?

F. Is there a summary? Given by whom?

G. Is the tempo of the lesson too slow, too brisk, hurried, sustained?

H. Is the native language used judiciously (where feasible, when, why, how)?

I. Additional comments (grouping, individualization, etc.)

LESSONS WITH SPECIAL EMPHASES

A. Pronunciation
1. Is attention given to helping students hear and distinguish sounds and contrasts before asking them to produce them orally?
2. What aids are used (diagram of speech organs, expla-

nation of points of articulation, arrows or dots for intonation, etc.)?

3. Are all new sounds used in context after they are taught?

B. Structure

1. Is there relationship to known material (familiar English or native-language structure)?

2. Are examples modeled by the teacher? How many? What is their quality? How many times is each example given?

3. Is repetition done chorally first, then by subgroups, then by individuals?

4. How is the recurring feature clarified, emphasized, and described (diagramed on board, elicited)?

5. Pattern-practice activities

a. Are the most appropriate chosen?

b. Is the type of activity varied (substitution, replacement, question-answer, transformation)?

c. Is the type of pupil participation varied (teacher asks pupils, pupils ask teacher or other pupils, chain drills)?

d. How is the new structure used in authentic communication (dialogue dramatization, reading, action series, writing of experience chart)?

C. Reading and Word Study

1. Motivation (related to students' lives; to longer story)?

2. Clarification of difficulties (cognates, pictures, objects, paraphrases, dramatization, native-language equivalent, other)?

3. Oral reading by the teacher (tempo, phrasing, rhythm)?

4. Techniques to ensure comprehension (questioning to elicit the main thought and to note cause-and-effect relationships, completion exercises, true-false questions)?

5. Summary given? How elicited?

6. Word study (antonyms, synonyms, words of same family)?
7. Oral reading by students (Are able students called on first? How much class time is spent? How are errors corrected?)
8. Is the homework assignment based on what has been done in class (answers to questions, outline, summary)?

Some Concluding Remarks*

The teaching of English as a second language to speakers of other languages is now recognized as an important discipline with a philosophy and set of principles of its own. These principles are drawn from many sciences—particularly linguistics, psychology, anthropology, and sociology. While everyone would agree that good teaching in this area embodies desirable approaches involved in the teaching of any other curriculum area, several underlying premises, which often cause misunderstanding, may warrant further clarification and restatement. Let us repeat a few of these very briefly:

1. TESL (teaching English as a second language) is *not* the same as teaching English to native English speakers. On the contrary, it embodies the principles and methodology of teaching a foreign language.

2. TESL in an English-speaking community is *not* the same as teaching English as a foreign language in a non-English-speaking community, although basic principles of teaching in both situations would have much in common.

a. Some of the features of the sound system, structures, and vocabulary that might be deferred in a non-English-speaking country would have to be given priority because of the necessity of students to participate actively and immediately in a completely English-speaking school or community situation.

---

* This is an adapted and expanded version of an article by the author which appeared in the *Florida Foreign Language Reporter,* January, 1965, issue and which was reprinted in the *TESOL Newsletter,* Vol. 1, Number 1, April, 1967.

For instance, vocabulary in other curriculum areas or vocabulary needed to look for jobs may have to be introduced early.

b. We may assume that students will pick up some features of the rhythm of English and some vocabulary because of the fact that they hear English around them.

c. The pace of introduction of language content would have to be accelerated. Students could not afford to spend eight to ten years in learning the features of the English language and in learning the communication skills.

But

3. TESL in a community that is peopled predominantly by non-English speakers is *not* the same as TESL to language learners who live in a predominantly English-speaking neighborhood. The important feature of motivation for learning is lacking or diminished when storekeepers, movies, and places of worship use the native language of the learners.

4. Language, by anyone over about the age of eight, is not learned "incidentally," even in a predominantly English-speaking community. Language learning involves skill development and habit formation. Skills have to be practiced consciously before they can be used unconsciously or without constant and conscious effort.

5. Learning a second language is not the same as learning one's native language as a child. Not only are factors of time and exposure to the language completely different but, depending on the learner's age, features of the first language (sounds, word form, word order) generally cause interference with the learning of the second language.

6. Language is a reflection of the culture (used in the anthropological sense) of its speakers. Thus, the discussions of educators and linguists about precedence of structures or of vocabulary versus situations are quite pointless. Features of language should *always* be taught within the cultural situations that help give them their meaning.

7. Although priority should be given to listening and speaking skills, reading and writing should be taught as soon as

feasible and appropriate. Older learners who have to fill out job applications may need to *see* the graphic symbols soon *after* hearing them and saying them a number of times, (even on the same teaching day).

8. While mastery is a much desired goal, we should not require complete mastery of any feature of English before proceeding to another one. Since language learning is cumulative, the same feature of sound, structure, or vocabulary will be met hundreds of times in the course of a well-planned English program. Our aim should be to give our students *progressively* better control of any language feature.

9. It goes without saying that more intensive practice and thus greater, more immediate control should be given to those pronunciation items that would impede understanding; e.g., *live, leave.*

There are many methods and techniques in language teaching. The good teacher uses *all* of them at different times, not only to lend variety to his teaching, but also in the hope that one of them will give his students insight into the item or pattern being taught. Pupils have different learning modes just as teachers have different teaching styles.

1. The memorization of *lengthy* dialogues, containing utterances which are not of high frequency and which do not generate new, similar utterances, may prove time-consuming and basically unproductive. On the other hand, it is an excellent idea to have the pupils learn and dramatize many dialogues containing common formulas and basic utterances that duplicate the authentic speech of native speakers of their age level. Learning of dialogues should be achieved through their frequent dramatization, through many variations of them, and through combinations with other dialogues. It should not be attempted by overnight memorization.

2. While no one would recommend that the native language of the speakers be used as a constant crutch in the special English classroom, the occasional brief, *judicious* use of the stu-

dent's native language (by the teacher, student buddy, native informant, or teacher aide) may save minutes of class time, ensure practice with greater understanding and motivation, and give learners needed emotional security.

3. No one intended pattern practice to be the ultimate objective of language learning. The ultimate goal is "free" communication. On the other hand, *some* pattern practice (the amount depending on the learner's ability, age, knowledge, etc.) is necessary to give students reasonable and eventually habitual control of the important features of English.

While it is true that varied teaching methods and techniques in the hands of a skilled, sympathetic teacher may engender motivation in otherwise uninterested students, we should not fail to recognize (and provide for) the paramount importance of psychological and sociological factors in our pupils and of the numerous, often competing forces within the community that affect learning.

Far outweighing the most carefully planned steps in any phase of language development is the necessity for teachers to give students a sense of belonging to the new community and to the class, a pride in their cultural heritage and in their native language, a feeling of achievement, and many small successes. This means, of course, providing many integrative as well as differentiated experiences on the level at which the students happen to be.

It is only when language learners come to the English class and to school with a sense of pleasurable anticipation that we can hope to make their transition to and integration into the English-speaking community a smooth one, with a minimum of negative experiences. Only thus will the English-speaking society be enriched as it reaps the fullest benefits from the cultural gifts that these members can bring to it. These gifts will be proffered more freely as the speakers of other languages grow in their knowledge of the English language and in their appreciation of the culture reflected in that language.

A Glossary of Useful Terms

Note: Below you will find brief, simple definitions of terms as they have been used in this text or as you will find them in related books.

Action series.   A learning technique in which individuals perform a series of sequential actions and say what they are doing as they perform each action.

Active vocabulary.   Words that are taught so intensively that students can understand and say them and, later, read and write them.

Anthropology.   One of the social sciences. It studies the development and behavior of man as a social being and all the cultural features (including language) of a society. *See also* culture.

Area study.   The focus on various aspects of culture (including the language) of a given region.

Arrangement.   The order or sequence of the language items.

Articulation.   1) The smooth, continuous development from one level of language learning to the next. 2) The production of sounds by the meeting of the vocal organs.

Aural-oral.   *See* Audio-lingual.

Audio-lingual.   Listening and speaking. (The term is taking the place of *aural-oral*.)

Blending.   Change or omission of sounds in language spoken at conversational speed.

Center of activity.   An area of the classroom in which are concentrated materials related to a curriculum area (e.g., science, math) or to some facet of the language arts (listening corner).

Center of interest.   A topic, theme, or unit on which learning is focused for a length of time. The center of interest—self-identification, for

451

example—serves as the jumping-off point for the presentation, development, and practice of pronunciation, structures, concepts, vocabulary, and cultural information.

Chain drill. A technique for ensuring pupil participation in which one student asks a question or makes a statement to the student seated next to him, who in turn makes a statement or asks a question of the student seated next to him. The order of the chain is clearly specified by the teacher.

Cluster. The sequence or bunching together of consonants (e.g., ju*mps*) or of other language items.

Cognate. A word in one language that looks similar to and has an equivalent meaning to a word in another language.

Communication. 1) The transmission and reception of meaningful information. 2) The ability to understand, to speak, and to respond to the signals (in our case, vocal, and later, printed) of another individual.

Communication arts. Another term for language arts. Listening, speaking, reading, and writing.

Conflict. Interference or difficulty experienced by language learners because a feature of the new language is either not used at all in their native language or used in different combinations or ways.

Conscious selection. The step in the learning process in which students have learned two contrasting features of the language well enough so that they can now choose the correct one in a practice activity or in a communication situation.

Content word. One that refers to something in the world of reality—a thing, an action, a quality, a concept. Generally, a noun, a verb, an adjective, or an adverb. Content words and function words make up the vocabulary of the English language.

Context. A social-cultural situation; the surrounding words in an utterance that give a word or structure its particular meaning.

Contrast. Two different word forms or word sequences in a language that cause a change in meaning; e.g., rag, rack; talks, talked; convert (verb), convert (noun); bus station, station bus.

Cue. Anything that stimulates the desired response; e.g., a picture, an object, an oral word, a gesture, or a written word.

Culture. The pattern of the customs, traditions, social habits, values, beliefs, and language of any society of human beings. *There are no people without culture.*

Curriculum. The knowledge, information, skills, habits, attitudes, activities, and materials that are included in the teaching of any subject.

Derivational. Pertaining to the prefixes, suffixes, and infixes that change the meanings and function of words; e.g., trust, mistrust; bright, brighten.

Determiner. A word like "the," "a," "some," "each," "all," which is placed before the noun and which limits or modifies it.

Diorama. A miniature stage setting in which lifelike scenes are created through the use of appropriate objects and backdrops.

Diphthong. Two vowel sounds combined to form one sound; e.g., "i" in "ice" [a+i].

Equivalent. A word or expression in one language that conveys a similar meaning in another language. *Equivalents should not be confused with word-by-word translations.*

Experience chart. A series of sentences or utterances in the students' own words about any experience in which they have engaged. (Experience charts are generally used in beginning reading.)

Formula. An expression of greeting, thanks, agreement, disagreement, and so on habitually used by native speakers. "Good morning" and "Thank you" are formulas, for example.

Function word. One having little or no meaning by itself because it does not refer to an object or action in the world of reality. Function words are considered one of the four major meaning signals of English since they indicate relationships of content words to each other. Prepositions, auxiliaries, conjunctions are examples of such words. (See p. 36.)

Generalization. A statement describing the form, function, position, and meaning of the recurring feature or element of any language item or cultural concept; a "rule."

Inflection. The addition of an ending to express a grammatical relationship; e.g., *ed* added to "walk" to indicate past tense.

Informant. An individual who has native or near-native ability in a language and who uses the ability to "inform" learners or educators or scientists about features of language or culture needed to describe or to learn the language.

Integration. 1) The process of bringing together materials and skills that are related and that can be used concomitantly as in the language arts; 2) The feeling on the part of an individual that he participates and functions in another society while retaining his own sense of identity.

Internalize. To make some learning part of oneself; to achieve full control of.

IPA—the International Phonetic Alphabet (see p. 369).

Item. An element of language; e.g., a phoneme, a morpheme, a word, a structure.

Labial. Pertaining to the lips.

Language arts. Listening, speaking, reading, and writing components of the communication skills.

Language laboratory. A room or part of a room equipped with one or more tape recorders, microphones, listening and (sometimes) playback equipment with which pupils can listen to and imitate tapes and engage in varied practice activities for the purpose of reinforcing language skills.

Lexical. Pertaining to the vocabulary of a language (the content and function words).

Level. A stage of language learning; for example, beginning, intermediate, advanced.

Minimal pair. Two items that sound alike except for one difference; e.g., "rag, rack," "very, berry," "sheep, ship," "looks, looked." Minimal pairs are used to help students hear, distinguish, and produce the phonemes (the meaningful sounds) and the structures of the language they are learning.

Model. The "perfect," native production of a sound, word, or expression by a teacher or a tape for imitation and repetition by the students.

Morpheme. A minimal unit of meaningful speech; e.g., a word, "boy"; an inflection, "s," as in "boys"; a suffix, "ish" as in "boyish."

Morphology. The study of grammatical changes in the forms of a word; e.g., boy, boys; boy's, boys'; sure, ensure.

Native speaker. A person who has native or near-native command of a language because he was either born into that language community or has learned the language well enough to master it.

Passive vocabulary. Words which the learner can understand when spoken or recognize when read but which he cannot produce in speaking or in writing. (Also called *recognitional vocabulary*.)

Pattern. An arrangement of sounds, letters, or words that recurs systematically in a language and that is meaningful; the framework or design of an utterance; e.g., noun-verb (Birds fly).

Pattern practice. Drills, activities, and exercises that help give students control of patterns of language (word order, word form, function words, intonation).

Phoneme. The smallest unit of sound in a language that distinguishes one word from another. For example, "p" and "b" are phonemes because they make a meaning difference in words like "pit" and "bit," "peat" and "beat," or "pear" and "bear."

Phonemics. The study of meaningful units of speech.

Phonetics. The study of the sounds of speech and the way in which the sounds are produced.

Phonology. The study of the sounds, intonation, rhythm, stress, and pauses in the language. (Includes the study of phonetics and phonemics.)

Pitch. Contrasts in the relative height of the tone of voice. Pitch is an important component of intonation.

Programed learning. A method of learning that incorporates the following basic features: Students can proceed at their own pace; the items to be learned are presented in the smallest possible incremental steps; students learn immediately whether their response is correct. (This is referred to as confirmation.)

Pull-out program. One in which language learners (from one or more classes) are taken out of their regular rooms for a block of time daily for special instruction in English as a second language.

Self-contained classroom. One in which language learners are in regular classes with native English-speaking children. In many such classrooms, the teacher gives language learners special instruction while the rest of the class is occupied in other activities.

Slot. The position of a word or phrase in an utterance or sentence that can be occupied by words or phrases of the same class or type; for example, "the," "a," "some," "each" can fit into the same slot.

Spiral approach. A method of teaching in which the same language or cultural topic is presented in greater depth at each succeeding level of learning.

Stress. The prominence of syllables or words in speech. The stressed syllable in English is longer and louder than others.

Structure. 1) The grammar of a language. 2) The recurring patterns of a language as they occur in forms and arrangements of words.

Syntax. The arrangement of words in utterances and sentences. "I *always* go there," "I go there *in the afternoons*." Words like "always," "generally" and "never" are placed before the main verb whereas time phrases are placed at the end of a sentence.

System.   The recurring combinations and sequences of sounds and words into patterns that signal meaning. We talk of the sound system, the grammar system, the vocabulary system, the culture system of a language.

Utterance.   A word, expression, or sentence that conveys full meaning to a listener. For example, "no" is an utterance.

Unit.   1) A large subdivision of a subject. 2) A number of lessons or activities built around one topic. 3) One item of speech.

Voiced sound.   One produced with the vocal cords vibrating; e.g., "z" or "b."

Voiceless sound.   A sound made while the vocal cords are not vibrating; e.g., "s" or "p."

Resources and Texts

Note: Since books and articles in this field appear almost daily, we have considered it desirable to indicate names of agencies and a few periodicals which appear on a regular basis. Teachers and administrators should turn to them for guidance and for reviews or advertisements of new materials. The bibliographical entries are brief and represent, for the most part, those materials with which the author is personally familiar.

Resources for Teachers and Supervisors
Agencies and Service Bureaus

Association for Teachers of English to Speakers of Other Languages (TESOL), Georgetown University, Washington, D.C.

British Council, 65 Davis Street, London, England

Center for Applied Linguistics, 1755 Massachusetts Avenue, Washington, D.C.

Modern Language Association, 60 Fifth Avenue, New York

National Association for Foreign Student Affairs, United Nations Plaza, New York City

National Council of Teachers of English, Champaign, Illinois

UNESCO, United Nations Plaza, New York City (Will also have a European branch in Belgium in the near future.)

U.S. Department of Health, Education and Welfare, Washington, D.C.

United States Information Service, English Teaching Division, Washington, D.C. and

State Departments of Education in capitals of all states

British Council Bureaus and Immigration Agencies of all countries of the Commonwealth.

Periodicals or Professional Journals (Consult also other materials issued by Agencies listed above.)

English—A New Language, Commonwealth Office of Education, Sydney, Australia

English Teaching Abstracts, The British Council, London

English Teaching Forum, United States Information Service, Washington, D.C.

English Teaching News, The British Council, London, England

Grade Teacher, 20 Leroy Avenue, Darien, Connecticut 06820

Integrated Education, Integrated Education Association, New York, New York

Instructor, Owen Publishing Co., Instructor Park, Dansville, New York

Language Learning: A Journal of Applied Linguistics, 1522 Rackham Building, Ann Arbor, Michigan

Linguistic Reporter, Center for Applied Linguistics, 1755 Massachussetts Ave., Washington, D.C.

ML Abstracts, Fullerton, California

Modern Language Journal, Curtis Reed Plaza, Menasha, Wisconsin

NAFSA Newsletter, National Association for Foreign Student Affairs, United Nations Plaza, New York

TESOL Newsletter, Georgetown University, Washington, D.C.

TESOL Quarterly, Georgetown University, Washington, D.C.

Curriculum Bulletins and Newsletters issued by local and state Boards of Education and Commonwealth Offices.

Newsletters issued by publishing companies

Bibliographies

Allen, V. F., and S. Forman, *English as a Second Language: A Comprehensive Bibliography.* New York, Teachers College Press, 1967.

Baker, Hugh S., *A Checklist of Books and Articles for Teachers of English as a Foreign Language.* NAFSA, United Nations Plaza, 1959.

Broz, J., and A. Hays, *Linguistics and Reading.* Washington, D.C. Center for Applied Linguistics, 1966.

Dingwall, William Orr, *Transformational Generative Grammar: A Bibliography.* Washington, D.C., Center for Applied Linguistics, 1965.

English Teaching Bibliography, London, The British Council, English Teaching Information Centre.

English as a Second Language in Elementary Schools: Background and Text Materials. Washington, D.C., Center for Applied Linguistics, 1966.

Frank, Marcella, *Annotated Bibliography of Materials for English as a Second Language.* NAFSA, United Nations Plaza, 1960 and 1962.

Hammer, John, and Rice, Frank, *A Bibliography of Contrastive Linguistics.* Washington, D.C., Center for Applied Linguistics, 1965.

Johnston, M., and A. Jewett, *Resources for Teaching English: References for Teachers of English as a Foreign Language.* Washington, D.C., U.S. Dept. of Health, Education and Welfare, Office of Education, 1956.

Johnston, Marjorie C., and Catherine C. Seerley, *Foreign Language Laboratories in Schools and Colleges.* Washington, D.C., U.S. Dept. of Health, Education and Welfare, Bulletin No. 3, 1959.

Lado, Robert, *Annotated Bibliography for Teachers of English as a Foreign Language,* Washington, D.C., U.S. Government Printing Office, 1955.

Language Research in Progress, Report #3. Washington, D.C., Center for Applied Linguistics, 1966.

O'Hanessian, Sirarpi, *Interim Bibliography on the Teaching of English to Speakers of Other Languages.* Washington, D.C., Center for Applied Linguistics, 1963.

O'Hanessian, Sirarpi, *Thirty Books for Teachers of English as a Foreign Language.* Washington, D.C., Center for Applied Linguistics, 1967.

Ollman, Mary (ed.), *MLA Selected List of Materials for Teachers of Modern Foreign Languages,* New York, Modern Language Association, 1962.

Reference List of Materials for English as a Second Language. Part I, 1964 and Part II, 1966. Washington, D.C., Center for Applied Linguistics.

Rice, Frank, and Allene Guss, *Information Sources in Linguistics.* Washington, D.C., Center for Applied Linguistics, 1965.

Sanchez, George, and Howard Putnam, *Materials Relating to the Education of Spanish Speaking People in the U.S.* Austin, The University of Texas Press, 1959.

Selected Bibliography on Education, Cultural Backgrounds and Assimilation of the Foreign Born in the U.S. Washington, D.C., U.S. Dept. of Justice, Immigration and Naturalization Service, 1948.

Shen, Yao, and Ruth Crymes, *Teaching English as a Second Language,*

Honolulu, East West Centre Press, 1965.

University Resources in the U.S. for Linguistics and Teacher Training in English as a Foreign Language. Washington, D.C., Center for Applied Linguistics, 1966.

Visual Aids for English as a Second Language. Washington, D.C., Center for Applied Linguistics, 1965.

Wylie, Lawrence, and others, *Six Cultures: Selected and Annotated Bibliographies.* New York, Modern Language Association, 1961.

Texts (related primarily to language learning and teaching)

Abercrombie, David, *Problems and Principles: Studies in the Teaching of English as a Second Language.* London, Longmans, Green, 1964.

Agard, F., and R. DiPietro, *The Grammatical Structures of English and Italian.* Chicago, The University of Chicago Press, 1965.

Allen, Harold B. (ed.), *Readings in Applied English Linguistics.* New York, Appleton-Century-Crofts, 1961.

—— *Teaching English as a Second Language: A Book of Readings.* New York, McGraw-Hill, 1965.

—— *TENES. A Survey of Teaching of English to Non-English Speakers in the U. S.* Champaign, Ill., National Council of Teachers of English, 1966.

Allen, R., V. Allen, and M. Shute, *English Sounds and Their Spellings.* New York, Thomas Y. Crowell Co., 1966.

Allen, Robert L. *A Modern Grammar of Written English.* New York, Macmillan, 1965.

Anderson, Wallace, and Norman Stageberg, *Introductory Readings on Language.* New York, Holt, Rinehart and Winston, 1962.

Bach, Emmon. *An Introduction to Transformational Grammar.* New York, Holt, Rinehart and Winston, 1963.

Belasco, Simon, *Anthology for Use with a Guide for Teachers in N. D. E. A. Language Institutes.* Boston, D. C. Heath and Co., 1961.

Billows, F. L. *The Techniques of Language Teaching.* London, Longmans, Green, 1961.

Bloomfield, Leonard, *Language.* New York, Henry Holt, 1933.

Bond, G. L., and E. B. Wagner, *Teaching The Child To Read.* New York, Macmillan, 1966.

Bronstein, Arthur, *The Pronunciation of American English.* New York, Appleton-Century-Crofts, 1966.

Brooks, Nelson, *Language and Language Learning*. New York, Harcourt, Brace, 1960.

Buchanan, Cynthia D., *A Programmed Introduction to Linguistics: Phonetics and Phonemics*. Boston, D. C. Heath and Co., 1963.

Bumpass, Faye L., *Teaching Young Students English as a Foreign Language*. New York, American Book Co., 1963.

Carroll, John B., *The Study of Languages*. Cambridge, Mass., Harvard University Press, 1953.

———, *Research on Teaching Foreign Languages,* in Handbook of Research on Teaching (ed. N. L. Gage), Chicago, Rand McNally, 1963.

———, *Language and Thought*. Englewood Cliffs, N.J., Prentice-Hall, 1965.

———, *The Study of Language*. Cambridge, Mass., Harvard University Press, 1959.

Chomsky, Noam., *Syntactic Structures*. Mouton and Co. Gravenhage, The Netherlands, 1963.

Cornelius, Edwin, *Language Teaching: A Guide for Teachers of Foreign Languages*. New York, Thomas Y. Crowell Co., 1953.

Crowell, Thomas Lee, *Modern Spoken English*. New York, McGraw-Hill, 1961.

Dacany, F. R., *Techniques and Procedures in Second Language Teaching*. Quezon City, Phoenix Publishing Co., 1963.

Deterline, William A., *An Introduction to Programmed Instruction*. Englewood Cliffs, N.J., Prentice-Hall, 1962.

Devereux, E. J. P. (ed.), *An Introduction to Visual Aids*. London, Mathews, Drew and Shelbourne, 1962.

Dorry, Gertrude, *Games for Second Language Learning*. New York, McGraw-Hill, 1966.

Doty, Gladys G., and Janet Ross, *Language and Life in the U.S.A.* Evanston, Ill., Row, Peterson, 1960.

Finocchiaro, M., *English as a Second Language: From Theory to Practice*. New York, Regents, 1965.

———, *Learning to Use English: Teacher's Manual*. New York, Regents, 1967.

———, *Teaching Children Foreign Languages*. New York, McGraw-Hill, 1964.

———, and Harold McNally, *Educator's Vocabulary Handbook*. New York, American Book Co., 1965.

Firth, J. R., *The Tongues of Men and Speech*. London, Oxford University Press, 1965.

Fodor, Jerry A. and Jerrold J. Katz (eds.), *The Structure of Language: Readings in the Philosophy of Language*. Englewood Cliffs, N.J., Prentice-Hall, 1964.

Francis, W. Nelson, *The Structure of English*. New York, The Ronald Press Co., 1954.

———, *The Structure of American English*. New York, The Ronald Press Co., 1958.

French, F. G., *Teaching English as a Foreign or Second Language*. London: Oxford University Press, 1963.

———, *Teaching English as an International Language*. London: Oxford University Press, 1963.

———, *The Teaching of English Abroad*. London, Oxford University Press, 1950.

Fries, Charles, *Linguistics and Reading*. New York, Holt, Rinehart and Winston, 1963.

———, *The Structure of English*. New York, Harcourt, Brace, 1952.

———, *The Teaching of English*. Ann Arbor, Mich., The George Wahr Publishing Co., 1949.

———, *Teaching and Learning English as a Foreign Language*. Ann Arbor, Mich., University of Michigan Press, 1948.

———, and A. Fries, *Foundations for English Teaching*. Tokyo, Kenkynsha English Language Exploratory Committee, 1961.

Fries, Charles, and Robert Lado, *English Pronunciation*. Ann Arbor, Mich., University of Michigan Press, 1954.

———, *English Sentence Patterns*. Ann Arbor, Mich., University of Michigan Press, 1954.

———, *Lessons in Vocabulary*. Ann Arbor, Mich., University of Michigan Press, 1956.

Gatenby, E. V., *English as a Second Language*. London, Longmans, Green, 1944.

Gauntlett, J. C., *Teaching English as a Foreign Language*. London, Macmillan, 1957.

Gleason, Henry A., *An Introduction to Descriptive Linguistics,* Revised Edition. New York, Holt, Rinehart and Winston, 1964.

———, *Linguistics and English Grammar*. New York, Holt, Rinehart and Winston, 1965.

Gurrey, Percival, *Teaching English as a Foreign Language*. London, Longmans, Green, 1955.

——, *Teaching English Grammar*. London, Longmans, Green, 1964.

Hall, Edward T., *The Silent Language*. Garden City, N.Y., Doubleday and Co., 1959.

Hall, Robert A., *An Introduction to Linguistics*. Philadelphia, Chilton, 1965.

——, *Linguistics and Your Language*. Ithaca, N.Y., Ithaca Press, 1960.

——, *Sound and Spelling in English*. Philadelphia, Chilton, 1961.

Halliday, M. A. K., and others, *The Linguistic Sciences and Language Teaching*. Bloomington, Ind., Indiana University Press, 1965.

Harris, David, *Reading Improvement Exercises for Students of English as a Second Language*. Englewood Cliffs, N.J., Prentice-Hall, 1966.

Harris, Zellig S., *Methods in Structural Linguistics*. Chicago, University of Chicago Press, 1951.

Hayakawa, S. I., *Language in Thought and Action*. New York, Harcourt, Brace & World, 1949.

Hayden, Pilgrim, Haggard, *Mastering American English*. Englewood Cliffs, N.J., Prentice-Hall, 1956.

Hill, Archibald A., *Introduction to Linguistic Structures*. New York, Harcourt, Brace and Co., 1958.

Hockett, Charles F., *A Course in Modern Linguistics*. New York, Macmillan, 1958.

Hojer, Harry (ed.), *Language in Culture*. Chicago, The University of Chicago Press, 1954.

Hornby, A. S., *A Guide to Patterns and Usage in English*. London, Oxford University Press, 1954; reprinted, 1961.

——, *The Teaching of Structural Words and Phrases,* Stages I and II. London, Oxford University Press, 1959–61.

Huebener, Theodore, *Audio-Visual Techniques in Teaching Foreign Languages*. New York, New York University Press, 1960.

Hughes, Marie, and George Sanchez, *Learning a New Language*. Washington, D.C., Association for Childhood Education International, 1958.

Hughes, John, *The Science of Languages*. New York, Random House, 1962.

Jesperson, Otto, *Language: Its Nature, Development and Origin*. New York, W. W. Norton, 1922.

Jones, Daniel, *An Outline of English Phonetics.* Cambridge, Eng., Heffer, 1960.

Jones, Daniel, *Everyman's English Pronouncing Dictionary.* New York, E. P. Dutton, 1956.

Kenyon, J. S., and T. A. Knott, *A Pronouncing Dictionary of American English,* Second Edition, Springfield, Mass., Merriam, 1953.

Kingdon, Roger, *The Groundwork of English Intonation.* London, Longmans, Green, 1958.

Kluckhohn, Clyde, *Mirror for Man.* New York, McGraw-Hill, 1949.

Kreidler, Carol J., and M. Beatrice Sutherland, *Flash Pictures: A Set of 252 Cards Used as an Aid to Teachers of English as a Foreign Language.* Ann Arbor, Mich., University of Michigan Press, 1963.

Lado, Robert, *Language Teaching.* New York, McGraw-Hill, 1964.

————, *Language Testing.* London, Longmans, Green, 1961.

————, *Linguistics Across Cultures,* Ann Arbor, Mich., University of Michigan Press, 1957.

Lee, W. R., *Language Teaching, Games and Contests.* New York, Oxford University Press, 1965.

————, and Coppen, H., *Simple Audio-Visual Aids.* New York, Oxford University Press, 1964.

Lefevre, Carl A., *Linguistics and the Teaching of Reading.* New York, McGraw-Hill, 1964.

Levin, Samuel R., *Linguistic Structures in Poetry.* The Hague, Mouton and Co., 1962.

Mackey, W. F., *Language Teaching Analysis.* London, Longmans, Green, 1965.

Marckwardt, Albert H., *American English.* New York, Oxford University Press, 1958.

Marty, Fernand L., *Language Laboratory Learning.* Wellesley, Mass., 1960.

Miller, Bruce, *Sources of Free and Inexpensive Teaching Aids,* 25th and 26th ed., 2 vols. Riverside, Calif., Bruce Miller Publications, 1959–62.

————, *Sources of Free Pictures.* Riverside, Calif., Bruce Miller Publications, 1963.

Morris, I., *The Art of Teaching English as a Living Language.* London, Macmillan, 1964.

Moulton, William G., *Linguistics and Language Learning.* Chicago, The University of Chicago Press, 1960.

Nida, Eugene A., *Learning a Foreign Language: A Handbook Prepared*

Especially for Missionaries. New York, Free Press of Glencoe, 1950.

Palmer, Harold E., *The Teaching of Oral English.* London, Longmans, Green, 1940.

Pei, Mario, *A Glossary of Linguistic Terminology.* Garden City, N.Y., Doubleday, 1966.

——, *Language for Everybody.* New York, Devin Adair, 1957.

——, *An Invitation to Linguistics,* Garden City, N.Y., Doubleday, 1965.

Pepe, Thomas J., *Free and Inexpensive Educational Aids.* New York, Dover Publications, 1960.

Pike, Kenneth Lee, *The Intonation of American English,* 5th Printing. Ann Arbor, Mich., University of Michigan Press, 1953.

——, *Phonemics.* Ann Arbor, Mich., University of Michigan Press, 1947.

Potter, Simeon, *Modern Linguistics,* 2nd ed. New York: W. W. Norton, 1964.

Prator, Clifford, *A Manual of American English Pronunciation.* New York, Holt, Rinehart and Winston, 1960.

Roberts, Paul, *English Sentences.* New York, Harcourt Brace, 1962.

——, *English Syntax.* New York, Harcourt, Brace & Co., 1964.

Robins, R. H., *General Linguistics: An Introductory Survey.* London, Longmans, Green, 1964.

Ross, Janet, and Gladys Doty, *Writing English.* New York, Harper & Row, 1965.

Sapir, Edward, *Language.* New York, Harcourt, Brace, 1931.

Second Language Teaching in Primary and Secondary Schools, UNESCO. Vol. 13, No. 3, 1961.

Sledd, James, *A Short Introduction to English Grammar.* Chicago, Scott, Foresman and Co., 1959.

Smith, W. I., and J. W. Moore, *Programed Learning: Theory and Research.* Princeton, N.J., D. Van Nostrand Co., 1962.

Stack, Edward M., *The Language Laboratory and Modern Language Teaching.* New York, Oxford University Press, 1960.

Stevick, Earl W., *Helping People Learn English.* Nashville, Tenn., Abingdon Press, 1957.

——, *A Workbook in Language Teaching.* Nashville, Tenn., Abingdon Press, 1964.

Stockwell, Robert, and David Bowen, *The Sounds of English and Spanish.* Chicago, The University of Chicago Press, 1964.

———, ———, and John Maftin, *The Grammatical Structures of English and Spanish.* Chicago, The University of Chicago Press, 1964.

Sturtevant, Edgar, *An Introduction to Linguistic Science.* New Haven, Yale University Press, 1947.

Taylor, A., *Equipping the Classroom.* London, Nelson, 1953.

Teaching English to Puerto Rican Pupils. New York Board of Education, 1954–1957.

Thorndike, E. and I. Lorge, *The Teacher's Wordbook of 30,000 Words.* New York, Teachers College Press, 1944.

Trager, George and Henry Lee Smith, *An Outline of English Structure.* Washington, American Council of Learned Societies, 1957.

Trager, Edith Crowell, and Sara Cook Henderson, *The PD's: Pronunciation Drills for Learners of English.* Washington, D.C., English Language Services, 1956.

Valdman, Albert (ed.), *Trends in Language Teaching.* New York, McGraw-Hill, 1966.

Wallace, Betty, *The Pronunciation of American English for Teachers of English as a Second Language.* Ann Arbor, Mich., George Wahr, 1957.

West, Michael, *A General Service List of English Words.* London, Longmans, Green, 1953.

———, *Learning to Read a Foreign Language.* London, Longmans, Green, 1941.

———, *Teaching English in Difficult Circumstances: Teaching English as a Foreign Language.* London, Longmans, Green, 1960.

Zandvoort, R., *A Handbook of English Grammar.* London, Longmans, Green, 1961.

Texts, Pamphlets, and Long Articles (related primarily to teaching speakers of other languages or dialects)

These books include extensive bibliographies in this area:

Barron, Milton, *American Minorities: A Textbook of Readings in Intergroup Relations.* New York, Knopf, 1957.

"Bilingualism and the Bilingual Child: A Symposium," *Modern Language Journal,* April, 1965; September, 1965.

Educating Disadvantaged Children in the Primary Years. Washington, D.C., U.S. Government Printing Office, 1965.

Frost, Joe, and Glenn Hawkes, *The Disadvantaged Child: Issues and Innovations.* Boston, Houghton Mifflin Company, 1966.

Gittler, Joseph B. (ed.), *Understanding Minority Groups.* New York, John Wiley, 1956.

Improving English Skills of Culturally Different Youths, U.S. Department of Health, Education and Welfare. Washington, D.C., U.S. Government Printing Office, 1964.

Labov, William, *The Social Stratification of English in New York City.* Washington, D.C., The Center for Applied Linguistics, 1966.

Landes, Ruth, *Latin-Americans in the Southwest.* New York, McGraw-Hill, 1965.

Lanning, Frank and Wesley Many, *Basic Education for the Disadvantaged Adult,* Boston, Houghton Mifflin, 1966.

Loretan, Joseph and Shelley Umans, *Teaching the Disadvantaged.* New York, Teachers College Press, 1966.

Riessman, Frank, *The Culturally Deprived.* New York, Harper & Row, 1961.

Senior, Clarence, *Our Citizens from the Caribbean.* New York, McGraw-Hill, 1965.

Spodek, Bernard (ed.), *Preparing Teachers of Disadvantaged Young Children.* National Association for Education of Young Children, 1966.

Trager, Helen G. and Marion R. Yarrow, *They Learn What They Live: Prejudice in Young Children.* New York, Harper & Row, 1952.

Index

ABOUT THE AUTHOR

Dr. Mary Finocchiaro is Professor of Education at Hunter College of the City University of New York, where she is coordinator of programs in teaching English as a second language. She was formerly teacher of English as a second language, principal of an elementary school, and chairman of foreign languages in the New York City schools. As Fulbright Professor in Spain (1961) and Italy (1954 and 1968) and as Director, Consultant, or Demonstration Specialist at numerous government-sponsored seminars on language and language teaching in Poland, Yugoslavia, Israel, Spain, Morocco, France, and Germany, as well as in the United States, she has had many opportunities to test her ideas on learning and teaching both in the United States and abroad.

Professor Finocchiaro has been elected to the executive committee of the national organization devoted to teaching English as a second language—TESOL—and to the New York State Federation of Foreign-Language Teachers.

70 71 72 73 10 9 8 7 6 5 4 3 2